Heavenly Harmony

Malcolm Walker and David Davies have quarried the cathedral archives to tell the fascinating story of Exeter Cathedral's organs and organists. This is an exemplary account which enables the reader to enter into past controversies and triumphs, and to encounter various colourful characters along the way including Peter Pasmore, who was dispensed from his duties as organist in 1690 to defend the Devon coast against the French, and Wesley, who was described by an exasperated Chapter Clerk as 'The most to be avoided man I ever met with'. The authors are to be congratulated on an invaluable local study which feeds into the wider narrative of the history of English cathedral music.

Nicholas Thistlethwaite, Former Chairman of The British Institute of Organ Studies and author of *The Making of the Victorian Organ* (1990)

Heavenly Harmony

Organs and Organists of Exeter Cathedral

First published 2014
by Impress Books Ltd
Innovation Centre, Rennes Drive,
University of Exeter Campus, Exeter EX4 4RN

Typeset in Palatino by Swales and Willis Ltd, Exeter, Devon

Printed and bound by Short Run Press, Exeter, Devon

British Library Cataloguing in Publication Data

A catalogue record for this book is available from the British Library

ISBN: 978 1 9076056 5 9

The Friends of Exeter Cathedral

Contents

Foreword by Andrew Millington, Director of Music, Exeter Cathedral, 1999–2015

The view from the west end of Exeter Cathedral down the length of the nave and beyond to the east window is one of the finest architectural sights in the land. The feast of English decorated style would be enough in itself, but it is punctuated by the magnificent seventeenth-century organ case, imperiously situated on the stone pulpitum and seemingly almost reaching the vault above. The date of the Loosemore case, 1665, is a significant milestone in the history of the Exeter organ, but the story of its evolution is a complex and colourful narrative spanning several centuries. Previous attempts to chronicle this story have been worthy and enthusiastic, but, for the first time, this volume provides a comprehensive and meticulously researched study of the instrument, from the earliest records to the current and extensive restoration (2014). In addition, the long procession of organists and masters of choristers is described in detail, as well as the various organ specifications down the centuries.

The publication coincides with the return of the refurbished instrument in all its glory. During the time that the organ has been dismantled, much has been learned about its history from close inspection of the empty case and the precise evidence which that has provided.

I am sure that this book will appeal to organ enthusiasts far and wide, and to all those who work and worship at Exeter Cathedral. Our warmest thanks go to Malcolm Walker for his exceptional eye for detail, his passion for scholarly and accurate information, and for his support for the music of Exeter Cathedral and the Diocese. We are also indebted to David Davies for his skilled and supportive contribution to the project. Long may the organs and organists of Exeter Cathedral continue to make 'Heavenly Harmony'.

Foreword by The Very Revd Dr Jonathan Draper, Dean of Exeter

Andrew Millington's description of the place of the organ in the architecture and the worshipping life of Exeter Cathedral is a fitting description and needs no embellishment. Deans come and go in cathedrals, but music and its making remain central to the cathedral's life and witness. This organ, in its various developments, has served the cathedral in Exeter for 350 years, and the current work, undertaken by Harrison & Harrison of Durham to a very high standard, will give it another generation or two of excellent service. We are grateful to them and to the main funders of the project – Viridor Credits, the Friends of Exeter Cathedral, the Music Foundation Trust and the many individuals who have contributed to the funding of its restoration – for bringing our organ back to life.

Music remains central to the ways in which we worship God and this book tells an important part of the story of music at Exeter Cathedral. I hope many people will enjoy reading it.

Acknowledgements

The origins of this book lie in a work by the late Betty Matthews published in 1965, *The Organs and Organists of Exeter Cathedral*. Nearly half a century on, Betty's booklet needed at least to be updated. More than that, some of the material in it raised questions which could not be answered in so short a work, with many of its thirty pages taken up with specifications of organs. What really happened to the instrument in the English Civil War? How much has the magnificent case been altered since it was made in 1665? How badly damaged was the organ when a bomb struck the cathedral in 1942? What does the splendid Tudor memorial in the north nave aisle tell us about an organist who was only seventeen years of age when he died? To what extent have organists been responsible for changes in specifications over the years? A book proposal was born. Our very grateful thanks go to the Dean and Chapter of Exeter for approving the proposal, Impress Books Ltd for agreeing to publish the book, and the Friends of Exeter Cathedral for their generous support.

During the research phase of the project, many people provided assistance. In the Exeter Cathedral Library and Archives, Ann Barwood, Peter Thomas, Angela Doughty, Stuart Macwilliam, John Draisey and Ellie Jones were very helpful, especially Ellie, who supplied document after document and answered many queries. And staff of Harrison & Harrison Ltd, the organ-builders who have cared for the Exeter Cathedral organ since the early 1930s, welcomed us to their factory at Durham and not only allowed us access to their archives but also provided a number of illustrations for the book. We are particularly grateful to Christopher Batchelor, Dot Henderson, Jim Reeves and Carole Jeffery.

Specific queries have been answered by many people, in particular: John Allan (Exeter Cathedral archaeologist), Mike Dobson (Exeter Cathedral lay vicar), Todd Gray (historian, Exeter), Toby Huitson (archivist, Canterbury Cathedral), Jo Bartholomew (curator and librarian, Winchester Cathedral), Gill Rushton (archivist, Hampshire Record Office), Frances Lansley (searchroom supervisor, West Sussex Record Office), Julia Wood (archivist, Wells Cathedral), Robin Darwall-Smith (archivist,

Magdalen College, Oxford), Eleanor Fleetham (archive and records manager, Keble College, Oxford), Peter Horton (deputy librarian, Royal College of Music), Erin McHugh (museum assistant, Royal College of Music), Kathryn Adamson (librarian, Royal Academy of Music), Anna Wright and Geoff Thomason (librarians, Royal Northern College of Music), John Henderson and Trevor Jarvis (Royal School of Church Music), Peter Privett (assistant secretary, Friends of Exeter Cathedral), Mary Neale (daughter of Alfred Wilcock), Lucian Nethsingha (former organist of Exeter Cathedral), Renée Jackaman (collections development manager, Devon Heritage Centre), Anne Maskell (assistant librarian, House of Lords Library), Martin Cottam (freelance artist), Sarah Beedle (editor, *Organists' Review*), David Wyld (managing director, Henry Willis & Sons Ltd), Ian Payne (music editor, Severinus Press), Mark Stoyle (professor of early modern history, University of Southampton), Laura Elliott (library assistant, Lambeth Palace Library), Tom Corfield (assistant organist, Derby Cathedral), and William Hunt (Windsor Herald, College of Arms).

A number of other people helped us get the story right, notably Eddie Sinclair (Exeter Cathedral conservator), Paul Morgan (Exeter Cathedral organist emeritus), Stephen Tanner (assistant organist of Exeter Cathedral and head of music at Exeter Cathedral School), Stuart Blaylock (archaeologist, Exeter), Richard Parker (archaeologist, Richard Parker Historic Buildings Recording and Interpretation, Exeter), David Conway (an Exeter Cathedral worshipper for many decades), Philip Hickman (former chorister of Exeter Cathedral), and Philip Hobbs (former lay vicar, Exeter Cathedral). We are very grateful to them all.

It has been a great pleasure and honour to have two advisors for the book, Andrew Millington (director of music, Exeter Cathedral) and Dominic Gwynn (director, Martin Goetze and Dominic Gwynn Ltd, organ-builders). Their guidance and support are hugely appreciated.

Our thanks go also to Conrad Donaldson (chairman, Friends of Exeter Cathedral) and Richard Willis (director, Impress Books Ltd) for their support and encouragement and to Ann Barwood and Ellie Jones for permission to reproduce documents in the Cathedral Archives. We are grateful, too, to Norman and Linda Hart, Naomi Hart and Geoffrey Morgan (friends of David) for their assistance and support; and finally, we acknowledge with many thanks Malcolm's beloved wife, Diane, who has not only taken a very close interest in the story of Exeter Cathedral's organs and organists but also shown extraordinary skill in unearthing obscure facts.

Malcolm Walker and David Davies
August 2014

Figures

The authors and publisher are grateful for permission to reproduce illustrations from the Dean and Chapter of Exeter (Figures 1.1, 2.1 and 2.2), Martin Cottam and Dominic Gwynn (Figure 2.3), Diane Walker (Figures 5.2, 5.3, 5.4 and 5.5), University of Aberdeen (Figure 5.6), Harrison & Harrison Ltd (Figures 6.1, 6.5 and 6.6), Todd Gray (Figure 6.2), Mary Neale (Figure 6.3), Mike Dobson (Figure 6.4), the Royal School of Church Music (Figure 6.7), Lucian Nethsingha (Figure 6.8).

Plates

The authors and publisher are grateful for permission to reproduce colour plates from Harrison & Harrison Ltd, Andrew Millington, the Royal College of Music.

1 Matthew Godwin memorial, north nave aisle. Photograph by Malcolm Walker.
2 Inscription on Matthew Godwin memorial. Photograph by Malcolm Walker.
3 The keyboards that were taken out by Henry Willis in 1891. Note the reversed colour of the keys (ebony naturals and ivory sharps), the rounded sharps and the elegantly carved key cheeks. Photograph by Malcolm Walker.
4 Spiral stone staircase to the organ loft. Photograph by Malcolm Walker.
5 The organ as it now appears from the quire. Notice that the relative heights of the Chair and main cases are now the same as they were before 1870. The main case was raised five feet when Henry Willis rebuilt the organ in 1891. From a photograph by Harrison & Harrison Ltd.
6 The lowest sixteen pipes of the Pedal Organ's Contra Violone rank were moved to the south transept in 1891. Note the ingenious calculation that enabled the longest pipes to fit so neatly within the architectural constraint. Although not particularly loud in terms of volume, the rich harmonic development of the notes produced by these pipes means that the notes can be heard and felt throughout the building. Three of the sixteen pipes are behind the pipes which are visible in this picture. Photograph by Malcolm Walker.
7 Part of the Exeter Blitz commemoration window by Christopher Webb in the south nave aisle, showing a stone mason and an organ-builder. Photograph by Malcolm Walker.
8 The Chair case today, with the inscription above it: 'John Loosemore made this organ 1665'. The lettering of the inscription was gilded in 1965. Photograph by Malcolm Walker.

9   Pipework of the Minstrels' Gallery division. The principal and flute ranks can be seen in the foreground, while the pipes of the impressive Trompette stop occupy the middle. Note how the larger pipes are tied with black cotton tape to support the body of the pipe structure, and also how the largest pipes are 'mitred' (not dissimilar from an orchestral instrument where the resonating tube is folded over to lend rigidity and to save space). One of the wind reservoirs, complete with metal weights, can be seen behind the Trompette on the left. Note the wooden enclosure of the whole division on the back, top and sides to promote sound projection and climatic control. Photograph by Malcolm Walker.

10   The organ under construction in Durham in the Harrison & Harrison workshop during 2014. Here we are looking from the south side to the north. The different levels upon which the organ departments will sit can be clearly seen. Sited prominently on the left is the Solo division that occupies the Willis case on the lower order of the west façade of the organ. Here we see it side on. The height from floor level to the top of the organ is 8.1 metres (26.6 feet). Photograph by Malcolm Walker by kind permission of Harrison & Harrison Ltd.

11   The restored console in 2014, showing the small revisions of some of the stop jambs and piston designations.

12   The Solo and main cases from the nave. Photograph by Malcolm Walker.

13   The chamber organ built by Kenneth Tickell & Co Ltd in 2007. The details of the display pipes and of the wood carving were designed to complement the existing colour and woodwork patterns of the quire. The organ has four stops: Fifteenth (2), Chimney Flute (4), Principal (4), Stopped Diapason (8). Photograph by Malcolm Walker.

14   Andrew Millington (director of music since 1999). Behind him, the organ in the Lady Chapel, purchased in 1959 through the generosity of the Friends of Exeter Cathedral. The organ, which has one manual and no pedals, was built in the nineteenth century by Samuel Parsons of 2 Little Russell Street, Bloomsbury, London. It has six stops: Fifteenth (2), Principal (4), Stopped Diapason Bass (8), Twelfth (2⅔), Stopped DiapasonTreble (8), Open Diapason (8). Photograph supplied by Andrew Millington.

15   Samuel Sebastian Wesley in the 1830s. Courtesy of the Royal College of Music, London.

16   Detail on the east face of the organ case built by John Loosemore in 1665. Photograph by Malcolm Walker.

CHAPTER 1

A Rich and Lofty Organ

The year was 1635. Lieutenant Hammond was in Exeter. Though a voluntary member of the Military Company in Norwich, he was not in Exeter on military business. He was there as a tourist, pursuing his interest in the great churches of England. The organ in the cathedral impressed him greatly. It was, he said:[1]

> A delicate, rich and lofty organ, which has more additions than any other, as fair pipes of an extraordinary length, and of the bigness of a man's thigh, which, with their viols and other sweet instruments, the tunable voices and the rare organist, together make a melodious and heavenly harmony, able to ravish the hearer's ears.

Who built this organ, and when? Where in the cathedral was it? Who was the 'rare organist'? What 'other sweet instruments' were used, and why? How long had there been an organ in the building? To answer these questions, we begin the story of Exeter Cathedral's organs and organists centuries before the Lieutenant's visit.

Early Organs and Organists

There were pipe organs in churches across Europe more than a thousand years ago, including, in England, Malmesbury Abbey, Ramsey Abbey and Winchester Cathedral. The earliest record of an organ in Exeter Cathedral so far discovered dates from 17 July 1284, when the Bishop of Exeter granted a tenement in Paignton to a bell-founder, Roger de Ropford (or Ropforde), on condition that he and his wife Agnes, their son Walter and their heirs made bells for the cathedral, or caused them to be made. They were also to repair the cathedral's organs and clock as often as necessary (*fieri facient organa et orologium quociens opus fuerit reparabunt*). The grant was made with the consent of the cathedral's Chapter, who agreed to bear all costs.[2]

Another reference to *organa* can be found in the cathedral's fabric accounts for 16 February 1286/87, this being, in the words of Audrey Erskine's translation, 'expenses concerning the closing [encasing] of the organs' (*in expensis circa organa claudenda*).[3] The use of *organa* seems to refer to organs in the plural but in old usage meant one instrument. Encasement of pipes was a mediæval development.

In the thirteenth century, *organa* could mean pipe organs in particular or musical instruments in general. The record in the fabric accounts appears to confirm that *organa* in 1284 referred to a pipe organ, for it is unlikely that any other instrument would have been encased. Payments were also made on 16 February 1287 to 'Roger the bell-founder and his son' (i.e. Roger and Walter) for work on the bells, from which it is reasonable to assume that they were the people who encased the organ.

Construction of the building which was seen by the Lieutenant from Norwich began about 1270 and took a hundred years. Built in the Decorated Gothic style, this cathedral replaced one that had been built in the Romanesque (Norman) style between *c*.1114 and *c*.1200. This, in turn, had replaced the Anglo-Saxon minster in which, in the year 1050, Leofric had been installed as the first Bishop of Exeter. Though no reference to an organ in Exeter Cathedral before the 1280s has yet come to light, we should not be surprised if we find some day there had been one in the Romanesque cathedral or even the Anglo-Saxon minster. There were boy choristers in Exeter Cathedral in Leofric's time.[4]

The organ seen by the Lieutenant was on the pulpitum (the screen or platform at the western end of the quire). However, the organ(s) of the 1280s could not have been there, for this pulpitum did not then exist. It was built between 1317 and 1325. The supposition is that services were held in the nave of the Romanesque building while construction of the Lady Chapel and other eastern parts of the Gothic cathedral took place. This being so, we may wonder if the instrument of the 1280s was in the nave of the Romanesque cathedral. On the other hand, the Lady Chapel may have been sufficiently complete by 1284 for the *organa* to have been situated there; and we may speculate further to wonder if the instrument in question was a brand new one and encased for the first time by Roger and his son.

After 1287, the next record of an organ that has so far come to light appeared in a document dated 8 Edward II (i.e. July 1314 to July 1315), in which it was stated that Robert, son of Walter le Belleyetere (bell-founder), was to 'retain a messuage and land in Paignton which Roger le Belleyetere his grandfather acquired from Peter [Quivil] late Bishop of Exeter and the Chapter for making and repairing, at the expense of the Chapter, all the bells, organs and clocks of the Cathedral Church'.[5] And there was a further reference to Robert, son of Walter, in January 1318, when he was appointed to ring the bells and repair the organs and clocks.[6] Responsibility for the cathedral's bells, clock and organs was indeed being passed down to the heirs of Roger and Agnes.

After 1318, there was no mention of an organ until 11 December 1389, when there was a payment of 12s 4d for mending the organs in the Lady Chapel at the Cathedral Chapter's expense.[7] There is in the fabric accounts for 1353, however, a tantalizing entry which has long exercised the minds of scholars but never been explained satisfactorily.

In the first week after Trinity, i.e. the week beginning 20 May 1353, new work began in the cathedral before, or in the vicinity of, the great cross (*fuit incept' novi operis ecclesiæ beati Petri coram magna cruce*). For the following nineteen weeks, masons, carpenters, sawyers and labourers were employed on the work, assisted for a week and a half by Master Richard Farleigh, the cathedral's architect. Audrey Erskine discussed in her translation of the fabric accounts the possible nature of the 'new work' and concluded that 'the only guess which it seems reasonable to hazard is that the new work was a structure on the pulpitum itself, where the organ now stands, to raise and enhance Thomas of Witney's original design'.[8]

Unfortunately, the nature of the new work was not specified in the fabric accounts, and the accounts for the seventeen years beginning Michaelmas (29 September) 1353 have not survived. However, we may speculate that the work possibly involved modifications to the pulpitum for an organ to be placed on it. Exeter's bishop at the time, John de Grandisson, possessed great enthusiasm for music and indeed introduced at the cathedral liturgical reforms which involved polyphony and both vocal and instrumental music.

The pulpitum appears to have been made sturdy enough to support an organ from the outset, as it is recorded in the fabric accounts that the weight of iron which was purchased for it in 1319 and 1320 specifically for making into bars exceeded 1,220 pounds. The existence of iron bars an inch and a quarter square set horizontally and vertically into the pulpitum was revealed by the architect Sir George Gilbert Scott during his restoration of the cathedral in the 1870s, and a simple calculation shows that the weight of iron purchased in 1319 and 1320 matches almost exactly the weight in the bars which Scott revealed.[9]

There was certainly sufficient height for an organ of the fourteenth century to be placed under the great cross. Two small remnants of iron brackets that appear to have supported a beam on which the cross was mounted are visible to this day, projecting from the walls north and south of the eastern side of the pulpitum about 25 feet above its upper surface. The length of the longest pipe of an organ of the 1350s was unlikely to have been more than about ten feet. It is a further point that an organ took up a considerable amount of floor space, not least for the bellows, which would have been at the side of the instrument. The upper surface of the pulpitum would have made an ideal location for an organ, but whether one was first placed there in 1353, or one had been there before, we may never know for sure.

Nicholas Orme has stated in his article 'The early musicians of Exeter Cathedral' that this cathedral, 'like the other great churches of mediæval England, cultivated the art of music on a large scale to enhance and dignify its worship'.[10] Organs were important elements of that music-making, and it is likely that a great church like Exeter Cathedral possessed more than one, as it certainly did in the early sixteenth century, when there were organs in the Lady Chapel and on the pulpitum. We have already seen that an organ existed in the Lady Chapel before 1400, and we may suspect that another existed on the pulpitum at the same time.

As with the early organs, we know little of the early organists. Indeed, as Orme has stated in his article, there was 'in mediæval Exeter no office of organist with its own title or salary'. The organ would have been played by clergy 'as part of their ordinary duties, a custom followed elsewhere'. In this respect, the earliest specific mention of an organist comes on 28 March 1393, when a deacon, Thomas Hop, was admitted by the Dean for his pleasing ability to play the organ.[11] However, as Orme has pointed out, this does not refer to the appointment of an organist as such. He explained that, 'in the fifteenth century, as organ-playing developed and most of the English cathedrals acquired specialised organists, it is likely that the task devolved on the Clerk of the [Lady] Chapel'. He listed all the known clerks of the chapel who served Exeter Cathedral between 1276 and 1547, the latter being the year when the office was abolished and the post of organist created. The modern office of organist at Exeter was therefore instituted soon after the English Reformation began.

A Large Organ on the Pulpitum

Organs were tuned (*modulando*) in 1416, and a new organ was made in 1429 (there being a record of expenses *pro novis organis faciendis*).[12] We find, too, that repairs to an organ were carried out in 1480. As was the case with organs before the fifteenth century, however, we lack information about cost, location or specification.

Another new organ was made in 1513, this one certainly on the pulpitum, as we know from the account roll for the building of the instrument, a document which has survived by chance, attached to the cathedral's fabric accounts for that year.[13] The document states that the organ was a new one on the pulpitum (*pro novis organis in pulpito*) and tells us that it was built by Laurence Playssher at a cost of £164 15s 7¼d, a large sum in those days.

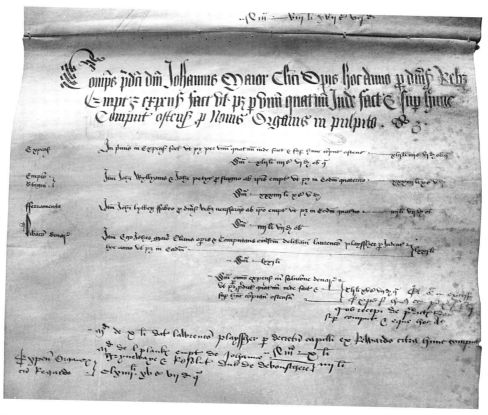

Figure 1.1   Account roll for the building of an organ on the pulpitum by Laurence Playssher, 1513.

Stephen Bicknell mentioned in his book *The History of the English Organ* that Playssher is known only from this organ in Exeter Cathedral and one in Glastonbury Abbey.[14] The total amount he was paid for making the organ at Exeter was £81, made up of £71 agreed in the indenture plus an additional £10 as a further reward granted by the Chapter. Thus, the payment to him accounted for nearly half the cost of the organ. The cost of tin, which would have been for organ pipes, was £64 16s 2d, and a payment of £4 0s 7½d was made to a blacksmith for ironwork. Another four pounds was spent on timber, while other unspecified costs accounted for the rest of the £164 15s 7¼d.

Bicknell concluded from a calculation based on the likely price of tin in 1513 that the instrument built by Playssher was 'very substantial and, despite lack of detailed information about its musical potential, the largest organ we know of in the British Isles before the Civil War'. Assuming a price of around 7½d per pound, the weight of tin purchased for the organ was nearly a ton. If this was the organ seen and heard by the Lieutenant from Norwich, it is not surprising he was impressed. Its bass pipes, made of tin, would have been at least twenty feet long and might well have been 'of the bigness of a man's thigh', as the Lieutenant put it.

But was this the organ the Lieutenant described? He visited Exeter Cathedral 122 years after Playssher's organ was built, which is a long time in the lifespan of an organ. Repairs and maintenance would have been required over the years. There is, however, no record of another new organ, from which we may suppose that the organ seen and heard by the Lieutenant was in essence the one built in 1513.

A Time of Uncertainty

After 1513, the frequency of references to Exeter Cathedral organs and organists increases for a few decades. In March 1527, for example, Lady Chapel organs were sold to the Vicar of Chagford for £5 6s 8d;[15] and in the 1540s we find there were two organs serving the quire: one on the pulpitum, the other standing in and on the north side of the quire (*stantes in et ex parte boriali chori*). The Chapter nominated Mr Holwel and Mr Raynold to supervise the organs in the quire but also instructed them to mend and sell the organs in the Lady Chapel.[16] Robert Bostocke was appointed keeper of the organs on 29 October 1547, with a salary of 16s 8d (*officium custodis organorum cum salario 16s/8d*).[17]

An inventory of Exeter Cathedral's possessions compiled in 1552 shows there were still then organs in the Lady Chapel, for it was recorded that the chapel contained 'two pair of organs, one greater, the other small'.[18] There were also, at the same time, 'two pair of organs in the quire, one great, the other less'.[19]

A letter dated 4 December 1554 from John Holwill to Exeter Cathedral's treasurer states that an agreement had been made with a Mr Chappington (no forename given) for 'the mending and keeping in tune of the great organs from time to time'.[20] He was to be paid forty shillings for mending the organs and thereafter 13s 4d yearly for keeping the instrument in tune. The organ was worth, the letter states, £200, which is consistent with the organ being the one built in 1513. 'Mr Chappington' was probably Hugh Chappington, an organ-builder from South Molton, Devon.[21]

Thomas Heath was appointed organist of Exeter Cathedral in July 1558.[22] After that, though, there is no mention of organs or organists for nearly thirty years. How long he remained organist, we do not know. He may have died in 1583, but, again, this is uncertain.

The Protestant reforms of the 1530s, 1540s and early 1550s brought about great change in churches all over England and Wales, including Exeter Cathedral. A fundamental aspect of this was rejection of the cult of the Virgin Mary, which had been so central to the worship and life of churches before the upheaval wrought by Kings Henry VIII and Edward VI.[23] A return to papal authority and Roman Catholic forms of worship during the reign of Queen Mary proved short-lived, as she reigned for only five years (1553–58), after which her successor, Queen Elizabeth, reasserted the belief that authority over the English Church belonged to the monarchy, not the Pope. However, Elizabeth proved to be a pragmatist who espoused Protestant principles and theological insights while, at the same time, showing herself comfortable with Catholic creeds and many aspects of Catholic liturgy and patterns of ministry.[24] Under Elizabeth, the Church of England became both Catholic and reformed.

Though exaggerated devotions to the Virgin Mary were rejected by the Church of England, her role in the Incarnation continued to be acknowledged. From 1561, the calendar of the Church of England included five feasts associated with Mary, these being Conception, Nativity, Annunciation, Visitation and Purification; and the Magnificat was retained in the service of Evening Prayer. Nevertheless, the place of worship became the quire and, as Nicholas Orme has put it in *Exeter Cathedral as it was, 1050–1550*, 'the Lady Chapel and other chapels were left empty and unused, their dedications forgotten, and some of them were turned into vestries or court-rooms'.[25] After Queen Mary's time, centuries were to pass before there was again an organ in the Lady Chapel of Exeter Cathedral.

In the time of Queen Elizabeth, there was a collective ambivalence in the Church of England. Some cathedral deans and chapters were strongly Calvinistic and therefore unsympathetic to the choral tradition. Indeed, canons at Norwich broke down the cathedral organ about 1570; and in the following year, as Alan Mould has put it in *The English Chorister*, 'the Bishop of Winchester banned polyphony from his cathedral and abolished the office of organist at Winchester College'.[26] In contrast, clergy in many churches and cathedrals retained Catholic sympathies, either covertly or overtly, and continued to encourage the centuries-old choral tradition.[27]

To what extent the clergy of Exeter Cathedral continued to encourage choral and organ music, we do not know. The bishops of Exeter in the 1560s and 1570s were William Alley (1560–70) and William Bradbridge (1571–78). Alley had Protestant leanings, while Bradbridge appears to have been equivocal. Maybe the religious conservatism of the South West in the Prayer Book Rebellion of 1549 was not yet a distant memory, causing the clergy of Devon to tread carefully. Whatever the truth of the matter, no reference to organs or organists at Exeter in the period 1558 to 1586 has yet come to light.

Two Organists from Canterbury

Matthew Godwin was appointed organist of Exeter Cathedral on 13 May 1586 but, sadly, died only eight months later.[28] Information about him is provided on a splendid memorial which is affixed to the wall of the cathedral's north nave aisle (see Plate 1).[29] It is believed to be the earliest surviving memorial to a musician in a British church.

The inscription on the memorial states that Matthew was seventeen years and five months old when he died and gives the date of his death as 12 January 1586, which was 1587 by today's reckoning (see Plate 2).[30] It states, too, that he was a clever youth and expert musician, which certainly appears to have been so. As the inscription says, he had been in charge of the music of Canterbury Cathedral and had also gained a bachelor's degree in music.

The records of Canterbury Cathedral tell us that, on 15 February 1584, Matthew was to be 'joined in patent with Mr William Selby in the office of organist and master of the children'.[31] Selby died four months later, whereupon, on 20 June, a patent was authorized for Matthew to serve alone as organist and master of the children. The Dean of Canterbury at the time was Thomas Godwin, who was given to finding posts for members of his family.[32] The International Genealogical Index shows that Matthew, son of Thomas, was baptized in August 1569 at Chartham, four miles west of Canterbury, where, at that time, the deans of Canterbury had a country residence. Thus, there is circumstantial evidence that Matthew was indeed the Dean's son, as a number of writers have suspected.[33]

Thomas Godwin was elected Bishop of Bath and Wells on 10 August 1584 and consecrated on 13 September 1584. We do not know what then became of Matthew, but it may be that he was, to quote Ian Payne, 'sent to the provinces, perhaps to widen his experience'.[34] On the other hand, he may have continued to serve as organist of Canterbury Cathedral. Be that as it may, he supplicated for the degree of Bachelor of Music at Oxford University on 2 July 1585 and proceeded to the degree twelve days later. In those days, the normal minimum period of study for a degree in music was seven years, and the candidate was expected to compose an anthem or motet in five parts. It was also customary for supplicants to state the number of years spent studying music. No composition by Matthew has ever come to light; and he claimed he had studied music for twelve years!

Part of the inscription on the memorial has long been debated: 'posuit (set up by) G.M. Fr.'. To identify G.M. Fr., we may note that Francis Godwin became Sub Dean of Exeter Cathedral on 11 June 1587, only five months after Matthew's death. Francis was a brother of Matthew, born in 1562 at Hannington, Northamptonshire, where his father, Thomas, was Rector, he being the same Thomas Godwin who later (1567) became Dean of Canterbury. Thus, it is plausible that G. stands for Godwin, Fr. for *frater* (Latin for brother), and M. for *maior* (elder) or perhaps Matthew. The shield on the memorial shows the Godwin arms used by Thomas when Bishop of Bath and Wells (1584–90) and by Francis when Bishop of Llandaff (1601–17) and Bishop of Hereford (1617–33) with the addition of a martlet, which indicates that Matthew was the fourth son.[35] It therefore seems clear that Francis set up the splendid memorial to his brother.

Carved on the memorial there are two lutes, a cornett and a natural trumpet. These instruments were used in churches across Europe in the sixteenth century, mainly for ceremonial music and processionals but also for accompaniment of liturgical texts. An organ is carved on the memorial, too, with Matthew praying in front of it. Thus, it would appear that there was no antagonism towards the use of organs in Exeter Cathedral in the 1580s.

Matthew Godwin was succeeded by Arthur Cocke (or Cox), who had also been organist of Canterbury Cathedral. However, there seems to have been no urgency over replacing Matthew, for Arthur was still organist and master of the choristers at Canterbury in 1588.[36] He was admitted organist of Exeter Cathedral on 19 April 1589 and made a lay vicar on 21 June 1589.[37]

There is uncertainty over Cocke's subsequent career. The records of Exeter Cathedral indicate that he was 'deprived' on 22 December 1593 'because he did absent himself a longer tyme than Mr Deane gave him leave'.[38] Two months later, though, on 25 February 1594, he supplicated for the Oxford University degree of Bachelor of Music and, in so doing, described himself as 'Organist of Exeter Cathedral'. As Ian Payne has said in his article about Godwin and Cocke, 'there is nothing to suggest that Cocke was ever re-instated after his expulsion, though this cannot be ruled out completely'.[39] 'It is known', he said, 'that many decisions of the Chapter at Exeter were either never carried out or reversed later.'

An entry in the Exeter Cathedral Register of Baptisms records the baptism of 'Elizabeth Cocke, d[aughter] of Art. Cocke' on 13 June 1597, which suggests he was then still in Exeter. Four years later, though, on 1 November 1601, an entry in the Canterbury Cathedral Register of Baptisms records the baptism of 'Elenor d[aughter] of Arthure Cocke', which suggests that he had by then returned to Canterbury from Exeter (assuming he was the same Arthur Cocke). On the other hand, to quote from a manuscript preserved among the muniments of the Chapel Royal, 'Arthur Cock from Exon' was appointed the chapel's organist on 8 March 1602, having the previous year, on 3 March 1601, become a 'gentleman in ordinary and organiste (without pay) in her Majestes saide chapple until an organiste place shalbe come voyde'.[40] He died on 26 January 1605.[41]

Musical Progress

The next known organist of Exeter Cathedral was appointed towards the end of 1602 or in early 1603. He was John Lugge, a man in his early twenties, baptized at Barnstaple on 24 October 1580. The first reference to him in the cathedral's records comes in the Ordinary Solutions (register of regular payments) for the quarter ending on Lady Day (25 March) 1603, when he was paid 50s as 'organiste'.[42] At the same time, an *ex gratia* quarterly payment of 6s 8d from the Dean and Chapter was made to John Paunchard (or Panchard) for serving as the 'custos organorum, campanarum et horologii' (guardian of the organs, bells and clock). Lugge was admitted a lay vicar on 24 June 1605.

After Lady Day 1603, quarterages (quarterly payments) of 50s to Lugge and 6s 8d to Paunchard were made regularly up to and including St John's Day (24 June) 1608. Then, among the quarterages paid at Michaelmas (29 September) 1608, we find one to Edward Gibbons, for sharing the duties of organist with Lugge.[43] Each was paid 25s.[44] Lugge's salary had been halved.

In the list of payments made at Christmas 1608, Gibbons was not mentioned. John Lugge and Peter Chambers were each paid 25s under the heading of 'organiste', and John Paunchard received 6s 8d for being custos organorum, campanarum et horologii.[45] A year later, though, at Christmas 1609, Gibbons appeared again, this time as 'informator choristarum' (master of the choristers). He and Lugge were each paid 25s, and Paunchard again received 6s 8d. Thereafter, quarter after quarter for many years, Gibbons and Lugge were each paid 25s, the former as informator choristarum, the latter as organist; and a payment of 6s 8d was made *ex gratia* by the Dean and Chapter to a 'custos organorum, campanarum et horologii'.[46]

The first reference to the cathedral's organ since 1554 came in 1618, when, on 4 November, the Chapter decreed that 'Mr Gibbons should inquire for a sufficient man to amend the organs, but to certify the Dean and Chapter what the cost will amount unto for doing the same before any work be begunne herein'.[47] It would appear from this that a significant amount of work on the instrument was required if the cost needed to be known before permission to proceed could be granted. The choice of the master of the choristers rather than the organist may seem curious for a matter that concerned the organ specifically. However, Gibbons had held the office of Succentor (sub-chanter) since 12 February 1616 and was therefore officially deputy to the Precentor, who was the person in charge of the music.[48] It thus appears that Gibbons was considered senior to Lugge.

To carry out work on the organ, a Mr Chappington was approached, as in 1554, but it was now Ralph Chappington (who was probably a nephew of Hugh, who had long since died).[49] If no substantial maintenance or renovation work had been done on the organ since 1554, it would have been long overdue, and evidence that this was indeed so is provided by the fact that the Chapter decreed on 19 June 1619 that 'the little organs be amended with all speed', which suggests a degree of urgency.[50] The Chapter decreed on 25 September 1619 that 'the great organs be amended by Mr Chappington'. Here, though, there is an inconsistency in the sources, because one says 'new organs', while another says 'great organs'.[51] This may be a measure of how much work was needed, with the word 'new' meaning substantially overhauled, not a completely new instrument.

Ralph Chappington did not carry out the work. He died in late 1619 or early 1620, and the Chappington dynasty of organ-builders thereby came to an end.[52] The Dean and Chapter turned to Thomas Dallam, an organ-builder of national repute who had repaired and altered the organ in the Chapel of St George at Windsor and built new organs for the cathedrals at Norwich and Worcester and the chapel of King's College, Cambridge.[53] It is recorded that the Dean and Chapter decreed on 15 January 1620 that 'the Chapter Clerk do write to Mr Dallam to come hither to amend the organs this year'.[54]

But it seems that Dallam did not come in 1620, for the Chapter agreed on 16 March 1621 that 'the organs should be amended according to an order formerly made in that behalf, and the last sortition to be performed according to the tenor thereof, or to such of the Chapter as will lay down their money for the parcels therein mentioned, and the Chapter Clerk to disburse such money out of their quarterages and other profit of such as shall be absent at such time as Mr Dallam shall come about the same work'.[55] In other words, a drawing of lots (sortition) was to be carried out to determine which members of the Chapter should pay for the work on the organ; and those who were absent had no option but to pay. Today's Chapter members may well be appalled by the very idea!

Nearly two years passed before there was any further reference to the organ. Then, on 22 February 1623, the Chapter decreed that 'the organs be used with the psalms before and after morning prayer', from which we may infer that the organ was in use and the work on it completed.[56] The following year, in the Chapter Acts for 17 January 1624, the name of the organ-blower is given, John Mills.[57] He was not, however, mentioned in the context of blowing the organ. Together with one Edmund Meredith, he was to 'receive and collect money for seats about the pulpit'. The first specific reference to the organ since 1621 suggests that its condition was not wholly satisfactory, given that the Chapter decreed on 29 April 1625 that 'Mr Dallam should be sent unto for new settling of the organs'.[58]

Dallam appears to have cured the problem, as there was no further mention of the organ until the latter part of 1636. We may conclude that the instrument which was seen and heard by the Lieutenant from Norwich was that built by Playssher in 1513 as renovated by Thomas Dallam in the early 1620s and 'settled' in 1625.

A Rare Organist

'The long and close collaboration between Edward Gibbons and John Lugge made the music at Exeter Cathedral some of the finest in the country.' So wrote the distinguished organist and musicologist Susi Jeans.[59] As she said, though, Lugge was overshadowed by Gibbons, who had been 'called to Exeter by Bishop Cotton to reorganize the Cathedral choir'.[60] Both men remained in their posts until 1646 and were therefore, as organist and master of the choristers, respectively, the musicians who were entitled to the credit for the 'melodious and heavenly harmony' which so impressed the Lieutenant from Norwich. But Gibbons was no longer Succentor by 1635. He had, on 15 December 1627, 'relinquished all his right in the sub-chantership which he hath from the Archbishop of Canterbury and acknowledged to hold under Mr Chanter Cotton'.[61] His appointment, made in 1616, had been declared invalid.

It was increasingly common from the time of King Henry VIII onwards for cathedral choristers to be taught to play the organ and other musical instruments, and Exeter was no exception.[62] Gibbons taught the Exeter choristers composition and also to play instruments which were used during services. These would have been the viols and other sweet instruments mentioned by the Lieutenant.

For the most part, Lugge seems to have been well regarded by the cathedral authorities. The Dean and Chapter decreed on 18 October 1617 that he be allowed the profits of a vacant clerkship to supplement his income, and in 1622 they granted him permission to live in his house in Kalendarhay with his family until their deaths.[63] They also appointed deputy organists, among them Peter Chambers (1608), Greenwood Randall (1610–12), Hugh Facy (1618) and Thomas Gale (1628).

There were doubts about Lugge, though. A letter to him written by his brother Peter in December 1617 was intercepted by the Bishop of Exeter. Peter had been brought up in Lisbon and become involved in a religious and political plot. Suspected of harbouring Roman Catholic sympathies, John Lugge was examined by Bishop Cotton in January 1618, the outcome being that he was exonerated. Doubts lingered, though, and his house was searched three years later, whereupon he was again found innocent. The possibility that John did indeed harbour Roman Catholic views is suggested by the fact that his son Robert resigned as organist of an Oxford college (St John's) in early 1639 and then, in John Lugge's words, 'went beyond the seas and changed his religion for that of Rome'.[64]

Hugh Facy was also not beyond suspicion. He was granted a year's leave of absence without loss of stipend by Exeter's Chapter on 6 November 1619 and a further year of absence on 4 November 1620. It is not known where he went or what he did during the two years, nor is it known what happened to him thereafter. However, as Susi Jeans has pointed out, he set the plainsong *Ave Maris Stella* for organ and used a Latin text for his *Magnificat*, something, she said, 'no good Anglican would have done'. On the other hand, as Christopher Maxim has pointed out, Latin had not been altogether forbidden in worship as part of the English Reformation.[65]

The Lieutenant from Norwich called John Lugge a 'rare organist'. He was indeed. He was not only an accomplished player of the organ; he also composed anthems and plainsong settings and pieces for the organ and virginals, including three voluntaries for double organ.[66] He was, as Ian Payne has said, 'one of the most talented English provincial composers of the period'.[67]

The Lieutenant found that musical standards were high in Exeter Cathedral in the middle of the 1630s. There could be every expectation that the 'tunable voices' (as he put it) and one of the finest organs in Britain, if not the very finest, would 'make a melodious and heavenly harmony' (as he further put it) for many years to come.

CHAPTER 2

Turmoil and Triumph

Prince William of Orange landed at Brixham on the coast of Devon on 5 November 1688 and entered Exeter four days later. Then, in the words of a contemporary account by John Whittle (a chaplain in the Prince's army), 'His Highness was pleased to go and render his hearty thanks to Almighty God in the Cathedral Church for his safe arrival', adding that 'the organs played very sweetly as he came all along the body of the church'.[1] The historian Lord Macaulay wrote even more approvingly of the organ heard by the Prince:[2]

> William repaired in military state to the Cathedral. As he passed under the gorgeous screen, that renowned organ, scarcely surpassed by any of those which are the boast of his native Holland, gave out a peal of triumph.

This was not the organ which had impressed the Lieutenant from Norwich. That one no longer existed. What had happened to it, and why? Who had built the organ heard by the Prince, and when? To answer these questions, we continue the story of the organs and organists through one of the most unsettled periods in Exeter's history.

Dissent and Discontent

Throughout the 1630s, John Lugge continued to be organist and Edward Gibbons informator choristarum. Only once was there an exception. A new name appeared in the quarter ending on Christmas Day 1635, when William Wake was paid as informator choristarum and Edward Gibbons was not mentioned.[3] There were also quarterly payments to a custos organorum (who was never named); and there was expenditure from time to time on the repair and purchase of sackbuts, cornetts and viols.

Lugge was paid 10s 0d on 21 March 1637 'for mending the organs' and 2s 8d in the spring of 1638 for four candlesticks, two snuffers and mending the organ's bellows.[4]

From this, it appears that he carried out repairs himself. However, he was paid £3 8s 4d on 12 December 1638 'for John Loosemore's horse-hire charges, and payment for ten daies in mending and tuning the organs', which suggests that the work on this occasion was carried out by someone else. Loosemore was an organ-builder who lived at Barnstaple. Perhaps Lugge and the custos organorum were able to carry out minor repairs but needed to send for specialist help when work of a substantial nature was required.[5]

The mention of Loosemore is noteworthy, being the first reference in the records of Exeter Cathedral to a man who would gain a central place in the story of the cathedral's organs.

There is nothing in the records to suggest that the cathedral's musical provision was anything but routine in the 1630s. However, trouble was brewing in the city. Puritanism had been increasing in Exeter since about 1600, and ancient rivalries between the City Chamber (the City Council) and the cathedral's authorities had intensified. And nationally, relations between Parliament and King Charles I had been growing ever more strained.

Lugge and Gibbons would have been aware of all this, especially in 1638, when a cathedral porter defied the city's authorities and a riot ensued near the cathedral. Furthermore, there were protests in Exeter in February 1639, when the King ordered his troops to march to the north, showing, as Mark Stoyle has pointed out in his study of the city in the first half of the seventeenth century, 'just how much national politics had begun to influence local affairs'.[6]

Mobs appeared increasingly frequently outside the cathedral, and the Chapter eventually took action, decreeing on 8 April 1640 that, 'whereas we find dayly the Church be much abused and prophaned by the standing open of the doors all dayes, the Church and Cloisters shalbe kept shutt and not opened but in the tyme of divine service and sermons'.[7] Nationally, relations between Parliament and King Charles I continued to deteriorate. When the Civil War began (on 22 August 1642), the City Chamber had a large Puritan majority and sided with the Parliamentarians.

Troubled Times

Lugge was paid as organist throughout 1641 and 1642 and twice received payment in 1642 for work on the organ.[8] William Wake was paid as informator choristarum in the first two quarters of 1641 and all four quarters of 1642, and Edward Gibbons was paid for carrying out the duties of that post in the third and fourth quarters of 1641.[9] The musical life of the cathedral appears, therefore, to have continued untroubled through the unsettled times of the early 1640s.

A hint of problems to come can be found, however, in the Chapter Acts for 12 November 1642, when it was recorded that the Mayor of Exeter had pressed the Dean and Chapter 'to contribute something towards the fortification of this citty'.[10] And the fears of the municipal authorities were realized in December 1642, when an army of Royalists approached the city. The Westminster Parliament responded. A decree was issued on 12 December:[11]

> It is this day ordered, by the Lords and Commons in Parliament assembled, in regard of the great and imminent danger the City of Exon is now in, the same being threatened to be besieged, and sacked, and plundered, . . . that such part of the Common Prayer and Service as is performed by singing-men, choristers, and organs, in the Cathedral Church there, be wholly forborn and omitted; and the same to be done in a reverend, humble, and decent manner, without singing, or using the organs.

The city's authorities acted immediately. The cathedral was locked and services were banned.

Parliamentary reinforcements reached Exeter on 6 January 1643 and repelled the Royalists who were trying to take the city. Soon afterwards, a mob of Roundheads and Exeter citizens demanded the keys of the cathedral and went on a rampage, breaking windows, damaging monuments and effigies, and defacing and destroying decorations they considered 'popish'. Members of the cathedral's clergy and others were forced to pay large sums of money towards the Roundhead cause, among them Edward Gibbons, the master of the choristers, who was, as noted in Chapter 1, a wealthy man. He was ordered to pay £50.[12]

In a counter-offensive, Royalists besieged Exeter for nearly three months and took the city on 4 September 1643. At some time that year, most likely during the rampage in January, the organ in the cathedral was damaged. In the words of a Royalist propaganda tract, *Mercurius Rusticus*, written by the Rev Bruno Ryves, chaplain to King Charles I:[13]

> They brake down the organs, and taking two or three hundred pipes with them, in a most scornefull, contemptuous manner, went up and down the streets, piping with them: and meeting with some of the choristers of the church, whose surplesses they had stolen before, and imployed them to base, servile offices, scoffingly told them 'Boyes we have spoyled your trade; you must go and sing hot Pudding Pies'.

This was written towards the end of 1643 and may have exaggerated events in Exeter, but it is essentially correct, and is supported by other contemporary reports.

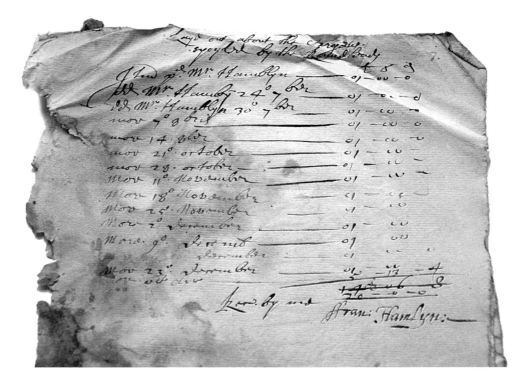

Figure 2.1   Document headed 'layd out about the organs spoyled by the
Roundheads', showing weekly payments totalling £20 for repairing the organ in
the last three months of 1643.

Ryves stated that 'the Holy Liturgie lay totally silenced for the space of three
quarters of a yeare'. This is borne out by the Chapter Acts. The Chapter met on
17 December 1642 and did not meet again until 9 September 1643.[14] Interestingly,
though, payments to the organist, informator choristarum and custos organorum
continued to be made while the cathedral was closed. John Mayne was the organist
paid in March 1643, not John Lugge, but the latter was paid in June and September
of that year.[15] Edward Gibbons was paid as the master of the choristers throughout
the period of closure.

The organ was repaired soon after the cathedral reopened, but we do not know by
whom. A document which is headed 'Layd out about the organs spoyled by the
Roundheads' shows that the work of repairing the organ took three months (mid-
September to mid-December) and that weekly payments totalling £20 were made
to Francis Hamlyn.[16] The damage sustained by the instrument had clearly been
substantial.[17] The Chapter decreed on 27 April 1644 that Mr Hamlyn was to receive

the £20 which he had claimed 'for mending of the organ' and that Henry Foster was to be paid 'ten shillings for blowing and attending the organ'.[18] Thus, it is clear that the organ was repaired in the latter part of 1643.

The Westminster Parliament ordered on 9 May 1644 that:[19]

> All Organs, and the Frames or Cases wherein they stand, in all Churches and Chapels aforesaid, shall be taken away and utterly defaced, and none other hereafter set up in their Places; whereunto all Persons within this Kingdom whom it may concern are hereby required at their Peril to yield due Obedience.

This was ignored in Exeter. The city was then in Royalist hands.

John Lugge was paid as organist throughout 1644 and 1645 and in March 1646; and payments were also made to the master of the choristers, who was sometimes shown as William Wake but more often than not Edward Gibbons. A 'service book for the organ' was bought in the autumn of 1645;[20] and a payment was made to the choristers on 5 April 1646.[21] It therefore appears that choral services with organ accompaniment continued into the early part of 1646.

The Organ Silenced

Parliamentary forces began a blockade of Exeter in late 1645. Eventually, on 9 April 1646, with the city bankrupt and disease-ridden and its citizens starving and demoralized, a surrender was agreed. The New Model Army entered Exeter four days later.

Chapter meetings did not cease immediately. The last was held on Saturday 6 June 1646, when the Dean and Chapter considered a demand that they hand over to the Parliamentary authorities their books of accounts, rentals and other documents.[22] They refused and, indeed, managed to spirit them away. A great many have survived to this day.

We may wonder what happened to the organist and the master of the choristers after choral services were abandoned in 1646. Both Lugge and Gibbons were elderly by then, Lugge in his mid-sixties, Gibbons nearly eighty. Lugge died sometime in the period 1647 to 1655 and Gibbons in 1649 or 1650.[23]

Many believe the organ was destroyed in 1646, citing the report by Bruno Ryves quoted above. However, the report was but one of a series published as a compilation in 1646 with a title page which stated that the events described had all taken place before 25 March 1646, when Exeter was still in Royalist hands. Moreover, Ryves made clear that the rampage he described had occurred during 'the space of three quarters of a yeare the Holy Liturgie lay totally silenced', i.e. December 1642 to September 1643.

It was agreed under the terms of Exeter's surrender (Article 5) that neither 'the cathedral church nor any other church within the city shall be defaced, or any thing belonging thereunto spoiled or taken away by any soldier or person of either side whatsoever'.[24] Those who assert that the terms of the surrender were quickly broken are contradicted by contemporary reports. There was no wilful damage to the cathedral after the surrender.[25]

We do not know what then happened to the cathedral's organ. No reference to it in the period 1646 to 1656 has yet come to light. We can only conjecture, but there are some possibilities for which there is a little circumstantial evidence.

It was recorded in an Act Book of the City Chamber on 18 November 1656, soon after the municipal authorities had taken over the cloisters to convert them into a market place, that 'Mr. Gandy and Mr. Slade or either of them are desired by this house to be assisting to Mr. Receiver in the disposing and sale of the organs lying in the cloysters'.[26] In the words of Cotton and Woollcombe, 'that objectionable popish instrument had been removed from the cathedral and stowed away in the cloisters'.[27] We do not know when or by whom it had been removed.

Presbyterians and Independents both used the cathedral church for their worship in the 1650s, but, to quote Cotton and Woollcombe, 'singing formed a leading feature in the services of the one, which was a practice abhorred by the other, and both desired to assemble for worship at the same hours'.[28] To overcome this difficulty, a wall was built in 1657 to separate 'Peter the East', where the Presbyterians worshipped, from 'West Peter', where the Independents worshipped. As minuted by the City Chamber on 11 August 1657:[29]

> Who doe alsoe agree that the partition of the Cathedrall Church of S. Peters bee made with a brick wall on the East parte of the Crosse Ile where the Organs stood closeing upp the bodye or midle Ile upon a foundacon which is already there.

Exactly where the wall was has long been debated. Was it close to the pulpitum or actually across its upper surface, where the organ had long stood?

Was the organ sold in 1656 or 1657? If so, to whom? An answer to this question may be provided by a licence issued by the Customs' Commissioners on 16 January 1656 'to permit an organ to be shipped and brought from Exeter to London by sea for His Highness's use'.[30] 'His Highness' was none other than the Lord Protector, Oliver

Cromwell, who was a lover of music and especially liked organ music. Indeed, he acquired the organ from the chapel of Oxford's Magdalen College and had it set up in the Great Hall of Hampton Court Palace, where his secretary, the poet John Milton, played it for the pleasure of His Highness. Puritans did not object to music and organs as such, only to their use in worship.

No evidence that the organ was indeed shipped from Exeter to London has been found. It has been suggested that it was either broken up as useless lumber in 1656, 'melted up in the Cloisters by night' or possibly shipped secretly by night.[31] If the organ did go to London, where might it have gone? An inventory of Hampton Court Palace made in 1659, after the death of Oliver Cromwell, shows there were then two organs in the Great Hall, 'one large Organ and a Chaire Organ which was brought from Maudlin Colledge in Oxford, value about £300'.[32] Perhaps these two organs were really two parts of the same instrument, the one acquired from Oxford. It is known that this instrument, built by Robert Dallam in 1631, was a double organ (i.e. an organ with two divisions).

Organ Music Returns to the Cathedral

If any of Exeter Cathedral's organ did go to London, was any of it then returned in 1660 after the Restoration of the Monarchy? We do not know. The Chapter gave 'a poore man two shillings for preserving four organ pipes' in October 1660 and the same day gave 'a poore man two shillings and sixpence for preserving the King's Arms formerly placed over the organs'.[33] These are the only records yet discovered of any parts of an organ being returned to the cathedral after the Restoration.[34] Magdalen College recovered their organ in 1660, paying the sum of £16 10s 0d for it to be taken back to Oxford.[35]

The first meeting of the Dean and Chapter after the Restoration took place in the Chapter House on 31 August 1660, and the work of repairing the cathedral soon began.[36] The first reference to an organ came on 1 October 1660, when Robert Blechyndon, the clerk of the works, was paid 1s 6d 'for a candlestick and carrying up the organ pipes'.[37] This suggests that work on building an organ had started in September 1660. It is unlikely this instrument was built on the pulpitum, for if the partition wall which had been built in 1657 was indeed there it had first to be removed. That demolition work was ordered by the House of Lords on 1 September 1660 and carried out in October, November and December 1660.[38]

An opportunity to investigate the upper surface of the pulpitum was presented when the organ was dismantled in 2013. An exciting discovery was made. Many of the decorated tiles which had been laid in the 1320s were found, along with a number of larger plain tiles of much later date. The latter were in a strip about three feet wide across the top of the pulpitum along its north–south axis. This may be evidence that the wall had been built across the top, with the plain tiles showing where the surface had been repaired when the wall was removed.[39]

The first specific mention of John Loosemore since 1638 came on 10 November 1660, when the Chapter ordered that he be paid £5 'towards the making of a sett of pipes to the organ which is to be used in this church'.[40] He was paid £5 'more' on 14 February 1661 'toward the perfecting of the organs' or, as it was put in the Chapter Acts, 'towards the repairing of his organs'.[41] Finally, on 2 April 1661, he was paid £40 'for perfecting the organs newly erected in the cathedral'.[42]

Son of Samuel Loosemore, an organ-builder, John was born in North Devon in 1613 or early 1614 and brought up in Barnstaple.[43] He carried out work on the organ in Hartland parish church from 1634 onwards and also tuned and repaired the organ in Tawstock House (near Barnstaple) in the latter part of the 1630s and early 1640s.[44] He relocated from Barnstaple to Exeter at some time between late 1642 and the summer of 1645 and resided there for the rest of his life.[45] He found employment as an instrument-maker and craftsman during the Interregnum, and also maintained the organ in Tawstock House.

It is not surprising that the Chapter turned to Loosemore to provide an organ when they repossessed the cathedral in August 1660. He was an experienced organ-builder who lived near the cathedral and had, as previously noted, worked on the cathedral's organ in 1638.[46] Moreover, he could conceivably have been the organ-builder who repaired the organ in 1643, possibly removing to Exeter for that purpose soon after the Royalists took the city. We may speculate further and wonder if he acquired any parts of the organ stored in the cloisters in 1656 and used them in the instrument he produced so quickly for the cathedral in 1660–61.[47]

Loosemore was allowed to use the Chapter House as his workshop and clearly overstayed his welcome, for on 12 April 1662, a year after the organ had been completed, the Chapter ordered the Chapter Clerk to give him notice to 'to remove his organs'.[48] Chapter meetings had been held in the Lady Chapel since the middle of September 1660, and the Dean and Chapter clearly wished to return to the Chapter House.

The Organists of the Early 1660s

The offices of organist, custos organorum and informator choristarum were included in the Ordinary Solutions for the quarters ending on Christmas Day 1660 and Lady Day 1661, with 'Nil' written against each office each quarter.[49] The first indication that choral services would soon be resumed came on 14 March 1661, when the Chapter 'ordered the two houses in the Cloisters appointed for the Singing School to be forthwith fitted for that use'.[50] Four days later, twelve choristers were admitted;[51] and on 30 March the Chapter 'ordered £20 [*per annum*] to be paid quarterly unto Mr Thomas Moore for his paynes in teaching the choristers until either he or some other person be appointed sub-chanter'.[52] The Chapter ordered on 11 May 1661 'that gownes be provided for the choristers that soe they may be in a comely condicion to serve in the quire';[53] and salaries were paid to the organist, custos organorum and informator choristarum for the quarter which ended on St John's Day 1661.[54] After a break of fifteen years, choral services with organ accompaniment had resumed.[55]

The recipients of the organist and custos organorum payments in June 1661 were, respectively, William Hopwood and Richard Williams, and it is clear from additional payments to the latter on 25 May 1661 and a number of subsequent occasions that he was also the organ-blower.[56] We know nothing of his background, but he proved a loyal and reliable servant of the cathedral for many years.

Nothing is known of Hopwood's education, musical or otherwise. The first reference to him as a member of the cathedral community came in the Chapter Acts of 6 October 1660, when it was recorded that he be admitted into a lay vicar's place and installed by a priest vicar who was also called William Hopwood.[57] The new lay vicar was then a young man, baptized in Exeter Cathedral on 4 November 1641, and we may wonder if family influence played any part in his appointment as organist. The priest vicar was his father.[58] On the other hand, the young man may have been the most competent organist available at the time, given the scarcity of organists after the church music deprivations of the Interregnum.

Though employed first and foremost as organist, Hopwood was paid £5 on 12 October 1661 for 'teaching the boyes, one quarter before Mr Moore took the employment on him'.[59] This suggests that Moore had not taken up the post of informator choristarum straightaway when appointed at the end of March 1661. However, the Ordinary Solutions show that he was in fact paid the quarterage due to him as master of the choristers in both June and September 1661.[60] Perhaps Hopwood had taught the boys before Moore was appointed and only now, several months later, received payment.

Hopwood remained organist until the autumn of 1664, when, on 25 October, he was admitted a gentleman of the Chapel Royal.[61] His job at Exeter went to Thomas Mudd, who had in fact been one of the cathedral's organists for several months, appointed by the Chapter on 5 March 1664 'to be one of the organists, and to sing in the quire, and to have £20 *per annum* for his salary *quam diu se bene gesserit* [provided he conducted himself well]'. He was also paid '£4 for his clothes and charges'.[62]

A person called 'Mudd' was first mentioned in the records of Exeter Cathedral on 9 February 1661, when the Chapter ordered 50s 0d to be given to him 'to be paid by 2s

6*d* a week'.[63] Only two months later, though, on 6 April 1661, the Chapter ordered £3 to be given to him 'and the remainder of the money formerly given to him to bear his charges in his journey for London'.[64] No reason was given for the journey, but it would appear that he was not expected to return, for on 18 May 1661 the Chapter ordered that the Dean should 'have power to dispose of the house wherein Mudd lately dwelt'.[65]

It is believed that the Mudd who was at Exeter in 1661 in some unspecified capacity was the same man who returned as one of the organists alongside Hopwood in 1664, having been employed meanwhile at Peterborough Cathedral in 1662 and 1663 and, briefly, Lincoln Cathedral in 1663.[66] He was paid as organist at Lincoln but dismissed for unruly behaviour and drunkenness, which may explain why Exeter's Chapter felt it necessary to include in the Acts *quam diu se bene gesserit*. Employing a man who had previously behaved disgracefully was evidently and understandably considered a risk.

In the event, Mudd did not stay long in Exeter. He was paid his quarterage of £5 on 15 March 1665 but the same day received an additional £3 15*s* 0*d* 'by way of augmentation this quarter and in full of all dimands', which suggests he had been dismissed.[67] The Chapter voted him a further £20 on 26 August 1665 for some unspecified purpose, after which he was never again mentioned in the Exeter Cathedral records.[68] Theodore Colby was appointed organist on 25 March 1665, with a salary of £50 *per annum* and 'a house to be provided for him'.[69]

By then, a new organ had been built in the cathedral, but before we turn our attention to it we note that the Chapter ordered on 31 December 1664 that £10 'be remitted unto John Loosemore (of the £30 he oweth to the church) for his charges in his London journey about the churches business'.[70] The nature of the business was not stated, but it has been suggested that it concerned the appointment of a new organist.[71] If so, the uncharacteristic vagueness of the Chapter Act could show that the Dean and Chapter were not satisfied with Mudd and did not wish to be open about it if they were minded to dismiss him once a suitable successor had been found.

Colby seems to have been unemployed at the time. He had been organist of Oxford's Magdalen College from 1661 until he resigned sometime in 1664 and may have resided in London thereafter. Exeter's Chapter ordered on 1 April 1665 that '£5 be given to Mr Colby towards his charges in coming from London and ryding upp'.[72]

Loosemore's Masterpiece

Since completing the organ he built in 1660–61, Loosemore had built another in the cathedral, this one certainly on the pulpitum, where its magnificent case remains to this day. Work on it began in 1663.

The Chapter ordered on 7 February that year 'that Mr Loosemore shalbe sent into Cornwall unto my Lord of Bath att the common charge of the Chapter to make choice of Tyn for the new organs to be made in this church', and he clearly went quite soon, for the Chapter ordered on 7 March that 'the horsehire for Mr Loosemore and his man be paid for their journey into Cornwall'.[73] The Earl of Bath was Lord Warden of the Stanneries and therefore the person who controlled the price of tin from the mines of Devon and Cornwall.[74]

The Chapter further ordered on 4 April 1663 'that the seiling and other tymber work for the Organ shalbe speedily taken in hand by Mr Loosemore and others', their weekly wages 'not exceeding 50s 0d or £3'.[75] And later that year, on 17 October 1663, the Chapter agreed to pay Loosemore's 'charges in riding to Salisbury to see the organ there, the better to informe himselfe to make the new organ of this church'.[76] The organ of Salisbury Cathedral had been dismantled in 1643, to save it from destruction, and re-erected in 1661.[77]

There was no further mention of Exeter's organ until 5 December 1664, when it was recorded in the Extraordinary Solutions (book of quarterly and occasional payments) that the sum of £407 10s 10d had been paid 'towards the great organs over and beside the £500 parte of Staverton fine and £2 odd money for shavings of lead'.[78] Thus, the Chapter seemed to think the cost of the organ was £909 10s 10d.

However, Loosemore's own account, dated 13 December 1664, made 'the total sume the Organ cost' £847 7s 10d; and he grumbled that he could have obtained a better deal if he had purchased tin before the Earl of Bath arrived in Cornwall.[79] Furthermore, he said, costs which were nothing to do with the organ had been included in the Chapter's account. As he put it:

> In not bying tinne in Seson thare was in every hundred[weight] lost 46 shillings for I could have bought a littell before the Erle of Bath came downe in the Cuntrey for £4 a hundred 6 score and 2 [lb] to the hundred, and wee paide afterward £5–17s for 5 score and 12 to the hundred so that thare is lost 4 score pounde or upward in this. When wee had measured the wenscot and counted how many thousand foote was in it wee found it 3 score pounde to deare. Mr Wriet [Mr Wright, the Cathedral's Treasurer] had the account. Then thare's eused in the Seats of the Church with the Maiors Seat above £30 worth of this timber which stands yet at the accounte of the Organ. Then the building of the Chimley and the inclosing of the worke house is all in this account. So thare is an £170 at least to be subtracted out of this account which is –
>
>   £   s   d
> 847-07-10
> 170-00-00
> 677-07-10

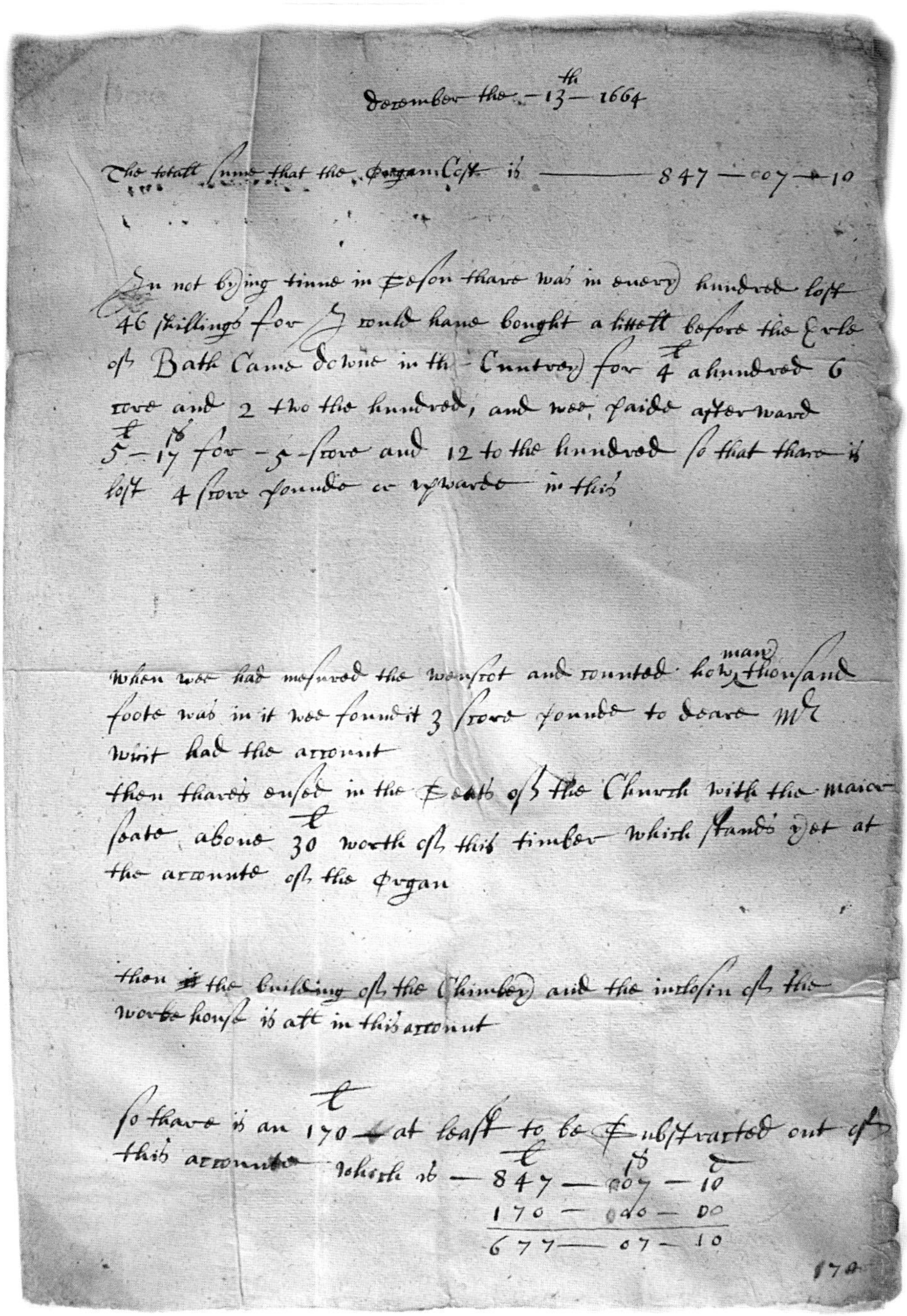

Figure 2.2   John Loosemore's account for 'the total sume the Organ cost', 13 December 1664.

We do not know exactly where the chimney and work-house were, but they were probably in or very close to the cloisters. The indenture for the premises let to Loosemore by the Dean and Chapter on 26 January 1661 included the words 'messuage tenement and house with the appurtenances lately erected and built upon part of the cloisters'.[80] Thus, the dwelling house which he rented in the cloisters had an outbuilding and adjacent land assigned to its use. He would presumably have used the outbuilding as his workshop, and the chimney would have been associated with a furnace which was used to melt tin.

Loosemore said in his account that he had paid £5 17s 0d for every hundredweight of 112 lb, whereas he could have bought tin at £4 per hundredweight of 122 lb before the Earl of Bath arrived.[81] By so doing, he had paid at least '4 score pounde' (£80) more than he need have done. When added to the wainscoting being £60 too dear and the £30 cost of timber being included incorrectly in the organ account, the £80 excess for tin accounted for the £170 'to be subtracted'. However, the higher price for tin should not have formed part of the £170, because it had already been paid and therefore could not be recovered or transferred to another heading in the cathedral's accounts.

We may never know the true cost of the new organ, but we can calculate from Loosemore's statement that he purchased about 1.8 tons of tin, which was roughly twice the amount Playssher had bought for the organ he built in 1513. Unfortunately, no specification of Loosemore's organ has been found, so we can do no more than rely on a description of the instrument by a visitor in the early 1680s, clues in the Chapter Acts and accounts, and inferences based on modifications made by later organ-builders.

The new organ was first used in divine worship sometime in the spring of 1665. The Chapter ordered on 27 May 1665 that 'the old organ be taken down att the charge of the Chapter, and delivered to such as Mr Archdeacon [Edward] Cotton shall appoint'.[82] Payments for making good where the organ of 1660–61 had stood were made on 5 November 1665, when Mr Robbins was paid 'the Mason's bill dated 30 August for worke donne where the syde-organ stood', and on 14 November, when Mr Blechyndon was paid 'germaine the Hilyar's (tiler's) bill dated 6 November for worke where the syde-organ stood'.[83]

The magnificent case that was built in 1665 towers above the pulpitum to this day and remains essentially the product of Loosemore.[84] Its features have been described thus by Andrew Freeman:[85]

> The case presents several points of interest, amongst which may be mentioned the treatment of the central flat tower of the east front, in which the middle pipe of the five which compose it is made to project beyond the others – the

V-shaped additions to both bracket and cornice thus rendered necessary, adding considerably to the effect. The end towers of this front are larger than semi-circles, while all three towers of the west front are semi-circular. In both fronts, the intermediate spaces are divided into tiers, but whereas the lower tiers are very similar, and both fronts have small circular compartments in the second stage, the east front has additional features in the form of two small towers placed high up between the circular compartments and the outer towers. . . . The instrument, which has overhanging sides, has a commanding appearance. The pipe-shades are cut so as to fit each pipe separately. Perhaps the only points that can be urged against this splendidly executed, and in all other respects finely designed case are that the caps of the two circular towers of its east front are rather too heavy, and the two diminutive towers somewhat fussy.

The main case was certainly made by Loosemore, but there are stylistic differences between it and the Chair case. This being so, we may ask a number of questions. Did Loosemore make the Chair case, or did he merely install his Chair Organ in a pre-existing case? Had that case remained in position over the doorway at the western end of the quire right through the Civil War and ensuing Interregnum? After all, removing it would have left an unsightly gap on the eastern face of the pulpitum. Moreover, organ cases bereft of their pipes and action were not uncommon during the Interregnum.[86] If Loosemore did not make the Chair case, who did? Could it have been Thomas Dallam in the early 1620s? We may never know.

The Chief among Craftsmen of His Kind

Soon after completing his masterpiece, Loosemore built two more organs. One was an instrument for the cathedral's Singing School, the other an organ for Nettlecombe Court, an Elizabethan mansion near Watchet, western Somerset.

The organ for the Singing School had one keyboard. Its pipes were all wooden and the ranks were, according to Hopkins and Rimbault: Stop Diapason, Open Diapason, Principal, Twelfth, Fifteenth and Flute.[87] The compass of the instrument was four octaves, from the C two octaves below middle C to the C two octaves above, with some sharp notes omitted from the bass section. The organ was still intact in 1847, when Sir John Sutton noted that it had been 'preserved more for curiosity than use';[88] and the organ-builder J.C. Hele noted in 1890 that it was then spread about above the vaulting of the nave (its natural keys black, the sharps white, and the whole instrument about the size of a harmonium). It appears to have disappeared sometime between the middle of the 1920s and the end of World War II.[89]

We do not know what happened to the organ that was built in 1660–61 and delivered to Archdeacon Cotton in 1665. It may have been moved to the Singing School.

Figure 2.3   Organ cases bereft of their pipes and action were not uncommon during the Interregnum. It is possible that the Chair case of the organ remained in position on the eastern face of the pulpitum throughout the Interregnum.

However, an entry in the Chapter Acts Book a decade later, on 1 January 1676, stated that the Chapter had 'ordered satisfaction to be given to Mr Loosemore for removing the organ given by Archdeacon Cotton into the Chapter House'.[90] The records of the cathedral do not shed any light on which organ this was or where it came from.

The organ on the pulpitum suffered a few teething troubles. A smith was paid 10s 0d in October 1666 for 'mending' it, and Loosemore was paid £5 on 16 March 1667 'for to buy tymber etc for the making a new paire of bellows for the organs'.[91] Over and above this, Loosemore was paid a further £7 15s 8d a month later (13 April) and £1 10s 8d on 20 August 1667 'for worke on the organ'.[92] Meanwhile, some of those who had been involved in the building of the organ in the first place had had to wait a while for payment. Robert Blechyndon was paid the large sum of £24 16s 9d on 16 February 1666 for the smith's bill dated 31 May 1665 in respect of 'worke donne on the great organs', and he was paid an additional 15s 8d the same day for the hilyar's bill dated 14 December 1665 'for worke donne on the stairs leading to the organ loft'.[93]

After 1667, the organ appears to have functioned trouble-free for many years. The Chapter Acts and accounts contain no mention of any unusual expenditure on it. The only payments were to Loosemore, for tuning and routine maintenance, for which, as we see from the Chapter Acts on 9 September 1671, £15 was paid yearly to him 'for repaireing and keeping in tune the Organ of the Church, *vizt* tenn pounds to be allowed for the rent of his house (wherein he now lives) and five pounds to be paid him in mony'.[94] The Extraordinary Solutions confirm that he was indeed paid £1 5s 0d each quarter 'for tuning the organ'.[95]

Loosemore was clerk of the works by 1671, having been appointed successor to Robert Blechyndon on 8 January 1670. For tuning and maintaining the organ, he was already being, or would soon be, assisted by John Shearme, who became his son-in-law in 1675. The marriage settlement, dated 9 March 1675, showed Shearme's occupation as 'organ maker' and stated that his father-in-law was to hand to Shearme 'all the tooles that belong to the saide trade'.[96] Moreover, Loosemore promised that he would 'not for the future take upon him any further newe worke but leave the same wholy unto the said John Shearme except the mending and repearinge of such worke ashallbeen heare to fore perfected of which the said John Loosemore is to hand the moytie'.[97] Under the settlement, Loosemore agreed to make over to Shearme his house in the cloisters, with the exception of one room for himself.

A further agreement between Loosemore and Shearme was signed on 15 April 1676, this one binding them to tune and maintain the organ at their own cost and charges during the term of the lease for £15 a year.[98] Now, for the first time, we find a reference to a specific stop, for Loosemore and Shearme agreed to add 'a new stopp or sett of mettle pipes in imitation of an humane voice', with the Dean and Chapter providing the tin for the purpose. The stop appears to have been a Vox Humana, but we do not know if it was in fact added. It was not mentioned by any of the organ-builders who submitted tenders for renovation work on the organ in the early eighteenth century.

The Dean and Chapter proposed in the late 1670s that the organ pipes be gilded. However, the Bishop of Exeter rejected the idea. He noted in his response to the Chapter (dated 29 December 1679) that the work would be paid for out of a legacy from a Mr Bold but said that he could not 'be justly charged with any intention to burthen either you or your successors'.[99] His view was that the gilding would in due course need to be renewed, and he did not wish to commit a future Chapter to that expense.

Payments to Loosemore continued up to and including the last quarter of 1680 and then ceased. An indication that his death was anticipated came in the Chapter Acts for 26 March 1681, when it was decreed that 'the Office of Overseer of the Works' be granted to John Caroll 'after the death of Mr Loosemore'.[100] In the event, though, the job went to Shearme, for the Chapter decided on 30 April 1681 to grant him 'the Office of Clerk of the Works now voide by the death of Mr John Loosemore'.[101]

Loosemore died on 18 April and was buried in the cathedral two days later, at the eastern end of the nave, near the entrance to the south quire aisle, only a few yards from the organ he had created and maintained.[102] The following was inscribed on his gravestone:[103]

> Hic jacet Spe Resurrectionis Johannes Loosmore quondam Decano & Capitulo Huius Ecclesiæ Curator fidelissimus et inter Artifices sui Generis facile Princeps sit Organum hoc augustum prope situm Perpetuum illius Artis et Ingenii Monumentum. Obiit 18 Aprilis An: 1681 Aeta suae 68.

The Chapter showed their gratitude by agreeing on 14 May 1681 that 'the fees of breaking the ground' for Loosemore's grave 'in the body of the Church' be 'remitted'.[104]

Only two years after Loosemore's death, the Lord Keeper of the Great Seal (Francis North, Baron Guilford) visited the cathedral. He was clearly impressed by the largest pipes of the organ. In the words of the Hon. Roger North, one of his descendants:[105]

> His Lordship, agreeably to his great mastership of music, took great notice of the organ in the cathedral church at Exeter, where the two side columns, that carry the tower, are lined with organ pipes, and are as columns themselves. His lordship desired the dimensions of the great double diapason; and the account, as returned, is thus:-

	Feet.	Inches.
Speaking part, long	20	6
Nose	4	0
Circumference	3	11
Diameter	1	3

Baron Guilford gave the 'content of the speaking part' of this largest pipe as three hogsheads eight gallons (i.e. about 158 imperial gallons) and the weight of the pipe as 360 lb.[106]

Impressed though he was by the Double Diapason pipes, Baron Guilford was critical of their performance. He wrote thus of the largest pipe:[107]

Figure 2.4   Loosemore ledger stone, north quire aisle.

This is heard plainer at a distance than when near, as also louder: and behind
that, and the other large doubles, are placed large wooden pipes to help them
into their sound, which otherwise would come on very slow, or, perhaps, not
at all. One, being near enough, may by the touch of the hand, discern when
it speaks, and when not. How it is tuned, whether by measure or the beats,
we were not informed; and, bating their account of it, which was curious and
diverting enough, I could not be so happy to perceive that, in the music, they
signified anything at all, but thought them made more for ostentation than use:
for there are terms in sound which will not be exceeded; for, when the vibratory
pulses are so slow as may be distinguished, sound vanisheth; which is, nearly,
the case of this great pipe.

Baron Guilford did not know that the length of a sound wave is the speed of sound
divided by the frequency (pitch) of the note. The pipe whose dimensions he quoted
played the G three and a half octaves below middle C. The frequency of that note is
about 24 cycles per second, and the speed of sound at a temperature of 20°C is 343
metres per second. Therefore, the length of the wave produced by the biggest pipe

is 343 divided by 24, i.e. 14.3 metres (47 feet). To hear fully the note played by the pipe in question, the listener had to be at least that distance away. It is therefore not surprising that the pipes were 'heard plainer at a distance than when near'. Whether the wind supply was sufficient for the pipes is another matter, to which we return in Chapter 3.

The Organists of the 1670s and 1680s

By the time the Prince of Orange visited the cathedral, Colby was no longer the organist. He had left the cathedral's employ in the summer of 1674, in mysterious circumstances. He signed for his quarterage in June 1674, and his signature was as firm and clear as it had always been.[108] He certainly did not sign with a cross, as some have asserted.[109] Documents in the cathedral archives contain no hint of any problem over his conduct or competence. He was still in early 1674 teaching choristers and others to play the organ, as he had been paid to do since 1667. The only record that may be considered critical of him was the Chapter Act of 21 October 1671 which ordered him to 'remove his books and papers from the library and likewise to deliver the key of the said library which is now in his possession'.[110]

And yet, a new organist was appointed on 8 August 1674, when the Chapter 'pronounced the organist's place of this church to be void, upon Mr Colbie's absenting himself'.[111] It is possible he had died or become incapable through illness, for a payment of £30 to Mrs Colby for the use of his children was approved by the Chapter on 8 August and paid to her in September 1674. But if he had died or become ill, the Chapter Acts would surely have said so. Perhaps he had fallen on hard times. He had been lent substantial sums in 1668 and 1670 'towards the supplying of his present necessities'.[112]

The new organist was Henry Hall, whose name first appeared in the records of Exeter Cathedral on 6 December 1673, when the Chapter agreed to pay him £20 *per annum* to teach singing and organ-playing.[113] He was a young man, born in Berkshire in *c.*1656 and one of the Children of the Chapel Royal until late 1672.[114] He was an organist at Wells Cathedral in early 1674, and it is possible that he subsequently assisted at Salisbury Cathedral, for it was recorded in Exeter Cathedral's Extraordinary Solutions in the Midsummer to Michaelmas quarter of 1674 that £8 had been paid to Dr Cotton 'for so much layde out by him to Mr Hall organist to bring him from Sarum'.[115]

Hall did not stay at Exeter for long. He was dismissed in June 1679, for having 'deserted his place of organist of this Church'.[116] There appears to have been no problem before that year. He was paid his stipend every quarter up to and including December 1678 but then disappeared from the payroll. The Ordinary Solutions

list Charles Ford as organist in March 1679 and Peter Pasmore in June, while the
Extraordinary Solutions show that John White was paid in June 1679 for playing
the organ in Hall's absence.[117] The Chapter admitted 'Peter Pasmore (one of the lay
vicars of this church) into the place of organist' on 14 June 1679.

Hall was assistant organist of Hereford Cathedral by 27 June 1679 and progressed
to become organist of that cathedral on 15 September 1688, remaining so until his
death in 1707. He composed his first anthems while at Exeter and became well
known while at Hereford as an organist, composer and poet. Indeed, Bruce Wood
has called him 'the most distinguished among the lesser composers of Purcell's
generation'.[118]

While at Exeter, Hall may have felt uncomfortable or inadequate over Pasmore,
for the latter had been a chorister in Exeter Cathedral and had, in 1677 and 1678,
received organ lessons in London from the organist of Westminster Abbey, John
Blow. These lessons had been paid for, and his travel expenses defrayed, by
Exeter's Chapter.[119] On the other hand, Watkins Shaw has suggested that Pasmore
may have been 'influenced in this by Hall, who was himself an admiring pupil of
Blow'.[120] Be all this as it may, the link between Pasmore and Blow continued, for
on 6 October 1683 Exeter's Chapter agreed that a chorister, Robert Hodge, should
go to London to learn the organ and composition from Blow.[121] And in February
1685, it was recorded in the Chapter Acts that Pasmore was sick in London and
advised to remain there until he recovered his health.[122] It appears that he was
visiting Blow at the time.

The Chapter appointed John White assistant organist on 23 October 1680, with a
salary of £20 *per annum*, a decision made 'for the better supply of the quire in the
organist's absence and upon special occasions requiring the organist's presence in
his [vicar choral's] stall and for the honour of this church'.[123] He and Pasmore were
appointed on 24 July 1686 to 'tune and keepe the organs in the Cathedrall Church,
and allowed the salary of £15 *per annum* formerly allow'd to Mr Shearme for the
same, they undertaking the same'.[124] Shearme had recently died. Meanwhile, on
24 October 1685, 'upon the removal of the widow Crabb out of the Cloisters to an
hospitall of better provision, they [the Chapter] order'd that chamber in the cloister
to be given to Richard Williams the bellowes blower of the organ for his life'.[125]

White was probably the organist when, on 9 November 1688, the Prince of Orange
gave thanks in the cathedral for his safe arrival in England and sat in the bishop's
seat to hear read his declaration of peaceful intent to preserve the Protestant religion.
Besides reporting that 'the organs played very sweetly' while the Prince processed
along the nave to the quire, John Whittle stated that it was 'not the right organist
himself, he being gone aside on purpose, as I was inform'd there'.[126] Pasmore

had evidently chosen to absent himself, like most of the clergy and many of the choristers. Their flight from Exeter as a gesture of support for the catholic King James II proved, though, a lost cause. The Prince of Orange was crowned King William III of England in February 1689 and the Reformation which had begun in the 1530s was now complete. Henceforth, the place of music in the cathedral within a Protestant framework was assured.

CHAPTER 3

Defects and Decorations

After the visit of the Prince of Orange, life in the cathedral quickly returned to normal. The Dean and Chapter continued to support and encourage the musicians. There was a fine organ, and there were competent organists in post to play it. Musical standards in the cathedrals of England were generally low in the late seventeenth century, with organists and choristers frequently absent and badly behaved.[1] Exeter Cathedral had become an exception since the arrival of Peter Pasmore. Would it continue to be so?

A New Era

The need to appoint a new custos organorum arose quite soon after the visit of the Prince, for on 6 April 1689 the Chapter 'ordered Robert Bishop to have twelve pence per week for his paines in blowing the organ in Richard Williams's sickness and thought him fitt for the place of bellowes blower and custos organorum upon the death of Williams'.[2] The passing of the long-serving Williams occurred a few days later. He was last paid on 9 March 1689 and did not collect the payment in person. It was collected for him by William Humfrey.[3]

Bishop was appointed on 11 May 1689 and signed for his first quarterage (of £1 5s) five weeks later.[4] However, he held the post for only five years, passing away towards the end of October 1694. In the words of a Chapter Act on 10 November 1694: 'Robert Bishop custos organorum dying an month after Michaelmas they order'd half of the Christmas quarterage to be allowed his widow'.[5] As promised, she received 12s 6d on 21 December, and the other 12s 6d went to James Mortimore, the clock keeper.[6] The death of a custos organorum again seems to have been anticipated, for on 13 October 1694 the Chapter appointed Mortimore 'to perform the office of bellowes blower and custos organorum according to Mr Dean's and Mr Treasurer's request until they be further consulted'.[7]

Mortimore's appointment was short-lived. The Chapter 'admitted Henry Clase into the place and office of bellows blower and custos organorum' on 22 December 1694.[8] He was paid as such on 22 March 1695 and subsequently held the post for many years. Mortimore reverted to being clock keeper, a post he had held since 1690 and continued to hold until March 1744.[9]

Meanwhile, circumstances beyond Pasmore's control had prevented him from carrying out his duties as organist for a while. On 13 July 1690, in the course of hostilities between French and Anglo-Dutch forces, enemy ships had bombarded and partly destroyed Teignmouth, fifteen miles south of Exeter. Pasmore had been, in the words of a Chapter Act of 26 July, 'desired by the Deputy Lieutenant to take a commission and go towards the enemy and forme a party of the Posse'.[10] The Chapter had 'order'd leave to be given to him so to do and to have necessary supply'. Then, a week later, on 2 August, they had allowed him 'five guineas towards his expense in his commission pursuant to the act last Saturday, he having taken on him a commission of Cornet'.[11] He had not been away from the cathedral long. The invaders had soon been repulsed, and he had signed the Extraordinary Solutions book himself on 13 September 1690 when receiving his organist's stipend.

Pasmore and White were both paid for tuning the organ up to and including March 1693. Thereafter, however, until June 1694, Pasmore alone was paid for the tuning.[12] White was paid as an organist up to and including December 1693 and then appears to have retired or died, for it was recorded in the Chapter Acts on 17 February 1694 that 'the pension or salary of £20 *per annum* and formerly paid to Mr John White as organist shall for the future cease and be sunk together with the £5 *per annum* from the books of Extraordinary Solutions paid for tuneing the organs; and that £10 *per annum* be wholly allow'd to Mr Pasmore for tuneing'.[13]

Pasmore did not remain organist much longer. He was elected a priest vicar of Exeter Cathedral on 4 August 1694 and therefore had to seek holy orders and relinquish the positions of organist and lay vicar.[14] His last quarterage as organist was paid on 8 September 1694, but he remained at the cathedral for many years thereafter, not only as a priest vicar but also, from 1695, as clerk of the works.[15]

A Defective Organist

The Chapter appointed Richard Henman organist and lay vicar on 22 September 1694.[16] Baptized in Rochester, Kent, on 7 March 1669, he had sung in the choir at Rochester Cathedral from 1680 to 1682 and then in the choir of the Chapel Royal until 1692.[17] He had thus been taught by John Blow, then Master of the Children at the Chapel Royal, which raises the possibility that Pasmore, an organ pupil of Blow, had met Henman and recommended him to Exeter's Dean and Chapter. Regrettably, however, Henman proved a disappointment.

On 19 July 1695, after less than a year in post, he was ordered by the Chapter 'to be admonished to make himself capable and to qualify himself for his continuance in that place (complaint being made by the choir of his unfitness &c)'.[18] And dissatisfaction over the standard of his organ-playing did not end there, for he was again rebuked by the Chapter on 12 February 1698, when admonished 'to endeavour to improve and qualify himself better for the discharge of that office for the future, the choir having complain'd of his inabilitys to perform the same, *sub poena amissionis salarii* (under penalty of loss of salary)'.[19]

Dissatisfaction with Henman continued. He was reproved yet again on 15 July 1704, when the Chapter noted that he had been 'of late very negligent in attending the service of the church'.[20] They ordered that 'if at any time hereafter he be absent from Church without leave of the Dean or President of the Chapter and without providing some person to play the organ in his roome he shall for every such neglect forfeit tenn pence to be deducted out of his quarterly salary and paid to him that shall play for him, and if it should so happen that nobody plays the organ in the absence of Mr Henman then the forfeiture above specified to be to the use of the poor, and they admonished Mr Henman to take notice of this order and to attend the service of the quire in his lay vicar's place except on such days as the psalms are sung to the organ'.

Henman did not mend his ways. The Chapter reproved him on 2 November 1706 'for his ill language to Mr [John] Hicks and others of the choir and admonished him to behave himself more orderly for the future'.[21] And on 2 October 1714, for 'having absented himself for the space of two months past and upwards', the Chapter ordered him to be suspended *a beneficio* (without pay) and notice given him that if he did not 'forthwith attend and performe his duty in the Church' the Chapter would 'proceed to deprive him'.[22]

There was more to try the patience of the Chapter nine months later, as we find in a Chapter Act for 30 July 1715.[23] The Chapter noted that they had 'heard and examined the several complaints made in Chapter' against Henman and several other lay vicars concerning 'their continued refractoryness and disobedience in the performance of the services and anthems of the church from time to time and the aggravating circumstances thereof to the great dishonour of Almighty God and the disturbance of his service in this church, as well as in defiance of all order and good governance of the church'. Having 'weigh'd and well consider'd what the said offenders have been able severally to allege in the deniall or excuse of such their manifest offences', the Chapter 'did decree each of them severally guilty of the same and did suspend them *a beneficio* for a fortnight'.

Things had clearly come to a head now, for the Chapter put in place a new set of rules to govern the behaviour and duties of lay vicars and secondaries. The sub-chanter was ordered to be 'diligent in reviveing such services and anthems in this church as are valuable and have been disus'd and to lay before the Chapter on this day month a full account of all the musick in the church in order to his supplying such defects as may be found therein'. The lay vicars and secondaries were required to 'attend the sub-chanter at the Musick School as often as he shall summon them' and were also to receive the sacrament at least six times a year, of which Easter Day was always to be one.

Henman's attendance had left much to be desired over many years but worsened in the 1730s, when he was often reproved over it. The Chapter decreed on 8 February 1735, for example, that his pay be 'stopt till further order', without giving a reason.[24] Then, on 24 May, they relented a little and agreed that he should 'receive his pay which was formerly order'd to be stopt, deducting two guineas for John Sanders who has play'd the organ for him for one quarter'.[25] Later in the year, on 11 October, they ordered two guineas to be deducted out of his quarterage 'and paid to John Sanders the chorister for playing the organ as often as the sub-chanter appoints him to do it'.[26] And on 24 April 1736, the Chapter ordered three guineas per quarter to be paid to Sanders for playing the organ and deducted from the organist's pay.[27]

The Ordinary and Extraordinary Solutions show that Sanders was not the only person who deputized for Henman. Indeed, it was not unusual for two or even three people to be paid for playing.[28] From 1722 to 1735, either Edward Martyn or Anthony Martyn received payment nearly every quarter for doing so, and from 1735 onwards there were payments to either Edward or Anthony as well as to Sanders. William Doidge was paid in 1739, 1740 and the early part of 1741; Edward Collins was paid in two quarters of 1740; and Richard Holwell was paid in December 1739 and June 1741. Until January 1741, however, no one was formally designated as 'deputy organist'.

Henman seems to have been absent continuously in the latter part of the 1730s. On 10 June 1738, the Chapter 'order'd his pay to be stop'd till he gives his personall attendance on the service of the church'.[29] And on 19 May 1739, they 'order'd £4 to be paid quarterly to Mr Sanders for playing the organ in Mr Henman's absence and to be deducted out of the organist's pay'.[30] Indeed, the last time Henman actually signed for his quarterage was September 1737. No reasons for his absences have come to light.

Henman was eventually dismissed. As it was put in the Chapter Acts for 27 June 1741:[31]

They decreed that Mr Richard Henman (for his long absence and disorderly life) be removed from the place of organist and he is hereby removed accordingly. But they order'd that he shall still have the same sum out of the organist's salary that he now receives provided he continue to pay annually such debts as he hath charg'd his said place with the payment of, and that Mr John Silvester be admitted organist in his roome and receive the remainder of the pay, and they do now nominate and admit the said John Silvester to the place of organist of this Church.

Silvester had been appointed deputy organist on 24 January 1741, one of his duties being 'to teach all or any of the choristers instrumentall musick according to the orders which he shall receive from time to time from the Chapter'.[32] Baptized in Winchester on 25 September 1707, he had been a lay vicar in Winchester Cathedral since 26 July 1729 and was granted leave of absence by Exeter's Chapter on 31 January 1741 to settle his affairs in Winchester.[33] We know nothing of his musical education or training.

As we learn from the Chapter Acts for 23 February 1743, Henman retained a lay vicar's place after his dismissal 'by the Indulgence of the Chapter to find him subsistence'.[34] However, the Chapter decided to terminate the arrangement whereby he had continued to receive part of the organist's salary 'upon conditions no way concerning the service of the Church'. They ordered that, 'from Lady Day next, the whole salary belonging to the organist' would be paid to Silvester.

The Chapter Acts for 30 October 1731 state that the rooms in the cloisters lately in the possession of Henry Clase had been given to Mr Vinicombe the sub-chanter in consideration of his long service in the church.[35] Clase appears to have died or retired, after serving as custos organorum and bellows blower for nearly thirty-seven years. His health may have been failing latterly, for Benjamin Cornish was paid the quarterage of the custos organorum in December 1728, March 1729, December 1730 and all of 1731.[36] Clase was succeeded by Isaac Creswell, who was appointed custos organorum on 22 December 1731 and 'took the usuall oaths' at the Chapter meeting two days later.[37] Only three years later, however, on 12 October 1734, another new custos organorum was appointed, William Fieldhurst, 'granted the same salary and perquisites' which his predecessor 'had enjoyed'.[38]

As regards terminology, there were now inconsistencies in the cathedral's records. The genitive plural *organorum* was still being used in the Chapter Acts in 1734, whereas *organi* (genitive singular) had been used in the Ordinary Solutions since 1700 and the English expression 'organ keeper' in the Extraordinary Solutions since 1729. It appears that the practice of using the plural for an organ was passing, though it is possible that the organ keeper had responsibility for both the organ on the pulpitum and the organ in the Song School, in which case *organorum* would have been correct.

A Defective Organ

In the first decade of the eighteenth century, the state of the organ seems to have been such that renovation was considered necessary.[39] Opinions of organ-builders were sought.

One who responded was Thomas Swarbrick of London, in a proposal dated 25 May 1708.[40] He would repair the organ with the addition of two new sets of keys and three bellows and put the instrument 'in the proper pitch'. He would also 'put in' an Echo Organ of eight stops and add Trumpet, Cornet and Sesquialtera stops. The work would cost £580.

Another who responded was James Parsons, a Devon man, then in the early stages of his career as an organ-builder. He put forward 'A Proposall for making the Cathedrall organ more compleat & suitable to the largeness of the Church'.[41] His submission was not dated but is believed to be from c.1710. He proposed the following:

> 1st By altering that Great Defect which at present the Instrument labours under (*viz.*) the want of a Sufficient Supply & force of Air, by applying three good Sizeable Bellows which will be work'd with much more Ease than those two present.
>
> 2dly Those Grand Stops (*viz.*) the two Open Diapasons which compose both Fronts and are the foundation of the whole Organ, being at present little better than Mutes, will (with a few larger conduits) by this means have such a Supply of wind as is necessary to give them their true sound, and the whole Instrument a more Chearfull & Stronger Tone.
>
> 3dly All the other Pipes voic'd and compleatly tuned with the addition of a Bold Trumpet Stop all through the keys; the whole perform'd for Fifty Pounds, by me.
>
> The Organ shall be constantly kept in compleat Order for four pounds per annum.

Neither proposal was accepted. The Chapter decided to seek another opinion, ordering, on 28 March 1713, that 'the organ be mended, cleansed and made more tuneable and that My Lord Bishop [Blackall] with the other Canons now in London be desired to consult and contract with any person that they shall judge fit for such an undertaking'.[42] Eyebrows may be raised at the idea of a bishop and other senior clergy choosing and engaging an organ-builder without the involvement of the cathedral's organist, but the Chapter may have been wary of the judgements of Richard Henman.

An organ-builder with a fine reputation was invited to inspect the organ. He was Christopher Shrider of London, 'organ-builder to the Chapel Royal' since 1710, and he duly presented to the Chapter a quotation for putting the instrument into good repair. Thereupon, as it was put in the Chapter Acts for 6 June 1713, they 'order'd that a coppy of his estimate to be transmitted to the Dean whom they desire and authorize, in conjunction with the Chanter [Precentor] and Dr Atterbury [Archdeacon of Totnes] now in London, to treate, conclude and agree with the said Mr Shrider or any other upon such termes as they shall think fit for the effectual cleansing, repaireing and tuneing the said organ'.[43]

Word of this resolution soon reached Thomas Swarbrick, for a letter dated 12 June 1713 to the Dean from a Robert White of Bristol shows that Swarbrick wished 'to lay down his proposals at least in competition with another gentleman whom he is informed have been down at Exon to repair the organ'.[44] As no further mention of Swarbrick has been found in the records of Exeter Cathedral, we must assume he was rebuffed.

The next development came a few weeks later, when, in a letter to Nicholas Webber (Exeter Cathedral's Chapter Clerk), dated 6 July, Thomas Newey (Exeter's Canon Chancellor) reported that Shrider had agreed to waive an article of his proposals.[45] He would bear the cost of 'carriage of his organ when made'. Shrider confirmed this in a letter dated 18 July 1713, saying that he was willing to change the article for the sum of £10, and the way now seemed clear for a contract to be drawn up.[46] The Chapter agreed financial aspects of the work at their meeting on 1 August 1713, agreeing that Shrider would receive £200 in advance and £200 more when the work was completed.[47]

But there now came a twist in the story. Webber put to Shrider an idea rejected in 1679.[48] He suggested that the organ's display pipes might be gilded. Shrider replied enthusiastically on 13 August 1713, saying that he did 'mightily approve of having all those pipes in the front gilded, which certainly will preserve and look well'.[49] The cost would be 'about £100, more or less'. He believed it would be 'for the Chapter to find the gold and have a painter to lay it on'. Nothing came of the idea, though, which suggests that the Chapter declined to proceed, but as the Chapter Acts contain no reference to the proposed gilding, we may wonder if Webber had acted on his own initiative. He may have decided not to put forward the idea, knowing that the Chapter would reject it on grounds of cost.

Eventually, on 19 September 1713, a contract was concluded between Christopher Shrider on the one hand and the Dean and Chapter on the other.[50] In it, Shrider acknowledged receipt of an advance payment of £200 and promised and agreed to the following:[51]

> To make and put up a good new sounding board for the Great Organ in two parts. Have two Open Diapasons to speak, composed of the old pipes. Provide a new Stopt Diapason, a Principal of metal, a Cornet of metal, Twelfth, Fifteenth, a Nason of wood, a Sesquialtera of metal composed of three rows of pipes, and also a new set of keys with proper movements down to double Gamut long octaves. Make the work movements for drawing the stops new and make the Great Organ Gamut Proper.[52]

> To make and put up a new sounding board with its proper conveyances for the Chair Organ and a new Stopped Diapason, the Principal in the front to serve again but the trebles wanting to be new made. To make the Chair Organ Gamut Proper with a new Stopped Flute of wood, a Fifteenth and room for another stop of the old pipes and a new set of keys with proper movements.

> To make and put up two large pairs of bellows for the two organs, the materials of the said bellows to be entirely new, and the new bellows to have proper wind trunks made of the old wood if it be found good and sufficient for that purpose, or otherwise to make the said wind trunks or such part of them as cannot be had in the old work of new materials.

> To cleanse the front pipes of both organs as well as may be cleansed.

He also agreed that he would pay for the carriage of pipes and other materials from London to Exeter, 'either by sea or land', and would complete the work by Michaelmas 1714.

We now have more information about Loosemore's organ. From the proposals of Swarbrick, Parsons and Shrider and what was reported by Baron Guilford in the early 1680s, we know that his Great Organ contained a Double Diapason, two Open Diapasons and a Stopped Diapason, while his Chair Organ contained a Stopped Diapason, Principal and Stopped Flute.[53] We do not know what other stops were in Loosemore's organ, but we do know that it probably did not contain a Trumpet, Cornet or Sesquialtera. We can see from the proposals of Swarbrick, Parsons and Shrider and the comments of Baron Guilford that the wind supply of Loosemore's organ was inadequate for the larger pipes, and we can see, too, that the pitch of the organ was considered high by Swarbrick and Shrider. We do not know the compasses of Loosemore's Great and Chair Organs, but we can see that Shrider proposed to extend them.

The absence of any evidence to the contrary suggests that Shrider completed his work satisfactorily in 1714. Given that the instrument he produced was in many respects a new organ, it is testimony to his skill that nothing more than tuning and routine maintenance was needed for nearly three decades. Such work was carried out by James Parsons on at least two occasions. He was paid £16 in September 1726 for 'tuning and cleaning the organ' and three guineas in December 1740 for unspecified work on the organ.[54]

We can see from the foregoing that Shrider did more than simply renovate the instrument built by Loosemore. He also added stops. It was quite common by the early eighteenth century (and remains so today) for organs to be altered by the addition, extension or substitution of ranks of pipes in response to suggestions and requests of organists, organ-builders and sometimes clergy. Parsons wanted to give 'the whole Instrument a more Chearfull & Stronger Tone', and it seems from the changes in specification proposed by Swarbrick and made by Shrider that they tended to agree with him. The proposals of Swarbrick, Parsons and Shrider reflected technical and tonal developments in organ-building since the time of Loosemore.

The Organ Rebuilt Again

The first reference to the organ needing further attention came on 2 February 1741, when the Chapter asked the Dean to consult John Robinson, the organist of Westminster Abbey, and to 'send down a proper person to treate with the Chapter about mending and repaireing their organ'.[55] They also 'order'd the score books to be deliver'd to Mr Silvester the deputy organist and that only one key be allow'd to the organ loft'. Henman had not yet been dismissed, but it seems the Chapter had already decided to exclude him. On 7 February, the Chapter 'desir'd and implor'd Mr Dean and Mr Robinson the organist of Westminster to treat and contract with a proper person to repaire the organ and desir'd Mr [Richard] Hooper (a priest vicar) and Mr Silvester to inspect the work and see it well perform'd'.[56]

The person chosen to repair the organ was Abraham Jordan of London (c.1690–1756), son of an organ-builder whose name was also Abraham Jordan (c.1666–1716).[57] Tradition has it that the younger Jordan had worked with Shrider in 1727 when building an organ in Westminster Abbey for the Coronation of King George II; and he had certainly worked with him on other organ projects.[58] Thus, he was known not only to the organist of the Abbey but also to the man who had renovated the Exeter Cathedral organ in 1713–14. We may assume the reason Shrider did not carry out the Exeter repair himself in 1741 was that he was then quite old (about 65 years of age).

An agreement was concluded on 11 May 1741 between the Dean of Exeter and John Robinson on the one part and Abraham Jordan on the other.[59] This specified that Jordan would repair the organ and 'receive £200 on finishing and £200 more one year after, the gentlemen paying the caridge of the new worke & old'. He agreed to 'get the worke done by Midsummer 1742' and specified what he proposed to do in a letter to the Dean and Chapter dated 9 April 1741:[60]

> I propose to new work the Choir Organ and instead of the Twelfth to put a new Bassoon all throughout.
>
> In the Great Organ I propose to make entire new sound-boards of larger dimensions.
>
> And three new pair of bellows instead of the two at present; the movements and roller-board all new; and a new set of keys to D la sol in Alt: in short to use only such pipes as are good which in effect, I may say, is a new organ.[61]
>
> The Great Organ shall contain the following stops: two Open Diapasons, one Stopt Diapason, one Principal, one great Twelfth, one Fifteenth, a Grand Sesquialtera of five ranks or rows of pipes, the present being but of three; and a Cornett of five ranks mounted from the work with proper sound-board conduits &c the present being only on the sound-board & but three ranks or rows of pipes. And a Trumpet stop all through.
>
> I propose to make a new half-set of keys from C to D in Alt, to Echo and Swell, to contain one Open Diapason, one Trumpet & one Hautbois [oboe] stop.[62]
>
> This I will compleat in a durable and workmanlike manner for the sum of three hundred pounds, the Gentlemen paying the carriage.
>
> In case it shall not be thought an excellent instrument, when finisht, and well worth the above mentioned sum, I will oblige myself to put your work in the condition I found it, & be only pay'd my charges of coming & going my two journeys.
>
> P.S. I will undertake to make the two great pillars of pipes speak, as in their first condition, for the farther sum of one hundred pounds.

For many months thereafter, the organ was not mentioned in the Chapter Acts or any other cathedral documents. Then, in a letter dated 30 January 1742, Jordan appeared critical of Shrider, saying that 'so far as the Gentlemen [Dean and Chapter] were ill-used before, I shall make no use of any of the old worke of the Great Organ than the case & two fronts but let it be an entire new organ'.[63] He added in a postscript that his men would be 'ready to go to Exeter in little more than a month'.

Several weeks later, however, when his men had still not gone to Exeter, he said in a letter to the Dean dated 20 March that Mr [Richard] Bridge 'and our people' would go 'the 25th inst if the coach flyes'.[64] Part of the organ, he said, had gone to the carriers a little while ago and the rest had just gone. The Dean then asked the Chapter Clerk to revise the agreement with Jordan over payment for carriage. In a letter to Webber dated 28 March 1742, he noted that the Chapter had agreed to pay the carriage of the organ but now thought it would be 'for their interest to have nothing to do with the carrier who might impose upon us as he pleased'.[65] The Dean wished Jordan 'to agree with the carrier in his own name' and set it against the Chapter's account. Meanwhile, on 25 February 1742, the Chapter had ordered £100 to be paid to Jordan 'in part of the agreement for repairing the organ'.[66]

A letter from Jordan, undated but almost certainly written in late August or early September 1742, informed the Chapter that the organ was nearing completion and advised them that Hooper and Silvester had 'carefully perused the same' and would duly report.[67] He begged leave to lay before them extra work he had carried out beyond the agreement, saying:

> It was order'd for the benefit of the choir to transpose the whole organ, which at the lowest rate is £20.

> And the 14 Great Pipes by Agreement we were to make speak, to which as we were willing it should outdo any organ in England, and as they are much the largest, we made a large sounding board capable of receiving more pipes to follow those great Pipes, and stand withinside the Great Case, and is now a whole Stop containing 55 pipes instead of 14, called a Double Diapason, which with the Trumpet makes a most beautiful Clarion.

> The Swelling Organ is carried 5 keys lower than my Agreement which is 15 pipes I reckon nothing for.

> A new set of keys in the Choir Organ and added 2 keys and pipes all thro' stands in more than £10.

The Chapter heard on 13 September 1742 that Hicks (the informator choristarum), Hooper and Silvester were satisfied with Jordan's work and ordered that £200 be paid to him 'in part of the consideration money for repairing the organ'.[68]

Jordan had not in fact fulfilled his contract, for on 7 September 1743 the Chapter noted that he had 'not completely finished the Great pipes' and 'thought it reasonable that some abatement be made on that account and for other omissions'.[69] But he soon made good the omissions, and the Chapter agreed on 15 September 1744 that £100 should be paid to him for the remainder of his contract.[70] Nothing more was heard of Jordan at Exeter Cathedral, and no further renovation of the organ was necessary for a number of years.

Another Defective Organist

Silvester proved another disappointment. He was soon in trouble. On 19 February 1743, for example, the Chapter gave him 'a monition to attend the service of the church in the quire in his surplice on fast days when the organ is not play'd and to behave himself in a more dutiful and respectful manner to the members of the Chapter than he hath hitherto done'.[71] And there is more than a hint of dissatisfaction in the Chapter Acts for 23 February 1743, when it was recorded that the £6 *per annum* which had been allotted to him in June 1741 out of the pay of the informator choristarum (John Hicks) would, from Lady Day 1743, be paid to Hicks, who had 'received little or no assistance from Mr Silvester'.[72] Moreover, the Chapter ordered that 'if Mr Hicks shall at any time hereafter be hinder'd by sickness or otherwise, he shall have liberty to name his own deputy to be approved of by the Chapter'.

As with Henman, so it continued with Silvester. He was frequently absent. Quarter after quarter, part of the organist's salary was paid to deputies, with Anthony Martyn and William Doidge paid every quarter from June 1741 to March 1743 (respectively, £2 10s 0d and £1 out of the organist's quarterage of £6 5s 0d). Silvester did receive the whole amount after that, but only until September 1744. His full resumption of duties did not last. His signature did not appear again in the books of Ordinary and Extraordinary Solutions until June 1752.

The reason for Silvester's absence in the latter part of 1744 can be found in the Chapter Acts for 8 December, when it was recorded that 'Mr Silvester the organist being found to abscond for debt they allow'd him to be absent from the service of the church till Lady Day next to give him an opportunity in the mean time to make his peace with his creditors, and they order'd his deputy who plays the organ in his absence to be paid (out of his salary) after the rate of £12 *per annum* (as Sanders formerly had) from the first of this instant'.[73] The week before, on 1 December, the Chapter had ordered that Hicks would 'take the charge and care of the organ loft and books till farther order'.[74]

The absence of Silvester's signature from the Ordinary and Extraordinary Solutions should not be taken to mean that he was not still officially the organist. The Chapter clearly considered him so in the latter part of 1745, for on 9 November they 'order'd notice to be given to the organist to attend the Chapter next Saturday on paine of suspension';[75] and he was in trouble again four months later, when, on 1 March 1746, the Chapter noted that the sub-chanter had complained that Silvester had 'presumed to alter some of the service books and in many instances been guilty of irregularitys in playing the services'.[76] For this, Silvester was admonished 'not to be guilty of such malpractices for the time to come under paine of suspension'.

Problems over Silvester's conduct nevertheless continued. He was given notice several more times in 1746 and 1747 to attend Chapter meetings;[77] and then, on 5 December 1747, the Chapter 'order'd £16 *per annum* to be allow'd Mr Hooper for playing the organ during Mr Silvester's imprisonment [for debt] to be deducted out of his salary'.[78] William Hooper, son of priest vicar Richard Hooper, had been 'order'd and allow'd' by the Chapter on 3 September 1743 'to play the organ over a week such services and anthems as he is able to play';[79] and he had twice been paid thereafter for playing the organ (in December 1744 and March 1745).[80]

Silvester wrote to the Dean and Chapter soon after his release from prison. His letter, dated 26 March 1748, read as follows: 'During my confinement you were pleased to employ young Hooper to play the organ and to allow him out of my salary (as I apprehend) after the rate of £4 a quarter.[81] He hath rec'd £8 whereas he did not officiate full four months and therefore I humbly hope you'll be pleas'd to order him to pay over to me such part thereof as you shall think to be more than what he ought to have rec'd'.[82] The Dean and Chapter took Silvester's point and ordered at their meeting on 3 September 1748 that £2 13*s* 4*d* be refunded by Hooper and paid to the organist.[83] However, the money was in fact paid to Simon Westcott, not John Silvester.[84] Westcott, a lay vicar, had been one of the deputy organists for some time, paid £1 5*s* 0*d* every quarter since June 1745, with a chorister, John Richards, receiving the remaining £5 of the organist's quarterage.[85]

After Lady Day 1748, Hooper was never again paid for playing the organ. Westcott alone was paid every quarter from then until Lady Day 1752, when, lo and behold, Silvester resumed the duties of organist. As in 1745, though, he had been considered the organist in the interim, for on 3 September 1748 the Chapter reproved him and the bellows blower 'for neglect of duty (the organ not being played for one or two services in the last week)'.[86] They ordered him 'to waite upon My Lord Bishop and beg his Lordship's pardon for such his neglect', and they ordered the bellows blower 'to be suspended for one month and gave a monition to both to be more carefull in the discharge of their duty for the time to come'. As Westcott had been paid the organist's salary every quarter since June 1748, we are left with the impression that the Chapter did not know who was actually playing the organ.

In the same vein, the Chapter ordered on 24 February 1750 that '[Frederick] Warwell the chorister do attend Mr Silvester the organist in order to be taught to play the organ at such times as Mr Silvester shall appoint not interfering with his schooling or his attendance upon the service of the church'.[87] Moreover, a payment was made to Silvester three days later 'for mending the organ'.[88] If he was in fact in residence but not playing the organ, we may wonder how he was fulfilling his contract as organist. What was he doing to fill his time, and how was he making a living if he was receiving little or no income from the cathedral?

We have no answers to these questions, but they soon became academic. In the words of the Chapter Acts for 2 June 1753: 'Mr Silvester the organist being dead they appointed this day fortnight to proceed to the election of a successor.'[89] We do not know what caused his death or where he was buried.

By 1753, Joseph Densham had been bellows blower and custos organi for several years. However, cathedral documents tell a confusing story over his appointment. The Chapter appointed William Sanders bellows blower and custos organi on 28 June 1746 in succession to William Fieldhurst, who had recently died;[90] and the Chapter Acts for 10 January 1747 state that Sanders 'who was admitted bellows blower on 28 June last appeared personally in Chapter this day and took the usual oaths'.[91] Then, a week later, the Chapter 'allow'd Joseph Densham to be deputy bellows blower to William Sanders'.[92] Thus, it appears that Sanders was the bellows blower and custos organi and Densham his deputy. However, Densham had been paid as custos organi in September and December 1746, before he had been appointed by the Chapter, and Sanders never signed for quarterly payments to the custos organi, either in 1746 or at any time thereafter.[93] We do not know who Sanders was or why he never signed.[94]

An Organist and Composer

First Henman, then Silvester. For almost sixty years, the organists of Exeter Cathedral had been less than satisfactory, frequently absent and repeatedly badly behaved. Furthermore, the Chapter Acts show that there had been casual attitudes, disobedience and poor discipline in the choir, too. What kind of example had been set by Henman and Silvester? We have no information about musical standards in the cathedral in the middle of the eighteenth century, but our suspicion must be that they had fallen since the time of Pasmore and probably become as low as those in most other cathedrals.

The appointment of a new organist was made on 23 June 1753, when the Chapter 'elected and admitted Richard Langdon organist in the room of John Silvester deceased, the said Mr Langdon having first taken the usual oaths'.[95] He had been examined the previous week by the custos of the College of Vicars, and found to be 'sufficiently skilfull for the office of a lay vicar', as a result of which the Chapter had on 16 June admitted him 'to the place of a lay vicar choral of this Cathedral Church now void by the death of John Silvester, the last possessor thereof'.[96]

Born in Exeter in 1729, Langdon had been a chorister in the cathedral from the summer of 1738 to the spring of 1748, when he had become a secondary. As ordered by the Chapter on 1 December 1744, he had, in the absence of Silvester, been taught to play the organ by the sub-chanter (John Hicks).[97] His father, Charles, was a son of Tobias Langdon, who had not only been a priest vicar and sub-chanter of Exeter Cathedral from 1683 until his death in September 1712 but also a chorister of the cathedral in his younger days and master of the choristers from 1687 until his death.[98]

Langdon seems to have made a satisfactory start to his time as organist. There were no complaints about him or his competence; and as well as serving as organist he taught the choristers writing and arithmetic.[99] Then, however, throughout 1756, his salary was collected for him by one William Luscombe.[100] We do not know why he did not sign for the payments himself.

Evidence of his commitment to a high standard of musical proficiency came the following year, when, in the quarter ending on 24 June 1757, he was paid the large amount of £9 9s 0d for 'the first subscription for six volumes of Doctor Boyce's *Church Musick*'.[101] William Boyce was a celebrated composer and organist and had been, since December 1755, Master of the King's Musick. A second payment for music by Boyce was made to Langdon more than a decade later, when, in accordance with a Chapter resolution of 4 February 1769, he was paid £9 18s 0d for 'six copies of Doctor Boyce's Second Volume of *Church Music*, one of the copies to be bound'.[102] Meanwhile, on 13 November 1762, further evidence of esteem for the music of Boyce had become apparent when the Chapter 'order'd the Book of Dr Boyce's Services kept in the Exchequer Chamber to be deliver'd to Mr Langdon for the service of the church'.[103]

The only formal criticism of Langdon by the Chapter came on 3 March 1759, when they admonished him 'for his frequent absence from the Church and for not obeying the sub-chanter's orders'.[104] This was disappointing. Was he beginning to copy the poor example of his predecessors? A month later, however, on 7 April 1759, the Chapter granted him 'leave to be absent for five weeks', which indicates that he had this time applied for time off and not just absented himself without permission. But no reason for the absence was recorded.

There is no evidence that Langdon had any financial problems or other personal difficulties, and he never again after 1756 failed to sign for his quarterages. A possible reason for his absence may have been that he was devoting time to the advancement of his musical credentials. He took the Oxford Bachelor of Music degree on 18 July 1761, having matriculated five days earlier.[105]

This was not, however, the reason why he was granted leave of absence several more times over the years, including leave for three weeks granted on 25 August 1770 and a month granted on 13 April 1776.[106] On the latter occasion, a reason was given. The time off was to allow him 'to journey to Bath for the recovery of his health'. Whether or not his health problem was chronic, we do not know, but there may have been another reason for the leave granted in 1770: he married Susanna Evans on 28 August.[107]

Meanwhile, on 8 May 1762, Langdon had been appointed master of the choristers and (though not a priest) sub-chanter, in place of John Hicks, who had resigned because of great age and failing health.[108] The offices of organist and master of the choristers had thus been combined for the first time since 1608, with the exception of a few months in 1661, when William Hopwood had filled both offices.[109] Langdon also provided organ lessons for choristers.[110]

As well as carrying out the duties of organist and master of the choristers, Langdon composed and published songs, anthems, harpsichord sonatas, cantatas, glees and a collection of psalms and anthems called *Divine Harmony*. The last of these, which appeared in 1774, included twenty chants by various composers, all printed anonymously, one of them a double chant which is believed to be by Langdon himself and is still popular today (often used for the Benedictus). In his early years as Exeter Cathedral's organist, he published *Ten songs and a cantata*, *A collection of songs*, and a cantata called *Cupid and Chloe*. Later works included six sonatas for harpsichord, *Twelve songs and two cantatas*, and, after he left Exeter, *Twelve glees*.[111]

Langdon stepped down as organist, lay vicar, informator puerorum and sub-chanter on 4 October 1777.[112] No reason for his resignation has come to light. However, his successor, William Jackson, wrote as follows in his autobiography: 'I embraced an opportunity offered me by the then organist of Exeter to succeed him in his place, which he resigned, for a pecuniary consideration, in my favour, as I had in my early days regularly officiated for [John] Travers at the King's Chapel.'[113] The use of 'pecuniary consideration' is intriguing![114]

Langdon was appointed organist of Ely Cathedral on 25 November 1777 but held that post for only a week, as on 3 December he was appointed organist of Bristol Cathedral, where he remained until 25 June 1781, when he resigned.[115] He was next appointed organist of Armagh Cathedral in 1782 and remained there until November 1794, when he resigned because of poor health.[116] He retired to Exeter and died there on 8 September 1803. He was buried in St Paul's Church, and a plain white marble tablet was erected there to his memory. When this church was demolished in 1936, the memorial was moved to a church on the edge of Exeter's Cathedral Close, St Martin's, where it can still be seen.

The Organ Adorned and Repaired

While Silvester was the organist, and after the work by Jordan had been completed, the organ was mentioned in the Chapter Acts only twice. The Chapter ordered on 8 June 1745 that 'the quire service be performed in the body of the church whilst the quire is wainscotting and the organ be cover'd from the dust which must necessarily arise on this occasion';[117] and on 3 October 1747 they ordered 'the partition on the left hand of the organ loft to be removed, having been erected without order of Chapter and of no use'.[118]

Thereafter, the next reference to the organ came on 20 December 1760, when the Chapter 'having this day come to a resolution of accepting Mr Crang's proposals for the gilding and repairing the organ ordered that he be writ to accordingly to come and perform his contract as soon as he possibly can'.[119] John Crang was born in Devon c.1710 (at or near North Molton) and removed to London in the 1720s, possibly then becoming apprenticed to Christopher Shrider.[120] He was in business as an organ-builder and maker of harpsichords and other keyboard instruments on his own account by 1745.[121]

There was no further mention of work on the organ until 16 May 1761, when the Chapter 'agreed to accept Mr Crang's proposals for the further repairing the organ dated this day'.[122] However, no details were provided. Then, two weeks later, on 30 May, the Chapter ordered that Crang 'be paid £40 in advance towards repairing and gilding the organ'.[123] Again, though, details of the work were not provided. Eventually, in the Chapter Acts for 18 July 1761, information was given.[124] The Chapter 'accepted the following proposals of Mr Crang for gilding the things following':

	£	s	d
The crown and astragal under it on the centre at the top of the organ	1	15	0
Seventy-six fleur de lis on the six piers @ three shillings each	11	8	0
For gilding the King's and other Coats of Arms on the organ loft	11	0	0
The two irons that support the curtain rods at the end of the Dean's and the Chanter's seats in the Choir	0	10	6
	24	13	6

This was work additional to the gilding of the organ's display pipes.

On 25 July, the Chapter ordered Crang 'to be paid £60 in advance, towards repairing and gilding the organ;[125] and a week later they 'ordered the organ loft towards the quire to be painted'.[126] On 26 September, they ordered him 'to be paid £50 in part towards gilding the organ;[127] and on 19 December 1761 they ordered that he 'be paid £30 in advance towards gilding the organ', which suggests a further advance payment to him.[128] However, he was never again mentioned in the Chapter Acts, which contain only two more references to the organ in the early 1760s.

The Chapter ordered on 13 November 1762 that the west front of the organ loft be painted;[129] and they ordered on 4 December that 'some ornaments of papier mâché be put upon the cornice of the organ loft'.[130] There was, however, another reference to the organ in the early 1760s, this by John Wesley, one of the founders of Methodism. He attended a service in the cathedral on 29 August 1762 and afterwards wrote in his journal that 'such an organ I never saw or heard before: so large, beautiful, and so finely toned'.[131]

After the early 1760s, decoration of the organ and its immediate surroundings seems to have ceased, though the renovation and adornment of the interior of the cathedral as a whole, begun under Charles Lyttelton, Dean from 1748 to 1762, continued under his successor in that office, Jeremiah Milles. During the rest of Langdon's time as organist, attention on the organ focused upon repair work, entrusted to Paul Micheau, a native of Barnstaple.[132] He had learned his organ-building skills from George England, a London organ-builder.[133]

The first mention of Micheau in the cathedral records came on 14 March 1767, when the Chapter engaged him to repair the organ 'under the direction of the organist'.[134] He duly carried out this task and the Chapter ordered a month later, on 11 April, that his bill of four guineas for repairing and tuning the organ be paid.[135] Four months later, however, on 8 August, we see from the Chapter Acts that work of a more substantial nature needed to be carried out. The Chapter 'ordered that boards be placed to secure the lower part of the Great pipes of the organ'.[136] In the absence of any evidence to the contrary, we must assume that this work was carried out satisfactorily. The next reference to the organ in the Chapter Acts was brief but nevertheless indicated that there were still problems with the organ. The Chapter ordered on 27 February 1768 that 'the defect in the organ be repaired'.[137]

A resolution of the Chapter on 3 September 1768 shows that a defect of Loosemore's organ had still not been rectified:[138]

> Mr Paul Micheau having made a proposal to convey wind to the Great pipes of the organ, so as to give them their proper tone; & to put the same in good

order within the space of two months, for the sum of thirty pounds: and having, also, offer'd (in case it should be found necessary) to take the bruises out of the pipes, for the additional sum of five pounds. They agreed to his proposals on condition that he find all the requisite materials, & that he complete his undertaking in a workmanlike manner and to be completed in two months.

The wind supply to the Double Diapason and other large pipes was still not sufficient, despite the efforts of Shrider and Jordan to overcome this shortcoming.

Micheau agreed with the Dean and Chapter on 27 September 1768 that he would make 'the Great pipes of the cathedral organ speak in a proper manner', and also that if he did not 'compleat the above agreement in a proper manner' he did not 'desire to receive any thing for it'.[139] When, two months later, he had not fulfilled his contract, the Chapter decided (on 26 November) to defer the work to the following spring.[140]

We do not know if the work was in fact carried out, but, if it was not, the Chapter seem to have remained favourably disposed towards Micheau, for in their Christmas Audit of 1770 they agreed to pay him £10 'for taking care of the organ for one year'.[141] This appears to have been a speedy response to a letter from Micheau to the Dean and Chapter dated 20 December 1770:[142]

> Upon examining the organ I find it so much out of order as to require a great deal of time to repair it. . . . I hope for the future you will Gentlemen be so well pleased to consider me by fixing a salary for the care of so valuable an instrument. I have for those five years past tuned the reed stops & put the whole organ in good order whenever Mr Langdon has apply'd to me so to do, in which time I never received anything but once, when I clean'd the inside and tuned it, besides preventing the Great pipes from ciphering, which before were scarcely ever play'd without having that bad tendency, for which work I was paid four guineas. Had I not at this and several other times repair'd the organ, I presume Mr Crang or some other organ-builder must have been apply'd to for that purpose. I hope therefore Gentlemen you will be pleased to take this affair into consideration & I shall be ready to keep the instrument in good order by attending it once a fortnight or as often as Mr Langdon may think it necessary for the salary of ten pounds per annum.

During Langdon's years as organist, there were but few changes of custos organi and bellows blower. George Hayme replaced Joseph Densham in early 1756, and he in turn was replaced by John Bindon in the autumn of 1762.[143]

Retrospect

In six of the nine decades that followed the visit of the Prince of Orange, the behaviour of organists and other musicians of Exeter Cathedral left much to be desired, and it is likely, but nowhere stated expressly, that musical standards declined overall, as in so many other cathedrals. Alan Mould has referred to the 'Georgian nadir' of the English choral tradition, with casual attitudes by musicians and even clergy and a repertoire of bland anthems which did not extend choirs or inspire worshippers.[144]

Langdon seems to have endeavoured to reverse the decline during the 24 years he was organist. To what extent did he succeed? We do not know, but William Jackson was critical. On taking up the post of organist in 1777, he said, 'I found a bad choir, which I was determined, if possible, to make a good one.'[145] There was, it seems, scope for improvement. And we may wonder if Loosemore's Double Diapasons would ever be made to function satisfactorily.

CHAPTER 4

In Pursuit of Quality and Satisfaction

In the eighteenth century, as in the latter part of the seventeenth, clergy of Exeter Cathedral were often absent; and this was so in most English cathedrals. It was common for clergy to hold more than one benefice, often in places far apart. When William Jackson became organist, Jeremiah Milles was not only Dean of Exeter but also rector of parishes in Surrey, Sussex and the City of London.[1] We may wonder if the shortcomings of Exeter Cathedral's organists since the time of King Charles II had in any way reflected attitudes of clergy.

The practice of clerics holding benefices far apart continued throughout Jackson's time as organist, but he appears to have been unaffected by it.[2] He was diligent; and he endeavoured to raise the standard of music in the cathedral. Did those who succeeded him follow his example, and did the organ receive due care and attention? We now continue the story of the cathedral's organs and organists through a period when clergy were often away from Exeter but nevertheless consulted whenever important decisions had to be made.

William Jackson of Exeter

Son of a grocer, Jackson was born in Exeter on 28 May 1730 and received an education which, he said in his autobiography, began in his seventh year and continued till he was sixteen.[3] His musical studies began, he said, when his 'twelfth year had arrived'. Several sources state that he was a chorister in Exeter Cathedral in the early 1740s, but his name does not appear in the lists of choristers recorded in the Ordinary Solutions;[4] and he did not say in his autobiography that he had ever been a chorister. Some believe John Silvester was the person who introduced him to music.[5] However, Jackson himself did not mention Silvester. He wrote in his autobiography:

My master received my entrance fee and gave me my notes, which was all I was indebted to him for. From a subordinate member of the choir at Exeter I

> learnt two or three common airs such as are given to beginners. This was the whole of my instruction for three years which I received from others. By my own assiduous practice I could perform Handel's Organ Concertos and some of Corelli's Sonatas, in a wild irregular manner no doubt. As yet I was a stranger to any but my own poor performance.

Whoever 'my master' was, Jackson was not impressed. He had largely taught himself.

Jackson said that a violinist who 'played very finely' had 'lighted up a new flame' within him, and he went on to say that this man had persuaded his father to send him to London to advance his musical education.[6] He had been sent to study under John Travers, the organist of the Chapel Royal.[7] However, he had been forced to return to Exeter in 1747 or early 1748 and there try to make a living out of music. As he wrote in his autobiography:

> Being with Travers as a scholar, and not as an apprentice, the expense of my residing in London was too much for my father's finances, and he sent for me home. Under eighteen, I was obliged to practise my profession for a subsistence. My first year produced so little that the most severe economy could not prevent my having a debt of a few pounds. The next year I discharged it, and from thence to the present moment I have never owed a shilling, but have ever paid my bills as soon as delivered. I was early possessed with an idea that a debtor was in the most miserable situation in life, and to prevent being so was determined never to spend any money until I had not only earned it but had it in my pocket.

His wealth at death was £10,000, a large sum in 1803.[8]

Jackson's first published work, *Twelve Songs*, appeared in 1755, bearing on its title page, as on all his subsequent publications, the designation 'William Jackson of Exeter', to avoid confusion with a musician of the same name based in Oxford. By the time he became the organist of Exeter Cathedral, he had also published many secular songs and canzonets, two sacred vocal works, six sonatas for harpsichord accompanied by violin, and eight sonatas for harpsichord accompanied by violin, viola and bass.[9] Furthermore, he had composed the music for an adaptation of Milton's *Lycidas* performed at Covent Garden on 4 November 1767 and Bath three weeks later.

Jackson took up drawing at the age of eight and became, he said, 'deeply engaged' in astronomy and natural philosophy in his late twenties.[10] Painting in oil, however, became his principal interest in the 1750s, and he was introduced to the artist

Thomas Gainsborough about 1763. A close friendship between them developed, their common interests being painting and a love of music. By 1770, he was thinking of taking up painting professionally; and in 1771 he exhibited two paintings at the Royal Academy. However, he resisted Gainsborough's attempts to persuade him to leave Exeter and continued with music as his main source of income. He succeeded Langdon as organist of Exeter Cathedral on 18 October 1777, becoming also sub-chanter, master of the choristers and a lay vicar; and the Chapter 'allotted to him the house now inhabited by Mr Langdon, with the School and School Room to remain to him during his continuance in the said offices'.[11]

As noted at the end of Chapter 3, Jackson was somewhat disdainful of the choir he inherited from Langdon. Writing in 1801, again in his autobiography, he considered that he had succeeded in making it 'the best in the kingdom'.[12] Whether this was so, we do not know. An assessment of his life by Thomas Busby, published only six weeks after his death, made no mention of the choir but commended his keyboard skill:[13]

> When playing the organ or harpsichord, he seemed lost to everything around him. His performance was full, correct, and impassioned; and he had too just a taste, and was too much a devotee to the good old school, ever to destroy a single resident beauty in a composition for the sake of unnecessary and surreptitious embellishment.

Busby did not, though, wholly approve of Jackson's compositions, saying that 'his melodies were not always free from mechanical quaintness and rustic inelegance' and 'his basses not unfrequently chosen with but little art or design'. Others agreed, and William Husk, for example, wrote thus in 1890:[14]

> Whilst much of his music charms by its simplicity, melodiousness, refinement and grace, there is also much that sinks into tameness and insipidity; his church music especially is exceedingly feeble. Notwithstanding this, 'Jackson in F' is even now popular in some quarters.

Modern writers have concurred. Richard McGrady, for example, considered that Jackson's best music was found in his secular vocal works and called his cathedral services 'bland'.[15]

While organist of the cathedral, Jackson composed sacred and secular vocal works, as well as music for London stage productions.[16] He also wrote letters and essays and in 1792 helped found a society in Exeter for literary and philosophical discussion. He fulfilled his cathedral duties conscientiously and does not appear to have been absent very often. He was in London in late 1780 when his comic opera *The Lord of the Manor* was staged at Drury Lane, and he was absent from mid-July to late September 1785, when, as he put it, 'I interrupted the sameness of my life by making a little tour on the Continent.'[17] The only other absence we know of occurred in 1793, when, on 6 July, the Chapter granted him 'leave of absence for a fortnight' (but gave no reason).[18] Given his closeness to the cultural scene in London, though, it is likely that he was away from Exeter more often than records suggest; and his pamphlet entitled *Observations on the present state of music in London*, published in 1791, shows that he was no stranger in the capital.[19]

Jackson died of dropsy on 5 July 1803 and was buried in St Stephen's Church, Exeter, where a memorial was erected, with the following inscribed upon it:[20]

> In the science of music an eminent professor, whose genius united elegant expression, pure and original melody, with peculiar delicacy of harmonic combination. In painting, in literature, in every liberal study that enlightens the intellect or expands the heart his attainments were rare and distinguished: a writer, novel and acute in observation, a correct and discriminating critic, endeared to his select associates by a conversation and demeanour of impressive and fascinating simplicity.

Busby agreed, saying that Jackson was 'pleasant, social, communicative, dryly facetious, and abounding in useful and judicious remarks and entertaining anecdotes'.[21] Alexander Chalmers, on the other hand, considered him 'strongly alloyed by a mixture of selfishness, arrogance, and an insatiable rage for superiority', but these were his only critical comments in his otherwise positive assessment of Jackson.[22]

We end this biographical sketch with an anecdote, which concerns a bequest by Edward Young, the Dean of Exeter who died in 1663 and left £2 a year to the choristers of the cathedral, to be distributed annually by the Dean on 29 May.[23] According to George Townsend, Jackson was asked to 'prepare something by way of memorial of the bequest' and, in response, wrote 'a little poetical effusion, which he set to music, and which was sung by the boys in their music school in the cloisters':[24]

> We choristers young, with harps newly strung,
> And hearts overflowing with praise,
> How grateful are we, in music we see
> How good was Dean Young, whose praise is now sung, &c.

The man who succeeded Jackson as the cathedral's organist had been one of the choristers who benefitted.

Another Organist from Exeter

James Paddon was born in Exeter and baptized in the church of St Mary Major on 28 June 1768.[25] He became a chorister of Exeter Cathedral in 1775 or 1776 and subsequently a secondary (1786) and lay vicar (1793).[26] He attended William Marshall's School in Exeter, his fees paid by the Cathedral Chapter in 1779, 1780 and 1781.[27] He was admonished by the Chapter on 22 September 1798 'on account of his very frequent absence from the service of the church without leave', but this was not held against him.[28] The Chapter elected and admitted him the cathedral's organist and master of the choristers on 30 July 1803;[29] and they appointed him sub-chanter on 12 April 1804.[30]

Paddon became much involved in the musical life of the city and often conducted large-scale choral activities. On 21 April 1814, for example, a local newspaper reported that:[31]

> The amateurs of Sacred Music will learn with pleasure that a Musical Festival, on a grand scale, is now in preparation, and will be performed in the Cathedral Church of this city, some time in the month of August next. The superior advantage which this Cathedral possesses, in having one of the best organs in this kingdom, if not in Europe, would in itself be a great attraction; but when assisted as it will be, by an excellent band of instrumental performers, it will afford a treat indeed. The choir is universally known to be a very fine one; to this also will be added some stars of vocal celebrity from the metropolis, the whole forming a specimen of sacred harmony at once beautiful and sublime. It will be entirely under the direction of Mr Paddon, the organist.

Hyperbole this may be, but it is clear that the cathedral's choir was well regarded; and the organ seems to have been in good condition, too.

Paddon was a leading light in the musical life of Exeter and elsewhere in the South West for thirty years and also appears to have been well regarded by the cathedral's authorities, for on 20 December 1810 the Chapter agreed to give him 'an additional annual stipend of £5 a year besides his additional stipend as lay vicar as of the gift of the Chapter and to be continued as long as they shall think fit'.[32]

The only official reprimand Paddon received in all the years he was organist occurred on 28 December 1822, when he was reproved by the Chapter for 'not having attended or anyone for him at the Evening Service on Wednesday last'.[33] The Chapter Clerk was ordered to admonish him 'that no such neglect occur again'. This seems to have been an uncharacteristic lapse on Paddon's part. Perhaps he thought a deputy had agreed to play, but we should note that 'Wednesday last' was Christmas Day!

On 10 December 1830, the Chapter rejected Paddon's application for a salary increase, saying that he was entitled to ask a deputy to play occasionally, provided the deputy was 'fully competent'.[34] They did, though, conclude that he needed assistance in the Singing School and accordingly approved the appointment of an assistant informator puerorum with a salary of £20 a year 'without any diminution of Mr Paddon's present emoluments'. And they accepted Paddon's nomination of Philip Salter, a secondary, to fill the post.

Salter died four years later, as we find in the Chapter Acts for 30 December 1834, where it was recorded that 'his lamented death' had put an end to his instruction of the choristers and Paddon had agreed to 'undertake the entire charge of that instruction, as was his duty'.[35] The Chapter 'resolved to give to Mr Paddon *ex gratia Capituli* during the pleasure of the Chapter the yearly sum of £20', thus transferring to him the amount paid to Salter. Unfortunately, however, returning responsibility for choir training to Paddon did not prove satisfactory, as the Chapter Acts for 23 May 1835 show:[36]

> The Chapter find that the state of the Choir demands their interference – that the plan on which the instruction of the Choristers is now proceeding is not effectual to keep the Choir in that state which the Chapter think it their duty to require – and they therefore find it necessary to appoint some one person to undertake the instruction of the Choristers upon the terms which were adopted in the case of Mr Salter until Mr Paddon shall be able to resume his duties which they sincerely trust may be soon.

Paddon was unwell. He did not resume his duties. He died three weeks later, on 14 June 1835, at his home, 22 Southernhay, Exeter.

His obituary in *Trewman's Exeter Flying Post* was laudatory:[37]

> It has fallen to the lot of few men to have acquired greater honour for themselves, or to have seen the reputation of the choirs committed to their charge more firmly established, than has been the case with Mr Paddon. Disciplined under a gentleman with the correct ear and fine taste that were distinguishing qualities in Mr Paddon, the choir of the Cathedral of Exeter has attained a point of excellence that by universal consent places it among the foremost of similar establishments in Europe, and confers on him who has so eminently contributed to it a never undying fame.

These fine words suggest that the music of the cathedral had been rescued from the unsatisfactory state into which it had descended by the middle of the eighteenth century; and this appears to be the verdict of history.[38]

Paddon was buried in the south nave aisle of Exeter Cathedral on 19 June alongside his wife Elizabeth, who had died earlier in 1835.[39] The ledger which covers their grave can still be seen in the south nave aisle. It is the only known gravestone of an organist in the cathedral.[40]

For more than a decade, the Paddons lived in a house in the cloisters, but the house was then demolished. At first, as recorded in the Chapter Acts on 23 December 1814, it was ordered that part of the organist's house be taken down 'and the residue converted to two houses for the two virgers to live in'.[41] On 15 April 1815, however, the Chapter amended their previous order, deciding that 'part of the organist's late house which stands on the eastern side of the cloisters be pulled down immediately in order that the stones may be used in the repairs of the buttresses'.[42]

The house occupied by the bellows blower was also demolished, and the Chapter ordered, on 17 March 1815, that 'the annual sum of £7 paid to the custos organi or bellows blower in lieu of his late house in the Cloysters be continued only during the time of the present possessor of that office and not afterwards'.[43] This provision ceased on 20 December 1816, when the Chapter noted that the office of bellows blower was now 'void by the death of Mr Cook'.[44]

Caring for the Organ

Paul Micheau tuned and maintained the organ throughout Jackson's time as organist. On 14 May 1779, for instance, the Chapter ordered him to repair the bellows of the organ;[45] and on 15 February 1783, in response to a report he submitted on 5 October 1782, they ordered that the organ 'be immediately put in thorough repair'.[46] Micheau proposed to 'take out and new leather the bellows, take out and repair the Choir Organ soundboard (the purses in the wind chest being quite wore out), clean the whole instrument, and repair the springs of the reed work and many other things which follow of course at the expense of £60'.[47]

For the next 25 years, the organ seems to have been trouble-free. Then, in July 1808, Micheau had to carry out work on the bellows and 'movement of the Choir Organ', at a cost of £4 11s 0d.[48] Two years later, and apparently unexpectedly, the Dean and Chapter received a letter dated 15 March 1810 from George Du Chemin, carver and gilder of 73 Fore Street, Exeter.[49] It had nothing to do with the action or tuning of the organ. He was offering to re-gild the organ's display pipes. No action appears to have been taken, and nothing has come to light to confirm or otherwise that the Chapter then had it in mind to re-gild the organ. We must assume, therefore, that no official approach had been made to Chemin. Someone appears to have spoken out of turn.

Four years later, the state of the organ was giving cause for concern, and on 21 June 1814 Paddon wrote to George Pyke (or Pike) England, a London organ-builder.[50] In his reply, dated 23 June, England said that he felt 'much obliged by the order to tune the cathedral organ'.[51] However, he 'really was in hopes' that the work would have been carried out by Micheau and said that he did not wish to cause 'the Old Gentleman' any distress, 'as it would me under similar circumstances'. He was 'sure the instrument stands much in need of being taken to pieces and clean'd to put it in good order' and went on to say that he would send one of his men to Exeter around 18 July if Micheau could not carry out the work.

Micheau did not carry out the work. The Chapter ordered on 17 September 1814 that the organ be cleaned, repaired and tuned by England under the direction of Paddon and, moreover, that 'during the time of such work (to be commenced immediately) the service of the church be discontinued, namely the early prayers and the evening service on weekdays'.[52] For carrying out the work, England was paid £30.[53]

For subsequent tuning of the organ, William Brooking was contracted. As put in the Chapter Acts for 17 December 1814, he was '(in the room of Paul Micheau) to keep the organ in tune and clean for an annual salary of £25 without any additional charge on any account whatever and to commence from Christmas next providing the said William Brooking shall on trial prove competent and shall reside in Exeter by Lady Day next'.[54]

Micheau had not been ignored or dismissed. He was, according to the Chapter Acts for 17 March 1815, 'disabled from age and infirmity' and had been granted an annuity of £10 a year 'during the pleasure of the Chapter'.[55] The pension was paid quarterly thereafter until, on 12 November 1824, he died, aged 90.[56] His obituary in *Trewman's Exeter Flying Post* stated that his parents had intended him to become, like them, a woollen manufacturer.[57] Instead, though:

> He having displayed an early genius for music, and having made an organ without instructions, his friends placed him with Mr England, in London, the most celebrated organ-builder of that time, and under whose tuition he acquired a complete knowledge of his profession, which he afterwards exhibited in the erection of several organs in this county.[58] He built one at Tiverton, another at Dartmouth, and the organ in the Church of St Mary Major in this city, by which he acquired the friendship and esteem of that great musical genius Jackson, and of Mr Langdon, the organist of the Cathedral, who introduced Mr Micheau unto all the amateurs of music in this city and vicinity of Exeter; he had the care of the organ in the Cathedral for forty years. He was an honest, honourable, and a friendly man.

A report was received from George Pyke England in the last week of 1814.[59] Addressed to the Subdean, it was dated 26 December and began with an apology that he had not sent the estimate for repairs sooner. He had been ill, he said, since his son-in-law Nicholls had been to Exeter to inspect the organ.[60] The report said that the bellows were unsound and needed new corner pieces and gussets, and the soundboards were 'full of runnings'. Furthermore: the leather of the valves had become 'so hard as to be in danger of frequently ciphering'; the purses were 'much decay'd and losing wind'; the movements all rattled and were 'loose at their centres'; the keys were also 'very bad'; all the wires throughout the instrument were 'in a decaying state from age'; and the wind trunks were all too small. Many of the pipes did not speak well 'for want of sufficient wind', and, moreover, the Hautboy in the Swell was 'in a bad state and not of good quality'. 'Putting the organ in compleat order' would come, England said, to about 240 guineas.

He also suggested adding a Dulciana to the Choir Organ 'as far as gamut G in lieu of the Bassoon stop', which he believed was never used; and he proposed to take down, round, smooth and re-gild all the outside pipes in both fronts, as well as the large pipes around the columns. This would amount to an additional 150 guineas; and he added that the cost of scaffolding was not included in his estimate.

The instrument was clearly in need of an overhaul. Whether or not George Pyke England would have been employed to carry this out, we do not know. He died in February 1815.

A Dispute over Gilding

For more than three years after England's report was received, there was no further reference to the organ in cathedral documents. Then, in a letter dated 21 April 1818, from Ralph Barnes, the cathedral's Chapter Clerk, to a lay vicar, Charles Cole, carver and gilder of 270 Fore Street, Exeter, we find that gilding had become an issue.[61] Cole had offered to re-gild the organ's display pipes and then be paid for what had been done 'by a fair calculation'. This, Barnes said, was not a way of working the Chapter could accept.

Cole then wrote to Paddon, rather than Barnes, saying, in a letter dated 8 May 1818, that he had been as accurate in his estimate 'as the nature of the thing will allow'.[62] He had not made profit his object and had 'estimated for gold of a superior quality'. When the work was completed, he would agree to submit his charge 'to the judgement of any competent person the Chapter may employ'. Alternatively, he would contract that it should not exceed his estimate. No reply from Paddon has come to light.

The next development came on 6 June 1818, when the Chapter recognized that the erection of a new High Altar reredos would cause 'the service of the church to be interrupted' and thus provide an opportunity to re-gild the organ pipes, which they deemed necessary.[63] They instructed Barnes to write to the absent canons, to seek their 'approbation' for re-gilding the pipes and varnishing the woodwork, and they directed Cole 'to give a particular specification and estimate for the work which would then be examined and considered for the purpose of contracting with him for the same'.

One of the absent canons, John Francis Howell, made a suggestion.[64] 'If the organ could be bronzed instead of gilded', he wrote in a letter to Barnes, 'I should think it would assimilate better with the grave character of the church.' The interior of the cathedral had been colour-washed in the early 1780s, the walls then painted yellow and the columns brown. Nothing came of the suggestion.

Barnes wrote to Cole on 13 June 1818, saying that the Chapter wanted him to specify, for 'proper examination and consideration, the measurement superficial of the pipes and the mode in which that measurement is calculated and the number of respective sizes of the pipes – also the quality of the gold and a pattern exhibiting what it will be when finished, and showing the particulars of your estimate of the expense'.[65] Cole replied on 24 June, saying that, in square feet, 'the superficial contents of the gilded pipes of the cathedral organ' were: side pipes 577; east front 331; west front 272; Chair Organ 53 – total 1233.[66] The cost of covering this area would be, he calculated, £291 10s 0d. He advised that he would be 'able to lay before the Chapter' a specimen of the gilding at their meeting on 4 July and finish the gilding in four weeks.

The Chapter queried Cole's figures and on 19 September 1818, with Cole present, instructed the cathedral's surveyor, Robert Cornish, to check Cole's measurements.[67] Three weeks later, they rejected Cole's calculation of the amount of gold that was needed and accused him of overcharging by £136 10s 0d, 'the estimate still being subject to an examination of the correctness of the measurement which they directed Mr Cornish to ascertain'.[68] The Chapter Clerk was ordered to inform Cole that 'the said sum must be deducted from his estimate'.

Cole attended the Chapter meeting on 7 November 1818 and explained that the mistake in the quantity of gold had arisen 'from an erroneous calculation by Mr Carter who had made the calculation for him and who now attended to explain the same'.[69] The Chapter discussed the matter again a week later and ordered that Barnes must again write to Cole, which he did, on 16 November, telling him that he had 'stated the gold at three times its correct quantity'.[70] He added that the Chapter were 'much inclined to give him the preference and pay him fairly' but had 'no other alternative but to require the work to be completed at a deduction of the erroneous two thirds of the gold' or to pay him for what he had done already 'by a fair measure and value'.[71]

Cole advised the Chapter on 21 November that he was 'ready to waive the agreement and to finish the gilding work and to take such a sum as a competent judge should award'.[72] But the Chapter declined this proposal 'as too indefinite as well as expensive and not agreeable to their usual practice'. They considered that an agreement had been made and ordered Barnes to inform Cole that he had 'the option of giving up the work and being paid for what he had done at a fair valuation'.

As if the re-gilding matter had not taken up too much of the Chapter's time already, there were more twists in the story to come. A letter from Cole was read at the Chapter meeting on 5 December 1818.[73] In it, he said that 'it was difficult to say the exact quantity of gold required for gilding the organ, and the delay that had been occasioned by the Chapter would unavoidably increase the expense'. Therefore, he asked to be paid only 'for the quantity of gold he might actually use, as well as those extra expenses which had been unavoidably incurred, and subject thereto he would proceed with the work according to his original agreement'. The Chapter responded by ordering Barnes to inform Cole that he might proceed with the work but must now 'state to the Chapter the particulars and additional amount of the additional expenses', and he was to complete the gilding by Lady Day 1819.[74]

The Chapter ordered at their meeting on 23 January 1819 that Cole be paid £50 on account.[75] Thus, it may seem that the dispute over re-gilding had almost run its course. Alas, it was not to be, partly because the Chapter ordered, on 9 October 1819, that Cole was 'to paint the blue parts of the organ vermilion and to new gild the iron rods to which the branches [of the candelabra] are suspended from the roof – also the rods at the Dean's seat'.[76] A week later, Cole submitted his bill for the re-gilding work, including 'pinking in the carved work scarlet'.[77] Dated 18 October 1819 and submitted to Barnes on 30 October, it amounted to £214 4s 10d, plus sundry items which brought the bill to a grand total of £228 2s 10d.[78]

Cole's figures were again queried, so Barnes again wrote to him. Cole's reply, dated 4 November, showed indignation:[79]

> The quantity of gold charged in my bill has been all used in re-gilding the organ. To account for the surplus above my first calculation, I have been obliged to gild 23 of the pipes a second time. The Double Diapasons I had calculated upon gilding as I did the others in the Chapter House but was under the necessity of gilding them in their places. Those pipes contain nearly one half the organ. A considerable waste has been occasioned by laying on the gold from the books instead of the cushions. I have likewise paid the sum charged for labour to my workmen. The

difference in this item is occasioned by meeting with more difficulty in the work than I expected. The difference in gold size etc was occasioned by the delay which obliged me to prepare many of the pipes twice. This circumstance has likewise added to the labour, besides in the first estimate the removing, cleaning, taking out the bruises from the pipes, and replacing them in the case was not considered, being more properly the business of the organ builder.

Barnes wrote back on 6 November and informed Cole that the Chapter wished him to meet with Cornish 'and measure the work together'.[80] Cole replied two days later, saying that, 'if there be a doubt as to the quantity 1233 [square] feet and it be thought necessary to measure the organ again' he considered it would be 'more satisfactory to the Chapter that Mr Cornish measure it without my interference'.[81] Cornish did indeed measure the pipes on his own and calculated that the area to be gilded was 1222 square feet, not 1233.[82]

At last, the story of the gilding would soon be concluded. The Chapter resolved on 27 November 1819 that Cole be paid £223 0s 4d and instructed the Chapter Clerk to write to him, which he did the same day.[83] His letter read as follows:[84]

The Chapter have given your account much and repeated consideration. It appears by the report of their surveyor that the measurement is overstated but in a trifling degree, and making very liberal allowances for extra gold and labour the total sum coming to you would be £187. The Chapter however are very desirous that the settlement of this account should be to your satisfaction as far as they can possibly justify the acceding to your statement, and with this view disallowing only the 3 last articles of your bill £5-2s-6d they authorize me to pay you £223 – upon a receipt in full.[85] It is only necessary for me to add that if this is not agreeable to you, the offer is to be considered as not affecting any other mode of settlement more strictly agreeable to your contract, under which it appears to them that £187 is more than you would be entitled to.

Cole accepted this settlement, and the Chapter ordered on 4 December 1819 that he be paid the additional £5 2s 6d after all, making a total of £228 2s 6d.[86] He was paid immediately, the money coming from the Timber Fund.[87]

The Organ Repaired and Improved

While the re-gilding story was unfolding, other work on the organ was being carried out. The need for it was made clear at the Chapter meeting on 8 August 1818:[88]

Upon an inspection of the organ it appears that besides the new set of keys which have already been ordered, there are several improvements which may be made more advantageously at the present opportunity when the pipes have been taken out to be new gilded. They therefore directed Mr Paddon, the Organist, to enquire of Messrs Flight & Robson, Organ Builders in London, their terms for coming to view the organ.

The opinion of George Pyke England's son-in-law was not sought.

Paddon duly wrote to Flight & Robson, and a submission was received from James Flight, dated 1 October 1818.[89] The firm's proposals were as follows:

1st. To take the whole instrument in pieces, thoroughly clean it in all its parts, to put a new Dulciana stop in the Choir Organ, to take away the present old sets of finger keys and replace them with three new and complete sets – the price will be 200 guineas.

2ndly. In addition to the above estimate, to remove the old bellows from the instrument and put in new on our improved principle which combines the advantages of a much greater and more regular supply of wind, and a considerable diminution of the force requisite for working the same – 120 guineas.

3rdly. To make the interior wood work of the organ new throughout, including frame, soundboard and movements to the three organs (viz. Great Organ, Choir Organ and Swell) exclusive of the pipes, with new bellows on our improved principle and an addition to the Swell of a compass down to Tenor F with a composition of Stopt Diapason, Open Diapason, Principal, Flute, Cremona, and Hautboy to have an octave of pedals for the feet acting upon the present Double Diapason pipes of the organ from GGG up to GG including separate soundboards and conveyances for the same, the said pipes to be re-voiced to produce their full and requisite grandeur of tone, the whole to be completed in a good and substantial style of workmanship with all our latest improvements – price 800 guineas.

It was thus proposed that the organ would have a pedalboard, for the first time in its history.

There was, in fact, a fourth proposal by Flight & Robson, summarized thus at the Chapter meeting on 3 October:[90]

A new mechanical arrangement by which the three organs, viz. the Great Organ, the Choir Organ and the Swell, may be acted upon simultaneously by three separate performers and enabling the whole grandeur of the instrument to be displayed at once.

This was a promotion of the firm's new Apollonicon Organ, described by William Husk as a large organ 'of peculiar construction, comprising both keyboards and barrels', with many stops, as well as two kettledrums within the case which were 'struck, when required, by curiously contrived machinery'.[91] Perhaps we may regret that an Apollonicon was never installed in Exeter Cathedral. Kettledrums controlled by the organist would surely have added a new dimension to the accompaniment of anthems!

The Chapter ordered on 3 October that the Chapter Clerk should write not only to Flight & Robson, to ask for 'further explanation', but also to the absent canons, 'for their opinion'. A reply dated 6 October was received from James Flight, which added little to his firm's submission of 1 October.[92] The absent canons considered the proposed work unduly expensive, especially George Maximilian Slatter, a clergy musician and pupil of the organist and composer Samuel Wesley.[93] Writing on 8 October, he said that he had 'received from a competent judge' an assurance that Flight & Robson would prove very expensive and were 'not fit to undertake the improvement of an organ such as that at Exeter Cathedral'.[94] He said that he was 'well acquainted with Mr S Wesley, who was allowed by all musical professors to be the first organist and the best judge of organs in England; his opinion on this occasion would be highly valuable'.

In a further letter, dated 14 October, James Flight enlarged on the work his firm proposed to carry out and mentioned that the firm was currently working on the organ of Trinity College, Cambridge.[95] Barnes wrote to the college immediately, but the reply he received, from the college's organist, John Clarke Whitfield, was noncommittal. The work had not yet been completed, so it was 'impossible at that time to form an accurate judgement of Mr Flight's work'.[96] In a letter to Barnes dated 2 December, however, Whitfield was far from guarded.[97] Flight & Robson had entered into a written agreement with the college to make certain additions to the organ for 140 guineas and sent in a bill for 250 guineas. He regretted that the college had not employed Mr Lincoln, 'for whose integrity and reasonable charges' he could 'safely vouch'.[98] Meanwhile, Slatter had consulted Samuel Wesley and reported in a letter to Barnes dated 15 October that Wesley was also not inclined to favour Flight & Robson.[99]

Having been warned about the cost and quality of Flight & Robson's work, the Chapter resolved on 24 October that a decision over the organ be deferred to their audit at Christmas.[100] In the meantime, they sought the views of the Dean of Exeter, Dr Whittington Landon, who rarely attended Chapter meetings. He was normally resident in Oxford, where he was Provost of Worcester College.[101] Despite his extended absences, though, no major decisions about the cathedral were taken without his approval; and he took a close interest in the proposed work on the organ.

Barnes received three letters about the organ from Landon. In the first, dated 28 November, Landon said that he had heard the projected improvements of the organ were for the present suspended, and he confessed that he felt no regret that the Chapter had so determined.[102] 'Alterations in so very superior an instrument', he said, were 'perilous'; and although he felt it the duty of the Chapter 'to preserve the instrument in a sound state of repair, and to renew any parts decayed by time, yet novel additions and contrivances should be very maturely weighed before they are adopted at the hazard of incongruity if not of injury to the fabric of the whole'.

In his second letter, dated 6 December, Landon said that he had examined in detail the estimate submitted by Flight & Robson and consulted a friend 'who understands the structure of an organ well'.[103] As well as overcharging, he believed the firm was proposing to introduce 'ingenious and clever contrivances' which were not necessary. He went on to suggest that the London organ-builder Thomas Elliot be invited to give an opinion on the work that was needed. The gilding, he advised, should be carried out while the organ was being overhauled.

In his third letter, dated 18 December, Landon said that he had consulted 'both Lincoln's partner and Elliot' and was now convinced that the estimate submitted by Flight & Robson was greatly excessive.[104] He again advised that Elliot should 'examine the organ and give an estimate'. Wesley 'always recommends him', wrote Landon, and Elliot was 'said to be not only a very able but also very honest man'.

Landon did not attend the audit meeting on 22 and 23 December 1818, when the Chapter considered 'the proposal of Messrs Flight & Robson for the repair and improvement of the organ and the recommendation of Mr Lincoln as an organ builder by the Bishop and Dean and from Trinity College Cambridge'.[105] Why it was recorded in the Chapter Acts that the Dean had recommended Lincoln is curious, in that he had clearly preferred Elliot in his letters to Barnes. But this is by the way. The Chapter resolved:

> As the first and next step but without any decision of what is ultimately to be done to request Mr Lincoln to inspect the organ and make his proposal and estimate of what is necessary and proper to be done. His charge for coming to be first settled at not exceeding fifteen guineas and Mr Lincoln not to be made acquainted with any part of Mr Flight's proposals and the Chapter Clerk to request the Bishop to communicate this to Mr Lincoln and they ordered the Chapter Clerk to inform Messrs Flight & Robson that their proposals remain for consideration and that they should be paid fifteen guineas for their journey and trouble in case their proposals are not adopted

A letter from Landon to Barnes dated 21 January 1819 made clear that he 'should for skill, honesty and moderation very strongly recommend Elliot, in preference to either of the others', but he would not press the point.[106] He would abide by the Chapter's decision.

A proposal was duly submitted by Henry Cephas Lincoln and considered by the Chapter on 3 February 1819.[107] In his opinion, the following was 'absolutely necessary':

The case and frame to be substantially repaired, braced and strengthened;

To have new horizontal double bellows upon the improved principle;

The soundboards to be taken to pieces and worked over entirely anew;

The movements to be worked over also and the plan and construction of the same to be altered and improved;

To have three sets of new keys and key movements;

The present Swell front to be removed and replaced with one upon the improved new principle of Venetian Shades and the whole of the Swell movements altered and improved;

To place a Dulciana stop in the Choir Organ of metal pipes as low as the case will admit (*viz.* C below middle C) and the remaining 16 notes continued in stopped wooden pipes;

The tone and voicing to be reinstated and carefully regulated;

To rebuild the instrument and restore it to its original state of excellence with many desirable improvements for £500;

The addition of Pedals properly applied – with distinct pipes upon a full and proper scale with distinct soundboards, keys and their respective movements will amount to not exceeding £200. The additional Pedal pipes are proposed to be an Open Diapason of wood pipes and to contain an octave and a half or 20 notes, *viz.* from CCC to G.

The above sums would include, Lincoln said, 'all expenses attending the proposed work'.

Absent canons were again consulted, and Barnes mentioned in his letter to them that the Dean had recommended Thomas Elliot.[108] He also drew attention to Lincoln's proposals regarding the addition of pedals. Chancellor Thomas Johnes was 'inclined to close at once with Mr Lincoln to the extent of the £500', while Canon Thomas Heberden was 'inclined to think that it cannot be improper to take Mr Elliot's opinion'.[109] The Dean replied on 7 February, saying that he would 'certainly feel more easy with the organ in Lincoln's hands than in Flight & Robson's', and if the Chapter thought proper to 'give him an immediate order', they had his 'full assent'.[110] If, however, 'the Chapter should send for Elliot, he should be told that he must come immediately or not at all'.

Barnes then wrote to Elliot and received a reply, dated 17 February.[111] Elliot said he was unable to travel to Exeter at that time, 'owing to a bad state of health', but was willing to send his foreman. This offer was not taken up, and Elliot never again featured in the story of the cathedral's organs. The Chapter decided on 24 March 1819 that a contract with Lincoln should be drawn up for the sum of £500 and his proposal that pedals be added should not be adopted.[112] When the contract was drawn up, however, it did indeed include the addition of pedals, at an extra cost of £20. We do not know why the Chapter changed their minds over the pedals.

Lincoln's contract, dated 10 April 1819, was an almost verbatim copy of his proposal as recorded in the Chapter Acts on 3 February.[113] There were only two significant differences. The new Dulciana stop in the Choir Organ would, as proposed, extend to the C one octave below middle C, with the remaining sixteen notes continued in stopped wooden pipes 'to be placed in lieu of the Bassoon stop which will remain the property of the Chapter'. And the set of pedal keys and movements would 'operate upon or play the present Double Diapason to comprise an octave and half, *viz.* from GG to C above, seventeen notes'.

Meanwhile, Flight & Robson had written to Paddon, on 28 March 1819, to say that they had 'not yet been favoured with any decision respecting the Exeter organ' and wished to inform the Chapter that a dispute 'respecting the charge for some extra work' existed between them and Trinity College, Cambridge.[114] As a consequence, the college had 'expressed an intention of preventing as far as lay in their power the probability of our having the work to do to the Exeter organ'. The firm trusted the dispute would not count against them. Barnes responded by informing Flight & Robson, in a letter dated 31 March, that the Chapter had decided not to employ the firm.[115]

Lincoln carried out the work he had been contracted to do, and the renovated organ was first used for a service on 21 October 1819. Two days later, he attended a Chapter meeting and reported that he had completed the work as per contract for the sum of £520, plus ten guineas for replacing the Bassoon stop, making a total of £530 10s 0d.[116] The Chapter then ordered that he be paid £430 and Paddon was requested to inspect the work. Lincoln was paid £430 the same day, from the Timber Fund, and a further £100 10s 0d on 27 November, after Paddon had reported to the Chapter (on 30 October) that 'he had examined the work of the organ' and found it had been 'finished in the best workmanlike manner'.[117]

Problems with the Organ

For a while, the organ seems to have functioned satisfactorily. Then, however, on 10 November 1821, the Chapter Clerk was ordered to write to Lincoln 'to request him to attend as soon as possible to put into order such parts of his work as are defective and for the purpose of having the organ now tuned and arranging the best plan for keeping it in tune in future.[118] Three months later, Lincoln reported to a meeting of canons chaired by the Dean that the bellows and some of the movements needed to be repaired and the organ as a whole cleaned and tuned.[119] He was ordered to 'proceed to put the organ in order in these respects'. He was also told the Dulciana stop was 'considered insufficient in strength', and he agreed to replace it with a larger one, 'without charge to the Chapter'.

Lincoln further agreed to 'come himself twice a year to keep the organ clean and in tune and to keep the whole of the instrument in substantial and compleat repair and condition in every particular'. He proposed that the organ should be tuned on his behalf at other times 'by proper and competent persons for the yearly sum of £30'. On 16 February 1822, the Chapter agreed that this sum should be £35 and that any person appointed for the purpose 'should be employed under Mr Lincoln and not immediately by the Chapter'. In the first instance, they recommended that Price Turner, one of the secondaries, be employed to keep the organ in tune in Lincoln's absence, proposing the yearly sum of five pounds for that purpose.[120] His duties, the Chapter specified, would be to 'keep the reed work in tune' and be 'at all times responsible for every other defect of the instrument whenever the same may happen'.

The position over organ-tuning had been unsettled for some time. William Brooking had been dismissed in 1819, with the Chapter resolving, on 3 July, that he be paid for the quarter ending at Michaelmas, after which they would 'take into consideration the best mode of keeping the organ in order for the future'.[121] On 23 December 1819, Abraham Vicary had been appointed to succeed Brooking, at a yearly salary of £20 to commence from Christmas 1819 and be payable quarterly'.[122]

Brooking complained of the 'injustice' of his dismissal, saying, in a letter to the Dean dated 26 May 1820, that it appeared to have resulted from misrepresentations.[123] In the five years he had held the job, he said, he had performed his duties 'in a manner satisfactory to every impartial and competent judge', and Paddon had been satisfied with his work. It seemed to him that the situation which had brought about his dismissal had arisen as a consequence of Vicary becoming Paddon's apprentice, after which Paddon had 'changed his language from praise to calumny'. Brooking said that he had been given no reason for his dismissal, and incapability had not been proved. Furthermore, jobs which he had been promised before his dismissal had been given to Lincoln.

Nothing came of the complaint, but Vicary's tenure as tuner and cleaner of the organ proved short-lived. He resigned in 1821, saying in a letter to the Chapter dated 1 February that he would 'not be able to continue the tuning of the organ at the cathedral beyond the half quarter day'.[124] The Chapter noted at their meeting on 6 March that he had resigned 'in consequence of his leaving Exeter' and ordered the Chapter Clerk to write to Lincoln 'for his advice as to keeping the organ in tune in future'.[125] Turner was evidently mentioned to Lincoln, for he said in his reply, dated 12 March, that he was unable to give an opinion on Turner's suitability[126] For the time being, the organ was 'tuned by Mr Barnes', but whether or not he was Ralph Barnes the Chapter Clerk we do not know.[127]

The Chapter ordered on 23 February 1822 that Lincoln be paid £21 for carrying out his work on the organ.[128] However, only three months later, Paddon reported to the Chapter that the condition of the instrument was still not satisfactory. This time, Lincoln appeared mystified. In a letter to the Chapter Clerk dated 30 May 1822, he said that he could not think it possible, 'unless from some extraordinary cause', that the state of the instrument could in any way warrant the report made by Paddon.[129] He would 'take the earliest opportunity to attend the instrument personally'.

On 22 June, Barnes wrote to Lincoln again, telling him that the organ was 'in such a state that it must be immediately and thoroughly tuned'.[130] Moreover, he said, the Chapter had that day decided that unless he could come within a fortnight the arrangement whereby he cared for the organ would be terminated. Lincoln clearly disregarded the Chapter's warning, for on 14 December 1822 they ordered Barnes to inform him that it would 'probably be found necessary at the end of his present year's engagement for the care of the organ to make some new arrangement for its being effectually done'.[131] This turned out to be no idle threat, for at the Chapter meeting on 13 May 1823 Barnes was ordered to write to inform Lincoln that the agreement with him for the care of the organ would not be renewed and that he was, furthermore, required to 'fulfil his engagement for the year elapsed'.[132]

A letter from Lincoln to the Chapter dated 5 June 1823 shows that he had recently carried out work on the organ.[133] However, it is clear from the Chapter Acts for 7 June 1823 that the Chapter were losing patience.[134] Lincoln had been to Exeter only once in the past year and had 'failed to come a second time after repeated notices'.

If he did not come soon, 'they would make other arrangements for the care of the organ'.

An organ-builder from Bristol, John Smith, was asked to inspect the organ, and he produced a report, dated 18 June 1823, in which he drew attention to numerous faults. Some of the large pipes did not speak; the wind trunk and pallets in the sounding board needed to be larger; the Swell sounding board had runnings; the Great Organ was 'very imperfect in the construction of the pedals with the keys'; the bellows were not functioning properly; and the organ was 'shockingly out of tune', with, especially, the treble pipes of the Choir Organ 'not in tune with the bass'.[135] He was willing to do the necessary work but had other jobs he needed to complete first. The Chapter thanked him for his report and ordered Barnes to write to Lincoln yet again, to tell him that they considered him responsible for completing his part of the work 'in the most perfect and satisfactory way'. Meanwhile, they would not pay the £30 due to him 'for the care of the organ during the last year'.[136]

Lincoln's response was considered by the Chapter at a meeting on 23 July 1823.[137] He said that he could do no more to give the Great pipes 'better effect' and recommended that nothing more be done to them. The runnings in the Swell had been cured and the bellows were now 'complete'. The action of the pedals had been found 'imperfect' and Turner instructed to remedy this defect. The tuning of the Choir Organ was, he admitted, unsatisfactory, and he would endeavour to correct it. He promised he would 'now leave the organ in excellent condition' and indeed reported the following day that he could 'pronounce it in a complete and proper condition'.[138] He approved of the work Turner had carried out, but he was irritated over some of the so-called defects, saying that they 'were in part so frivolous and trifling as to be unworthy of being reported to the Chapter'.

The Chapter agreed on 26 July 1823 that Lincoln be paid the outstanding £30 if, in the view of Paddon, the defects had been 'satisfactorily removed'.[139] Paddon was indeed satisfied and wrote to Lincoln on 3 September 1823 to inform him that the money would now be paid.[140] The Chapter appointed Turner on 31 December 1823 to 'tune and take care of the organ', his yearly salary to be £20 'to commence from the present Christmas and be paid quarterly'.[141] Lincoln had been dismissed but had not yet made his last appearance in the story of the cathedral's organs.

The Chapter ordered on 29 October 1825 that 'the pipes called Double Diapason on the west front of the organ be removed and placed horizontal at an expense estimated by Mr Turner at £3'.[142] It was reported to the Chapter on 19 November, however, that the metal of one pipe 'had been improperly cut away and the pipe stopped with paper'.[143] The Chapter Clerk was ordered to write to Lincoln to accuse him of leaving the pipe 'in an improper state'. Lincoln was incredulous. In a letter to Barnes dated

26 December 1825, he called the charge 'ridiculous and false' and threatened that 'if any man breathing may dare charge me with such improper treatments of the organ, I will immediately proceed against him and prove by witness his villainy', adding that 'the person who has attributed this to me, I have no doubt is the perpetrator of that which you complain'.[144] He accused the Dean and Chapter of trusting 'that excellent instrument in the hands of inexperienced and ignorant persons' and alleged that the 'cutting and paper stopping was undoubtedly the result of some of their stupid experiments'. His tirade was ignored by the Chapter.

On 23 September 1826, the Chapter agreed to ask Flight & Robson to tune the organ and carry out 'whatever may be necessary' for the sum of thirty guineas.[145] Joseph Robson replied on 28 September, saying that Mr Robson Junior (Thomas Richard Robson), with an assistant, would in a few days attend for the purpose. This they did, and the Chapter ordered on 21 October that the firm be paid the agreed thirty guineas.[146] It was something of a volte-face that the firm had been called upon after all, but their re-appearance in the story of the cathedral's organs proved brief.

The Chapter ordered Paddon on 9 June 1832 to 'procure an estimate' from Flight & Robson for cleaning the organ.[147] The firm offered to undertake the cleaning for the sum of fifty guineas and stated that 'Mr Robson Junior would come for that purpose with an assistant'.[148] Barnes wrote to Flight & Robson on 25 June 1832 and asked the firm to undertake the work, saying that the Chapter wished it to be 'commenced immediately on the cleaning of the interior of the Church being finished, which would be completed on Saturday 14 July'.[149] It was understood, Barnes said, that the firm would commence their work on 16 July, 'the object being to interrupt the service of the Church as short a time as possible'. The firm agreed the date, and the work was carried out as requested.[150]

On 19 July, however, Thomas Robson reported to the Chapter 'the necessity of doing something effectual to the bellows' and proposed that they be made 'entirely over again using any of the materials fit and introducing all their latest improvements for blowing so as to make them as complete and perfect as if they had originally constructed them for the sum of fifty guineas, and they would make a new wind trunk to the Choir Organ in addition to the one already there'.[151] The Chapter accepted the offer and Robson carried out the work.

The next development came in the form of an 'Official Application in the Matter of Flight & Robson Bankrupts'.[152] Signed by George Green, 'Official Assignee to the said Estate', and dated 9 November 1832, it stated that the cathedral owed the estate £33 and requested payment without delay. Barnes queried the request on 14 November, asking for 'a statement from the ledger of Flight & Robson', and Green complied two days later, saying that the firm had received £52 10s 0d on 27 July 1832 and £30 0s 0d on 11 August, leaving a balance of £33 0s 0d.[153] The money was paid forthwith and the association of Flight & Robson with Exeter Cathedral thereupon ended.

Whither the Music of Exeter Cathedral?

When James Paddon died, only 58 years had passed since William Jackson had become organist and master of the choristers. In that time, musical standards in the cathedral had risen markedly. The organ had also received due care and attention, especially since 1813, when Whittington Landon became Dean of Exeter.

Though Landon was away from Exeter for much of each year, he nevertheless stamped his authority from afar. He was undoubtedly in charge. Other members of the Chapter took an interest in the cathedral's music, too, and readily made their opinions known whenever consulted. Moreover, Ralph Barnes was efficient, reliable and not afraid to take the initiative. A solicitor by profession, he had been Chapter Clerk since 1810 and played an important and effective part in implementing decisions made by the Dean and Chapter, thus helping ensure the cathedral's musical standards were raised and the fine organ was cared for.

Langdon, Jackson and Paddon had all been born in Exeter. Would Paddon's successor be another local man, and would he be able to continue raising musical standards in the cathedral? And who would care for the organ, now that Lincoln had been dismissed and Flight & Robson declared bankrupt?

CHAPTER 5

A Time of Change

Henry Hobart of Hereford Cathedral wrote to Ralph Barnes of Exeter Cathedral on 4 June 1835. The canon's letter to the Chapter Clerk read as follows:[1]

> The organist of our cathedral by name Wesley (whose family are well known in the musical world) hearing there is likely to be a vacancy at Exeter has requested me to make inquiries. . . . As an organist he is invaluable, and myself as one of the Body should be sorry to part with him; but as he has lately unfortunately clandestinely married the Dean's sister, for which act he has so displeased the Dean he fears should he remain here it will be unpleasant to both parties and therefore wishes to get away from the Diocese.[2]

Wesley was a son of the celebrated organist and composer whose opinions of organ-builders had been sought by Exeter's Chapter in 1818.

Choosing Paddon's Successor

The Dean of Exeter wrote to Canon Bull of Exeter Cathedral on 15 June 1835 to tell him Barnes had drawn to his attention Hobart's recommendation of Wesley 'as a fit person to succeed Paddon in case of vacancy in our organ loft'.[3] Being in Oxford, he had not yet heard of Paddon's death, which had occurred the previous day. Dean Landon said he had written to Canon Clutton of Hereford Cathedral to enquire about Wesley, adding that he had 'heard from another quarter a strong recommendation, with a little private history'. Wesley's marriage was, he understood, the only reason why the authorities at Hereford were 'disposed to part with him'. Landon wrote to Barnes a week later.[4] He now knew of Paddon's death, having 'seen it in the Exeter paper';[5] and he had also received a reply from Clutton, who had given a high opinion of Wesley.[6]

Landon commented in his letter to Barnes that, 'if no superior candidate offers', Wesley 'may be more eligible than any individual at or near Exeter'. He did not appear to know that the Chapter had decided to advertise for a new organist.[7] Applications had to be submitted to the Chapter Clerk by 18 July, together with 'testimonials as to professional attainments and general character and conduct'. For the first time, there would be open competition for the offices of organist and master of the choristers of Exeter Cathedral. As organist, sub-chanter and informator puerorum, the successful candidate would receive 'about one hundred guineas *per annum*', and as a lay vicar 'about £20 *per annum*'. He would be 'allowed to take one or two apprentices and employ his leisure time in general tuition'.

Twelve applications were received, including one from Wesley, one from Thomas Jones, the organist of Canterbury Cathedral, and another from William Dixon, deputy organist of Norwich Cathedral. A canon of Canterbury Cathedral stated in a testimonial that Jones was 'fully competent to restore your choir to its former excellence', a surprising comment, given the fine words about the choir published in obituaries of Paddon.[8] But Jones did not move to Exeter. He withdrew his application, saying, in a letter dated 30 June 1835, that he had been 'led to suppose the emoluments of the situation were much more lucrative'.[9]

A letter dated 3 August 1835 from Wesley to the Precentor of Exeter Cathedral shows that he had been interviewed and subsequently informed that 'the Chapter had postponed further consideration of the election of organist' pending receipt of an additional reference.[10] The Chapter wished to be reassured as to Wesley's moral behaviour, and he made clear in his letter that he was indignant over this implied slur on his reputation.

A letter from Landon to Barnes dated 5 August 1835 shows that the number of candidates for the post had by then been reduced to two: Wesley and Dixon.[11] Landon said that his enquiries had confirmed the personal respectability of Wesley. The name of Dixon was, he added, new to him; and, moreover, he did not have a high regard for the music at Norwich. He still thought Wesley should be appointed. The Chapter decided at their meeting on 8 August that they would elect Paddon's successor at their next meeting.[12] Wesley's further testimonials satisfied them;[13] and on 15 August 1835 they elected him organist (see Plate 15).[14]

Samuel Sebastian Wesley

Born in London on 14 August 1810, Samuel Sebastian Wesley was an illegitimate son of Samuel Wesley and given his second forename after Johann Sebastian Bach, his father's musical hero.[15] He attended the Blue Coat School for a short time in 1817 and then, in November of that year, became a chorister in the Chapel Royal. On ceasing to be a chorister, in March 1826, he was appointed organist of St James's Chapel, Hampstead Road, London; and he added two more church posts in 1829, becoming, in January, organist of St Giles' Church, Camberwell, and, in November, organist of St John's Church, Waterloo. He was then organist of three churches simultaneously until March 1831, when he resigned from both the chapel and St John's but remained organist at Camberwell. He took another post in November 1831, as organist of Hampton Parish Church, on the understanding that he played for services on Sunday evenings only. There was no evening service in St Giles'. He also took up residence in Hampton, attracted, it has been suggested, by the better fishing prospects offered by the River Thames than the Surrey Commercial Docks![16]

How Wesley gained his mastery of the organ is not known.[17] The organists of the Chapel Royal when he was a chorister were Charles Knyvett (until his death in 1822), George Smart (from 1822) and John Stafford Smith, while Thomas Attwood, a composer at the Chapel Royal, and William Hawes, the Chapel Royal's Master of the Children, were both competent organists. However, it is doubtful that any of these musicians gave him organ tuition. It is inconceivable that his father did not help him develop keyboard skills, but it seems that young Wesley came to be one of the finest organists in Britain largely by his own endeavours. The credit for introducing him to the music of Johann Sebastian Bach was surely due to his father. Bach's organ music was little known in England at the time.

Several of young Wesley's contemporaries studied at the Royal Academy of Music, but he did not. He never received a rigorous grounding in harmony, counterpoint, orchestration or musical form. However, he gained much practical experience and a form of apprenticeship through his involvement in musical activities in the English Opera House and other London theatres and concert halls, sometimes with his father. Moreover, he made the acquaintance of leading continental musicians when they visited London, particularly Spohr, Weber and Mendelssohn. He came to be known as a composer of songs, church music and instrumental movements for small orchestra, as well as piano and organ music.

By the early 1830s, Wesley had become well known in musical circles in the capital and farther afield. He could have been expected to remain in London and there build upon his growing musical reputation, but in the summer of 1832, to the surprise of many, he applied to become the organist of Hereford Cathedral. He was appointed on 10 July and succeeded John Clarke Whitfield, who had, in 1818, when organist of Trinity College, Cambridge, advised against employing Flight & Robson to repair the organ of Exeter Cathedral.

Wesley soon regretted the move to Hereford. Musical standards at the cathedral were low, and his salary was only £60 *per annum*, with fewer opportunities to supplement his income than in London. Hereford was, he found, a musical backwater. He continued composing, though, and wrote, *inter alia*, his anthem 'The Wilderness' to mark the opening of the rebuilt cathedral organ in November 1832 and another fine anthem, 'Blessed be the God and Father', for Easter Day 1834. But his marriage soured his previously good relations with the Dean, who had formerly been a curate at Hampton and may have influenced the decision to appoint him at Hereford. He resolved to seek pastures new and in April 1835 applied unsuccessfully to become organist of St George's Chapel, Windsor.

Though elected organist of Exeter Cathedral on 15 August 1835, he commenced his duties on 7 October, when he made a marked impression on a chorister, William Spark, then aged 12:[18]

> When I first heard him play on the organ, I was seized with reverential awe. It was at the close of the afternoon service in the cathedral. The choir men and choir boys were asked to remain in their stalls; and we all listened in rapt silence to Wesley's masterly playing – one or two pieces, but chiefly extemporaneous – for about forty minutes. . . . We now heard for the first time what organ playing was under the magic touch of a master like Wesley.

Son of a lay vicar, also called William, young Spark was to become one of Wesley's most loyal pupils. When Wesley left Exeter, Spark went with him as his articled pupil. Wesley was elected and admitted a lay vicar on 24 October 1835, installed by lay vicars Charles Cole and William Spark senior.[19]

For the most part, Wesley's early years at Exeter appear to have been happy. Sons were born in June 1836 and December 1837; and his home life at 9 Cathedral Close and his social life seem to have been agreeable. His working relationship with the Dean and Chapter was amicable; and he became involved in the musical life of the city, enjoying particularly his associations with the Devon Madrigal Society and the Devon Glee Club. He continued to compose and, in so doing, strengthened his position as the foremost composer of church music of his time. However, the death of his father in 1837 cast a shadow, and it is believed that financial concerns led him to take, at Easter 1837, an additional post of organist, at Holy Trinity Chapel, Exmouth.[20] His approach to that appointment was, though, perfunctory, and he resigned after only one year.

A prickly side to Wesley showed itself in January 1838, when he took offence over a letter about the state of the organ written by Abraham Vicary, a priest vicar and former apprentice of Paddon.[21] Worse was to come. Dean Landon died in December 1838 and the Precentor, Thomas Hill Lowe, succeeded him. As Peter Horton put it, Lowe was 'concerned to maintain closer control over the daily business of the cathedral than his elderly predecessor had done'.[22] Relations between Wesley and the cathedral's authorities deteriorated, and Wesley soon concluded that he needed to leave Exeter. He set his sights on a university career and to this end gained the

Oxford Bachelor and Doctor of Music degrees by accumulation, both on 21 June 1839. He was considered for a chair in the University of Edinburgh in 1841 but was not appointed and never did become an academic.[23]

The year of 1840 was particularly unhappy for Wesley: his baby daughter died in February; there were disputes over his conduct and attendance; he made an unprovoked attack on two choristers in the Singing School;[24] and the plates for a collection of his anthems were destroyed by fire in October. Tension between him and the cathedral's authorities can be sensed in the Chapter Acts. On 16 May 1840, for example, the Chapter ordered that he 'be informed that he is not to give lessons on the organ either to his apprentice or to any other person, the order not being meant to extend to a prohibition to the apprentice to practise any service for use in the Church';[25] and on 20 June 1840 they 'ordered that the Organist be informed that no private engagement should interfere with his attendance on the Chapter on Saturday mornings'.[26]

His absences increased in frequency, leading to a reprimand from the Chapter on 7 June 1841: 'Dr Wesley having been absent since Thursday the 27th May without previous communication to the Chapter, and having left the organ to a young and inexperienced pupil, they directed the Chapter Clerk to inform Dr Wesley that it is expected that the organist should have leave of absence from the Chapter.'[27] Soon, though, an opportunity to escape from Exeter arose. He opened the new organ of Leeds Parish Church on 18 October and was offered and accepted the post of organist and choirmaster of that church at a guaranteed salary of £200 *per annum* for ten years.[28]

Wesley's wish to resign was recorded in the Chapter Acts for 20 November 1841.[29] However, he did not hand in his notice for several weeks. That came on 4 January 1842, when he stated in writing that he would 'give up all further attention to the duties of my offices at Exeter Cathedral' in March.[30] Thereafter, he was rarely present, leaving the organ loft, without the Chapter's permission, in the hands of his apprentice. This of course displeased the Chapter, who, for this reason and others, appear to have been more than glad to see him go. Indeed, a wrapper around Wesley papers in the Exeter Cathedral Archives has on it, in the handwriting of the Chapter Clerk, 'The most to be avoided man I ever met with'.[31]

A letter dated 11 March 1842 shows that Wesley had already moved to Leeds, even though his last day at Exeter was officially 25 March.[32] From Wesley to Ralph Sanders (Registrar, Peculiar Court of the Dean), it concerned his 'account with the Chapter of Exeter Cathedral'. The reply from Sanders, dated 15 March, was polite and promised that the matter would soon be resolved, but it was not, and there followed a series of disputes over money he claimed was owed him. A letter from the Chapter Clerk to Wesley dated 26 September 1843 shows the extent to which exasperation built up:[33]

The Dean of Exeter received a note apparently in your handwriting – dated Leeds Aug 22. The Dean transmitted it to me to be submitted to the Chapter. I have so done. The insolence of the note is so surpassing that you can expect, assuredly you will receive, no other answer than that announcement. No future communication addressed to the Dean will receive any reply whatever. If you have any to make to the Dean & Chapter, I beg it may be made to me, if in terms fit to be communicated.

From Leeds, Wesley moved to Winchester Cathedral in 1849 and Gloucester Cathedral in 1865. In all of these places, he was often difficult and abrasive.[34] He last played for a service in Gloucester Cathedral on Christmas Day 1875, his health then poor and his condition deteriorating. He died in Gloucester, from Bright's disease, on 19 April 1876 and was buried in Exeter's Old Cemetery eight days later, beside the baby daughter who had died in 1840.[35] The organist of Exeter Cathedral and several of the cathedral's choir were present at the burial, along with four of Wesley's five sons, his brother and several friends, but few other people attended, and there was no music.

Further Work on the Organ

A report in *Woolmer's Exeter and Plymouth Gazette* on 17 October 1835 stated that the Dean and Chapter intended to put aside several thousand pounds for renovation of the organ, the work to be carried out by the London organ-builder James Chapman Bishop. However, the only work he carried out was a tuning of the organ in December 1835, which was not mentioned in the Chapter Acts and for which he was never paid![36]

William Brooking, an organ and pianoforte manufacturer of Gandy Street, Exeter, wrote to the Dean and Chapter on 14 April 1836 to say that he and his son would 'engage to repair, clean and tune the organ in the cathedral for the sum of £20 a year'.[37] They had evidently inspected the organ already, for Brooking went on to say that they had 'tried the force of wind the bellows have got now' and found they required 'fifty to sixty pounds weight on them to make the organ the same power it was before Mr Lincoln repaired it'. They proposed to fit 'a new pipe to the wind chest of the Double Diapasons' and to renovate 'the helpers behind the large pipes'.[38]

The Chapter ordered on 4 June 1836 that the organ be cleaned and tuned by Henry Crabb, an organ-builder of Sidwell Street, Exeter.[39] His appointment was, though, short-lived, for the offer of Brooking & Son to clean and tune the organ was accepted by the Chapter on 23 July 1836.[40] They were ordered to carry out this work and 'to keep the same in tune up to Christmas next for £24'. At the same meeting, the Chapter ordered that the employment of Henry Venn, the bellows blower since the dismissal of his predecessor, should be 'continued during the pleasure of the Chapter and receive the weekly sum of five shillings'.[41] John Newcombe succeeded Venn on 11 January 1842 and the Chapter then granted a pension of one shilling a week to Venn 'until further orders'.[42]

The original offer of Brooking & Son to repair the organ, not just clean and tune it, for the sum of £20 a year, was accepted by the Chapter on 6 May 1837. However, as Horton noted, 'something more fundamental was required, and questions about the instrument's capabilities began to be asked'.[43] Initially, as he put it, 'Wesley kept his own counsel, but the publication of a letter from the Revd Abraham Vicary, Custos of the College of Priest Vicars, listing all the improvements made during the previous quarter-century, was more than he could stomach'. Wesley considered Vicary's intervention interference, stating scornfully in two letters to the Chapter Clerk, both dated 6 January 1838, that he was an authority on organs and organ-building and did not need Vicary to help him judge the condition of an organ.[44] Furthermore, 'the unfavourable opinion' of the state of the organ had not come from him, as Vicary had implied, but from professional musicians.[45]

Accepting that the organ needed to be renovated, the Chapter invited a London organ-builder, John Gray, to inspect the instrument. He reported orally at the Chapter meeting on 3 February 1838 and subsequently wrote a report which was considered by the Chapter on 20 March, and the decision was then made that renovation be carried out, the estimated cost being £205.[46] The Chapter resolved that the work 'be done this year', but Wesley was sceptical that it would happen or that any significant improvement to the organ would result. He was proved wrong on both counts. The organ was reopened on 4 November, to the evident approval of *The Musical World*, which declared that the instrument, 'from being the worst, may now be reckoned one of the best in the kingdom'.[47]

While the work on the organ was being carried out in 1838, an alarming discovery was made. Loosemore's case was leaning. The cathedral's surveyor, Robert Cornish junior, reported as follows to the Dean and Chapter on 22 September:[48]

> From the manner of its outer framing and from its excessive weight, the east front is given out, drawing after it the west one, and beside which, for want of extra supports, the organ rocks very much. My attention has been thereby called to it by Mr Gray; and extra iron and wood, cross and angle bars are required, and to effect which an outlay of from ten to twelve pounds will be required.

As ordered by the Chapter on 29 September, the necessary additional support for the case was provided;[49] and the Chapter agreed on 9 March 1839 that 'Gray's account of £240 15s 0d for the organ be paid and the Chapter Clerk do express to him the satisfaction of the Chapter at the manner in which the work had been performed'.

After 1839, the organ appears to have needed little more than tuning and routine maintenance for nearly twenty years. Only one reference to the instrument has come to light, and that in a letter to *The Times* published on 9 September 1844, from N.B.T. of Cheltenham:[50]

> About three weeks ago, in passing through Exeter, I stayed a few hours to view its venerable cathedral and attend divine service there. The nave of the church was then undergoing repair and cleansing. . . . The continued repairs of the nave were not permitted to interfere with the usual performance of divine worship twice a day, notwithstanding the organ was completely enveloped in brown Holland to protect it from dust.

The writer went on to mention 'the beautiful strains of the powerful organ'.

Changes in the Organ Loft

Exeter's forthcoming vacancy was advertised within days of Wesley announcing his intention to resign, and enquiries were soon received, one of them from Alfred Angel, assistant organist of Wells Cathedral. In a letter to the Chapter Clerk dated 13 December, Angel asked 'what the emoluments of the situation amount to'.[51] Barnes advised him that, in total, taking into account salary and other sources of income, he could expect about £190 *per annum*. This clearly satisfied Angel, for on 22 December he sent a testimonial from the Dean and Chapter of Wells and asked for his application to be considered.[52]

The Chapter seem to have assumed that Wesley would depart immediately. However, his note of 4 January 1842 that he would go in March caused the Chapter to delay the selection process. They resolved at their meeting on 12 January that the choice of a new organist be 'postponed until the spring audit and the candidates informed thereof'.[53] After Wesley's departure, though, the Chapter moved quickly to appoint a successor, for it was recorded in the Chapter Acts for 2 April that 'the Chapter met on Thursday 31 March for trial of the candidates for the place of organist'.[54] Five of the eight applicants were shortlisted, and all five attended on 31 March, when they were 'tried in the presence of the Dean, Canon Martin, Canon Rogers and Dr Bull with the assistance of Dr (Stephen) Elvey, the Organist of New College, Oxford'.[55] Their unanimous choice was Alfred Angel.

The Chapter spelled out the duties of the organist in the Chapter Acts for 5 April. He was answerable to the Dean and Chapter; he was not allowed to absent himself

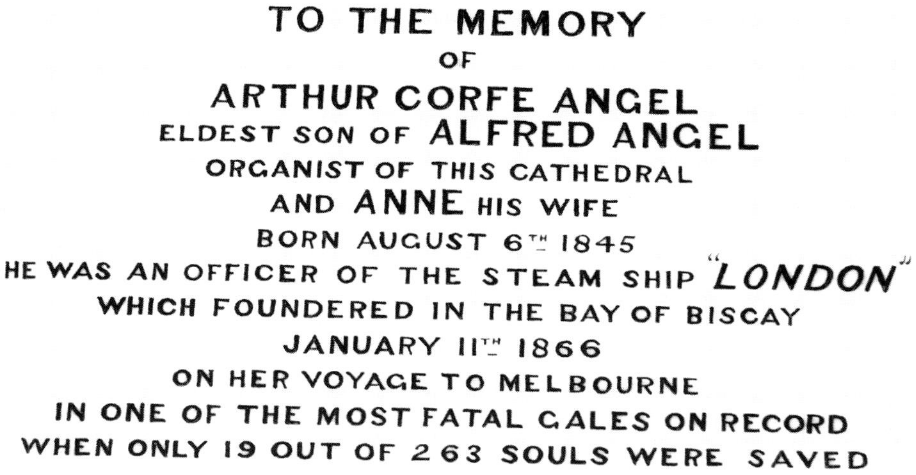

TO THE MEMORY
OF
ARTHUR CORFE ANGEL
ELDEST SON OF ALFRED ANGEL
ORGANIST OF THIS CATHEDRAL
AND ANNE HIS WIFE
BORN AUGUST 6ᵀᴴ 1845
HE WAS AN OFFICER OF THE STEAM SHIP "LONDON"
WHICH FOUNDERED IN THE BAY OF BISCAY
JANUARY 11ᵀᴴ 1866
ON HER VOYAGE TO MELBOURNE
IN ONE OF THE MOST FATAL GALES ON RECORD
WHEN ONLY 19 OUT OF 263 SOULS WERE SAVED

Figure 5.1   Angel memorial, north quire aisle

without leave of the Chapter or the Canons in Residence; he was 'to teach the choristers in all things necessary'; he was 'to assemble all the members of the choir, both men and boys, in the Music School and quire for the purpose of getting up new services and anthems and practising old ones'; he was required to attend Chapter meetings every Saturday; and he was allowed to use the cathedral organ 'at all hours of the day for his own improvement or the instruction of his apprentices'.[56] His emoluments would total about £190 *per annum*.[57]

Baptized in Chichester, Sussex, on 14 June 1816, Angel had been a chorister of Chichester Cathedral but was expelled in early 1828 'for improper conduct in this cathedral'.[58] He had been at Wells since 1829, as a chorister until 1831, organist's apprentice from 1832, and assistant organist and undermaster of the choristers since 1838.[59] When he moved to Exeter, the long tradition of the organist being also a lay vicar was broken.[60] Moreover, he did not become sub-chanter, being made instead a secondary.

Like his predecessor, Angel became involved in the city's musical life, keenly supporting the Devon Glee Club and the Exeter Madrigal Society.[61] He also composed a little, his anthem 'Blow the Trumpet in Zion' gaining him the Gresham Prize in 1842.[62] He married Anne Corfe of Salisbury on 23 September 1844, and they had two sons, both baptized in Exeter Cathedral, Arthur on 17 August 1845 and Edmund on 5 September 1847.[63] As recorded on a memorial in the cathedral's north quire aisle, Arthur perished in the Bay of Biscay on 11 January 1866, when the ship on which he was Third Officer sank in a tempest.

In the many years Angel was organist, mentions of him in the Chapter Acts were few and far between and concerned mainly with copying and purchases of music and appointments of organ apprentices. A significant change in his employment was, however, documented on 3 December 1849 when he resigned as a secondary, the Chapter deeming it 'inexpedient that he should continue to hold such a place'.[64] His good standing with the Chapter was evident, though, in the decision to continue paying him *ex gratia Capituli* what he had been receiving as a secondary and to increase his total emoluments from £198 8s 0d to £200 *per annum* while also reducing the rent he paid for his house from £42 to £20 a year. A further change in his employment came on 26 March 1864, when he became, after all, a lay vicar.[65]

The organ received attention in 1859 as a consequence of the Chapter's decision to hold Sunday afternoon services in the nave. Hitherto, all services had been held in the quire. On 21 December 1858, the Chapter 'ordered that the necessary alterations to the organ' be made.[66] Two in particular were proposed: that the organ be made adequate to support large congregations in the nave; and also that the keyboards be moved from the eastern side of the organ, between the main and Chair cases, to the

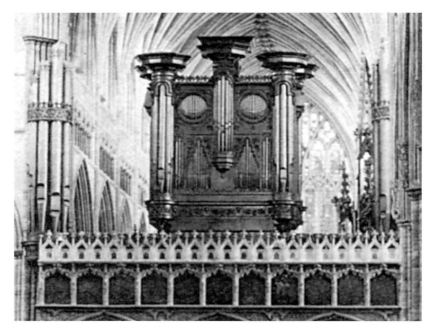

Figure 5.2   The organ from the nave in the 1860s, showing the large pipes clustered around the columns on the edges of the pulpitum, with the circular iron bands around the pipes fitted by Henry Willis in 1859.

southern side, so that the organist might hear the singing equally well at both quire and nave services.

Angel wrote to a London organ-builder, 'Father' Willis, soon after Christmas 1858 to ask him to provide a quotation for the proposed work. In his reply, dated 4 January 1859, Willis said that he was 'labouring under great pressure of work' and did not think he could commence work for about two months. Angel wrote back on 8 January, saying that the Chapter wished to advise Willis that the delay 'was thought likely to induce them to apply elsewhere'.[67] As the Chapter would discuss the matter further in a few days, however, he thought he would acquaint Willis with what he proposed should be done to the organ.

Angel pointed out in his letter of 8 January that moving the keyboards would render necessary an entirely new action and thus present an opportunity to effect a number of changes. He made several suggestions but quickly changed his mind, saying in a letter to Willis two days later that, 'upon a closer examination of the interior of our organ, I find there is not sufficient available space to admit any of my proposed extension of the Swell'.[68] In a letter to Willis the following day (11 January), he advised that the Chapter's intention was to 'open the nave for Divine Service of Easter Day, 24 April'.[69] If Willis could not complete the work by then, there would be no option but to approach another organ-builder.

Willis quickly provided a specification and estimate.[70] He proposed to clean the organ thoroughly and mount its internal pipes on new units, with the pipes 'made to speak their original tone and in tune to the present pitch of the instrument'.[71] He also proposed to provide three new sets of keys (with ebony naturals and ivory sharps) and a set of radiating and concave pedals of two and a half octaves from the C two octaves below middle C to the F above (a total of thirty notes). As requested, he would place the new keyboards on the south side of the organ, and he proposed to provide five new couplers and 'extend the compass of the Double Diapason of the Great Organ by adding new pipes, soundboard and movements so as to make it form one stop of 16 feet pitch'. He agreed to finish the work by Palm Sunday 'for the sum of £125 cash upon completion'. Angel then asked for additional pipes to be provided in the Great and Pedal divisions, and Willis advised him that the extra cost would be £20.[72] The Chapter approved the expenditure and the additional pipes were provided.

Willis completed the work to the Chapter's satisfaction and received £226, made up of £145 for his contract, £5 for extra keys, £4 for draw-stop knobs, £25 for re-voicing the organ, £40 for new reeds, and £7 for a new Clarabella (which replaced a Cornet).[73] A further £27 8s 0d was paid to Thomas Pridham & Son for ornamental circular iron bands, required to secure the pipes around the columns on the edges of the pulpitum.[74] An achievement of Willis's work was that he managed to overcome

Figure 5.3   View from the south-west, showing the large pipes around the columns and the organ case before it was expanded to its present depth.

a defect which had existed since Loosemore built the organ. He made the Double Diapason pipes speak properly. He also replaced the Trumpet in the Great Organ and the Hautboy (Oboe) in the Swell.

The Chapter resolved on 4 June 1859 that care of the organ be entrusted to Willis for the sum of £20 *per annum* and that payment to Brooking would cease after Michaelmas that year.[75] They further ordered on 17 June that 'in consequence of the alterations in the organ the bellows blower be paid for the present the additional sum of five shillings per week'.[76] Willis subsequently tuned and maintained the organ for several years and on 7 December 1861 was paid an extra £55 for 'new bellows and alteration of machinery in the organ'.[77] On 24 February 1866, however, without giving any reason, the Chapter ordered that 'the arrangement with Mr Willis for his tuning of the organ be discontinued'.[78] The job passed to Messrs Speechly & Ingram, organ-builders of London.[79]

Cathedral Restoration

In October 1866, as requested by the Dean and Chapter, the architect Sir George Gilbert Scott submitted 'suggestions as to a course of action' for both interior

Figure 5.4   The organ from the quire in the 1860s. Notice the relative heights of the Chair and main cases.

and exterior restoration of, and repairs to, the cathedral.[80] In this submission, he addressed a matter which had implications for the organ. Some people considered the case an eyesore and wanted it moved to a transept. A number of local architects were demanding something even more drastic: that the pulpitum be demolished altogether.[81]

Scott considered this demand 'the height of vandalism', and pointed out that the screen could not even be pierced, as had been suggested, without destroying the marble staircases which provided access to the organ loft from the pulpitum's passageways. These staircases were, he said, 'part and parcel of the structure'. In his opinion, the organ 'should retain its present position'. He acknowledged that the case was 'an obstruction to the "unbroken vista" of the view of the vaulting' but said that he was 'far from certain that the small height of the cathedral's interior might not be somewhat disappointing if the partial break in its length were to be removed'. He agreed that the central position of the organ was, musically, 'by far the best' and recognized that the position of the organist on the southern side of the instrument was advantageous for accompanying services in both the quire and the nave. He had only one objection to the organ case: 'the disproportionate dimensions of its cornices'.

Not until June 1870 did the Chapter decide to go ahead with a restoration of the cathedral, and then only when sufficient funds had been raised. Work began eventually on 1 May 1871, in accordance with revised suggestions and supplementary notes submitted by Scott on 25 April 1870.[82] His views on the positions of the organ and pulpitum remained the same as in 1866, and his view was supported by the Dean and most of the Chapter. The pulpitum would not be demolished and the organ would not be rebuilt somewhere else in the cathedral. But there was a compromise, agreed in September 1872.[83] The marble staircases would, after all, be removed and the arches of the screen opened up. The organ would remain where it had been for centuries and access to it provided by a spiral stone staircase built in the south quire aisle, its entrance in the southern passageway of the pulpitum (see Plate 4). It was built by Edwin Light Luscombe, a local contractor.[84]

There were jitters over the removal of the marble staircases, the concern being that they were part and parcel of the pulpitum and the screen itself and a necessary part of the cathedral's structure, without which the building might collapse. As early as 19 January 1871, the Chapter asked Scott if it would be 'possible and safe to remove the stairs'.[85] Scott was able to allay fears but decided, nevertheless, to provide extra support beneath the northern and southern limits of the organ case by bolting cast-iron frames to the walls and lintels inside the entrances to the pulpitum's passageways.[86] He also added four wooden pilasters to the western side of the case to improve its structural integrity.[87]

At their meeting on 19 January 1871, the Chapter asked Scott 'what it was proposed to do with the organ, as to the woodwork', this being a reference to his plan to replace the wainscot in the quire with stalls reminiscent of those originally in the mediæval building.[88] Scott replied that there was 'no intention of touching the present organ case, except making some modifications in the cornices which have undue projection'. Repairs to the case would probably be needed, however, and the Choir Organ case would 'have to be united to the new wood work below it'. When this uniting was eventually carried out, the Chair case was raised five feet. The height of the main case was not altered, but the cornices were indeed made smaller (by Edwin Light Luscombe).

Scott pressed for removal of the pipes from around the columns on the edges of the pulpitum. As the pipes were in poor condition, Henry Speechly remade them, using zinc for the largest four and a mixture of tin and lead called 'spotted metal' for the others, with much of the tin coming from the old pipes.[89] As instructed by Scott's son, John Oldrid Scott, the new pipes were placed inside the main case, and so also were the pipes that had been mounted horizontally on the upper surface of the pulpitum. To accommodate these pipes, the case was increased in depth (i.e. the east–west direction).

Many other pipes were found to be in poor condition, too. In the words of Thomas Worth, taken from his book about the restoration of the cathedral, published in 1878:[90]

> The whole of the pipes in both fronts of the organ, being found to be quite decayed and almost falling to pieces, were melted down; and, with the addition of new metal, remade to the original scales. They are of pure tin, and being burnished, present a brilliant appearance, contrasting finely with the grand old oak case.

Speechly advised against gilding the new pipes, saying in a letter to Angel dated 14 May 1875 that 'the pure metal will have the appearance of burnished silver and in such an organ case will present a very grand and imposing front'.[91] The gilded pipes were discarded; and no pipes have been gilded since.

Scott considered it 'vexatious that, in renewing the pipes of the Choir Organ, which were decayed, they have not reproduced the embossed patterns'.[92] Speechly had originally been 'anxious to try and leave some visible relic of the old Master's pipe work'. However, he had changed his mind, advising Angel in a letter dated 18 May 1875 that his opinion was now that the state of the pipes was such that they needed to be replaced, but doing so in embossed form would be unduly expensive.[93]

While restoration work was being carried out in the eastern half of the cathedral, all services were held in the nave. At first, the organ continued to be used, but when the need to rebuild the instrument became apparent and it was realized, moreover, that the organ needed to be out of action for a significant period of time while the pulpitum was being altered and restoration work was taking place in the western part of the quire, the Chapter ordered, on 14 December 1872, 'that an organ be obtained from Messrs Speechly & Ingram for the nave'. The charge, the firm stated, would be '20% of the value of the organ, *viz.* £150, 10% being for the use of the organ and 10% for its erection and for the carriage from and to London, the latter being remitted in case of the sale thereof in this neighbourhood'.[94]

In December 1872, Angel submitted to the Chapter suggestions respecting alterations to the organ on the pulpitum, and these were approved by the Chapter on 3 January

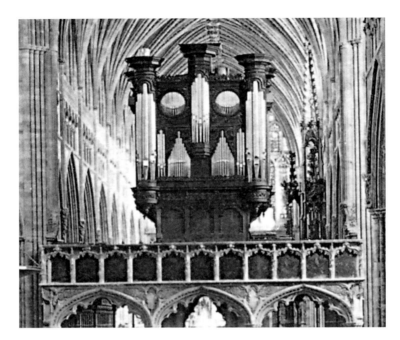

Figure 5.5   The organ from the nave, 1876, showing the tops of bass pipes protruding above the case. Notice that the burnished display pipes of pure tin presented a brilliant appearance. Notice also that the diameters of the cornices have been reduced since the 1860s and the cresting on the pulpitum has been removed. In addition, on the lower part of the organ case, four pilasters have been fitted and decorated carvings applied.

1873.[95] Speechly & Ingram thereupon considered Angel's suggestions and submitted a specification and estimate dated 29 January 1873:[96]

1. To provide and fix an entire new Swell sound board and Swell box, compass CC to F, in all 54 notes.[97]
2. To repair and reinstate the present wood and metal pipes excepting the Open Diapason.
3. To provide a new metal Open Diapason throughout the Swell CC to F, in all 54 notes.
4. To provide a new French Horn in the Swell throughout 54 notes in place of the present Trumpet.
5. To provide seven new pipes in the bass of each stop in the Swell, CC to F sharp.
6. To carry up the compass of the Great Organ from D sharp to F in all and provide new pipes for those notes in all stops.

7. To provide a new Harmonic Flute in the Great Organ GG to F, in all 59 notes.

8. To generally reconstruct all the mechanism necessary for the completion of the above works comprising new key action, new draw-stop action where necessary, and all necessary stands and stays for the arrangement of the 32 feet pipes which will have to be removed for the deepening of the case towards the nave.

9. The west front of the organ case to be moved by Speechly & Ingram 3 feet westward to give the required space for the additions according to Mr Angel's instructions. They are to make good also all stays and appliances connected with the Building Frame, but no additions or repairs to the case proper.

The work would cost £400, and, in addition, the Choir Organ would be 'lifted into a position to be chosen by Sir Gilbert Scott', with the organ left 'in playable and proper condition for the sum of £15, exclusive of case work'.

Speechly subsequently suggested changes to the specification of the Swell. As he put it in a letter to Angel dated 28 July 1873:[98]

The Swell soundboard is made for nine stops. I thought it would be a pity to make it for less as we should not be able to add any more stops to it after should it be required. I have planted it as follows: 1 Double Diapason (new); 2 Open Diapason; 3 Stopped Diapason; 4 Gamba or Keraulophon; 5 Principal; 6 Mixture; 7 Horn; 8 Oboe; 9 Clarion. We should very much like to complete the Swell at once, as it would be a great improvement to have soft 8 feet stops in the Swell, say Gamba or Keraulophon, and Clarion we should recommend having a new one for the Great which is wanted badly, and the old Great Clarion could be re-voiced which would do for the Swell. We have made sixteen new metal pipes for the upper notes of the 32 foot Open. The new work is all but ready to send off, but that we must put off until the work of the Cathedral has advanced enough for us to have it all clean.

The eventual specification of the Swell was: Double Diapason, Open Diapason, Stopped Diapason, Salicional from tenor C, Principal, Mixture (three ranks), Cornopean, Oboe and Clarion.[99] The pipes of the Double Diapason were made of wood, while some of the Stopped Diapason pipes were of wood, others metal. All of the other Swell pipes were metal. Many of the Stopped Diapason, Principal and Mixture pipes were new, and the pipes of the other stops were all new. Four composition pedals were also provided. An article about the restoration of the cathedral was published in *Trewman's Exeter Flying Post* on 28 June 1876, the day before the quire was reopened for divine worship. This listed twelve stops on the

Great Organ, six on the Choir Organ, and three on the Pedal Organ.[100] In addition, six couplers were provided, and the keys and action were new throughout.

The Chapter ordered on 18 March 1876 that £200 'be paid to Mr Speechly on account of the organ';[101] and they ordered on 2 September 1876 that a further £300 be paid to him, also on account.[102] Yet another payment was ordered on 3 February 1877, this one of £100.[103]

After 'ailing for some little time', as a local newspaper reported, Angel died on 24 May 1876, 'having taken a cold when attending the funeral of the late Dr. Wesley'.[104] He had returned home from the evening service on 23 May feeling unwell and passed away the next day, the cause of death being inflammation on the lungs. His funeral was a contrast to that of Wesley. It took place on 30 May in Exeter's Higher Cemetery and was attended, to quote the newspaper, 'by nearly the whole of the Cathedral

Figure 5.6   The organ from the quire as it appeared from 1876 to 1891. Notice that the Chair case was raised relative to the main case during Scott's restoration of the cathedral. Notice also that the tops of two of the longest bass pipes protrude above the right-hand side of the case.

Body, by all the leading organists and professional friends of the deceased, and by a large number of the citizens'. Speechly attended, and so, too, did a son of Wesley. Hymns and chorales were sung in the cemetery chapel and at the graveside by the cathedral choir, directed by the assistant organist and acting choirmaster, Edward Moxhay Vinnicombe.[105]

Problems

The first mention of any problem over the rebuilt organ came in the Chapter Acts for 28 October 1876.[106] Unfortunately, the nature of the problem is not known. The page which appears to provide details has been damaged by water, rendering illegible most of the record of the meeting in question. An organ-building firm was, however, consulted by the Chapter Clerk soon afterwards, William Hill & Son of London.[107] The firm's report, dated 17 March 1877 and written by Thomas Hill, focused on the work carried out by Speechly and on whether he had overcharged.

The report was addressed to the Chapter Clerk, Edwin Force, and showed there were gaps in the documentation for Speechly's work. As it was put in the report:

> We encounter a difficulty at the outset from the paucity of the information concerning the agreement entered into, which the papers afford. There is nothing from the late Mr Angel giving a clue to what his wishes and intentions were with respect to the improvement of the organ, the nature of which can only be partially gathered from the letters of the organ builders and their estimate of 29 January 1873. The latter provides for the extension of the Swell from G to CC, for new draw stops and key actions, the removal of the case 3 feet at back, and a general repair. A letter from Mr Speechly dated 28 July 1873 intimates that he has on his own responsibility added three stops to the Swell soundboard, making nine instead of six; another of 1 January 1874 refers to a wish of Mr J. Scott to have the large pipes removed from the pillars to inside the great case; and a third of 31 December 1874 suggests the remaking of the front pipes. Whether the proper authority was obtained for carrying out these various additional works we have no means of knowing except in the case of the Choir Organ front pipes, for which an order was given by you 29 May 1876.

Hill itemised expenditure and concluded that a number of charges should be reduced or disallowed. He advised that the overall charge of £555 for reconstruction of the organ should be reduced to the figure of £415 that had been quoted in the estimate of 29 January 1873; and he considered that the charge of £40 for remaking bellows, new action and reservoir should be disallowed because the bellows had not been remade. Indeed, he said, the bellows were now 'far too small and their action bad'.

Hill commented upon 'the act of melting up the old front pipes', which he could not believe were past repair. They were, he said, 'the last extant specimens of English seventeenth century art' and their removal 'much to be deprecated'. 'Their total destruction' was, he added, 'a most deplorable and unnecessary act, which could not be too strongly condemned'.

Speechly was annoyed, as his rejoinder shows.[108] It was dated 3 May 1877 and addressed to the Dean and Chapter. He considered that the report had been 'drawn up by Hill & Son in a most illiberal spirit, in shameful contradiction to their own mode of doing business and in utter ignorance of facts'. And he regretted that the Dean and Chapter had not seen fit to give him notice of Hill's survey, 'so that by the timely production of all letters and documents relating to the work any misunderstanding could have been avoided'.

Some of the work, Speechly pointed out, was 'never contemplated in the first idea', and effecting it had necessarily inflated the charge of £415. Hill 'knew nothing of this' and had 'made no effort to obtain information'. Three matters in particular had added to the cost. First, he had not anticipated that he would need to make the four large zinc pipes which now formed the lower notes of the Pedal Organ, or, therefore, their soundboards and connections. Second, the decision to remove the pipes from the columns at the edges of the pulpitum had rendered 'the ladders or gangways in their "towers" for tuning purposes and much other work useless'. Third, there had been additional labour involved in stowing the organ in the Chantry, then moving it to the Old Singing School when it was discovered that the Chantry could not be used as a workshop, and then removing everything back to the cathedral in consequence of the Singing School being required for conversion into a residence.

As regards the state of the Great Organ soundboard, Speechly said that 'it had always been an eyesore and source of dissatisfaction', and he added that he had told the Chapter so, but Angel had insisted that the old work be preserved. Furthermore, the arrangement of the Pedal Organ 'was entirely Mr Angel's' and he had not been 'allowed to depart from it'. He further complained that Hill had:

> . . . lost all sight of the fact that the work was spread over a period of more than three years, with every disadvantage to the organ builder; they do not know that I was not allowed to rebuild the organ in my own factory, that nearly the whole of the work was done at Exeter, that in consequence of alterations from time to time, by the architect, some portions of my work was done two and sometimes three times over.

When commenting on the condition of the old pipework, Speechly was scornful, saying that Hill's remarks displayed 'such an amount of ignorance they were unworthy of notice'. Their removal had been 'recommended by no less an authority than Sir Frederick Ouseley'.[109]

Speechly wrote to Force on 11 May 1877 to say that Hill had refused to discuss the matter with him and that he, Speechly, was not anxious 'to have any legal dispute in the matter'.[110] He pressed the cathedral's authorities to make him an offer to settle the matter. This the Chapter did, agreeing on 2 June 1877 that Speechly be paid an additional £300.[111]

Speechly had said in his letter to Angel dated 14 May 1875 that the tin pipes would have 'the appearance of burnished silver'. This was indeed so. When reporting the reopening of the nave in October 1877, *The Times* newspaper commented thus:[112]

> The great front pipes are, perhaps, unique. The tin of which they are composed is almost pure, there being hardly one part of alloy to 99 of pure metal. They have been burnished till they shine like silver, and are left, happily, without any enrichment.

From both the quire and the nave, the organ was a splendid sight.

Hill's criticism of the bellows was borne out by Edwin Light Luscombe, who reported to the Dean and Chapter on 5 February 1879 that the blowing apparatus was not only inadequate but also emitted 'a disagreeable sound'.[113] He recommended that the bellows be enlarged, or, preferably, made into two separate bellows. Moreover, he added, the lever of the blowing apparatus was in such an awkward and cramped position that the bellows blower could not exert himself fully. The apparatus needed to be reconstructed. No action was, however, taken, and on 11 December 1880 Luscombe wrote to the Dean and Chapter.[114] His opinion was that the organ should be blown by machinery, which he acknowledged would be expensive and 'involve the complete renewal of the blowing apparatus and also an engine driven by water or gas'. He had been 'in communication with an engineer in London during the past week' but was not yet in a position to make a definite proposal. And there the matter rested for several years.

Yet Another Rebuild of the Organ

Speechly's organ proved inadequate to meet the demands made upon it. Evening services in the nave were attended by huge congregations, and diocesan choral festivals often attracted more than a thousand singers. The organ needed more power and a greater variety of tonal resources. The Chapter decided on 16 May 1885 that if £3,000 could be raised, the Chapter would 'gladly sanction the renewal of the organ according to Messrs Willis' and Sons estimate' (which had been submitted on

30 April 1885 and amounted to £3,100).[115] A radical transformation of the instrument was proposed. The organ would 'consist of four complete manuals from CC to A (58 notes)' and thus have, for the first time, a Solo division.

An appeal for funds for rebuilding the organ was launched by the Dean in 1888 and the money was soon raised. And not only did the Chapter support renewal of the organ on the pulpitum; they agreed, too, on 2 June 1888, that an organ for the Singing School be purchased from Messrs Hele & Co of Plymouth.[116] This organ would cost £151 10s 0d and consist of one manual with three stops and a Pedal Division with two stops.[117] John Hele made clear in a note published in 1926 that the organ was entirely the firm's own work.[118] He had not, he said, used pipes from a previous Singing School organ, as some believed.

Willis's 1885 specification was re-submitted on 25 March 1889 and the instrument rebuilt in 1891 in accordance with it.[119] Fifteen stops were provided on the Great Organ, fourteen on the Swell Organ, ten on the Choir Organ, ten on the Solo Organ and eight on the Pedal Organ. New keyboards were provided (see Plate 3), extending upwards to A (58 notes), and the compass of the pedalboard remained from CC to F (30 notes). Twelve couplers were also provided, including two which incorporated ventils, and there were various accessories, too, among them five composition pedals to the Great Organ and four to the Swell Organ, as well as crescendo pedals to the Swell and Choir Organs, tremulants to the Swell and Choir Organs, extra reservoirs to the several organs for ensuring greater steadiness of tone, and a double-acting ventil to take off wind from all Pedal stops except the Bourdon.

Loosemore's case was further deepened (from east to west) and raised five feet, to make room for additional pipes, and a small projecting case of oak for the Solo Organ was added to the western side of the main case, corresponding to the Chair case on the eastern side. The lowest sixteen pipes of the Pedal Organ's 32-foot stop were relocated to the south transept, where they remain to this day (see Plate 6), and the action of the organ was altered to tubular pneumatic, described at the time as 'the most perfect of its kind yet invented, making the touch as easy and light as that of a Grand Pianoforte'.[120] A gas-engine blower was placed in the room below the Chapel of St James and wind conveyed in tubes through underground tunnels to the reservoirs in the organ. An era had come to an end. The bellows blower was now redundant.

The remodelled and reconstructed organ was first used at Evensong on 8 October 1891 and thereafter functioned satisfactorily for many years, cared for by Hele & Co, who later added a Choir to Great coupler and two reversible pedals. Tonally, Andrew Freeman said in 1926, the organ was 'very complete for its date, of excellent quality, and thoroughly distinctive of the great artist [Father Willis] who made it just ten years before his death'.[121]

A Modest and Dignified Man

The Chapter resolved on 22 July 1876 that the office of organist be offered to Daniel Joseph Wood.[122] Born at Brompton, Kent, on 25 August 1849, son of a boot-maker, he had been a chorister of Rochester Cathedral from 1859 to 1864 and then, simultaneously, organist of Holy Trinity Church at Brompton and an assistant organist of Rochester Cathedral. He had become organist of Cranbrook Parish Church in 1866, Lee Parish Church in 1868 and St Botolph's Church in Boston the following year; and he had gained his Fellowship of the Royal College of Organists (FRCO) in 1873 and an Oxford Bachelor of Music degree in 1874. His first cathedral post had come on 17 September 1875, when he was appointed organist and master of the choristers of Chichester Cathedral.[123]

The Chapter heard from the Dean on 29 July 1876 that Wood had accepted the office of organist and agreed at the same meeting that the salary paid to Vinnicombe for deputizing since the death of Angel be at the same rate as that usually paid to the organist.[124] Wood's conditions of service were identical to those of Angel and recorded in the Chapter Acts for 16 December 1876.[125] They were modified slightly by the Chapter on 20 February 1877, when it was agreed that 'a limited number of pupils in training for the service of the cathedral may be considered as apprentices'.[126] Wood wasted no time over obtaining pupils, reporting to the Chapter on 3 March 1877 that he had gained two already.[127]

Like his predecessors, Wood became involved in the city's musical life. He founded and conducted the Western Counties Musical Association, conducted the Exeter Orchestral Society, played the organ for festivals of the Exeter Diocesan Choral Association, and gave recitals on the organ of Exeter's Victoria Hall, an instrument he helped design (built in 1880 by Willis). He was a local examiner for the Trinity College of Music and further supplemented his income by directing choral music at The Maynard School in Exeter and teaching harmony at the Exeter Technical and University Extension College (now Exeter University). He was also an editor of, and contributor of tunes to, the Third Edition of the *Hymnal Companion to the Book of Common Prayer* and contributor of chants to the *Chant Book Companion to the Book of Common Prayer*.[128] He was honoured in July 1896 by the award of a Lambeth Doctor of Music degree.

A pen portrait of Wood published in 1899 mentioned that he was not highly paid.[129] In fact, Wood himself had drawn attention to this in 1885, when writing to the commissioners who were then inquiring into the condition of cathedral churches in England and Wales:[130]

> I venture to ask for a considerable increase in my salary as organist. This is at present £200 per annum, and a house, which however is too small for me, so that I am obliged to rent the adjoining premises.[131]

He went on to say that he performed the duties which were in many instances allotted to two separate persons and in some cases three, *viz.* sub-chanter, organist and master of the choristers; and he pointed out that he was 'responsible for all of these duties throughout the year without any assistance whatever, save such as I may myself be able to provide (of which I am not permitted to avail myself without express permission of the Chapter)'. The salary had not increased for at least fifty years, he said, even though the cost of living had increased greatly. He was 'obliged to take a considerable number of private pupils in order to realise an income such as my position requires'. His plea for a pay rise fell on deaf ears. He had to wait until February 1895 for an increase and was given it then, an additional £20, for only so long as he continued to direct practices of the Evening Choir.[132]

Wood's health declined rapidly in August 1919 and he died of a heart attack on the 27th, at his home in the Cathedral Close. The obituary published in *The Western Times* the day after his death repeated much of what had been written about him in the pen portrait twenty years earlier, noting particularly that he had been a modest and dignified man who was energetic, persevering and resourceful. As an organist, the pen portrait said, there was nothing showy in his style, and under his guidance the singing of the choir had been 'solid without being ponderous, bright without being procacious'.[133] The obituary added that he was 'a great disciple of Bach, of whose works he was an able exponent and acknowledged authority'.[134] In a tribute in the cathedral on Sunday 31 August, the Archdeacon of Exeter referred to Wood's 'loyalty to the core to those with whom he worked' and his 'sympathy and good comradeship with his colleagues and forgetfulness of self'.[135] He also mentioned Wood's 'meticulous care on simple and small detail'.

The funeral service was held in the cathedral on 1 September, the body having rested in the Lady Chapel through the previous night.[136] Many of the cathedral choir returned from holiday for the funeral, including some of the boys, and they were joined by several men and boys of the cathedral's voluntary choir. The Mayor of Exeter attended, along with numerous other local people and many organists, some of whom had been Wood's pupils. He was buried in Exeter's Higher Cemetery.[137]

Wood's death occurred less than a year after the Great War ended. Britain had changed as a result of that war. The certainties and complacency of pre-war times had been swept away. The modern era had begun. Attitudes to religion had changed. Would the new order affect the musical life of the cathedral? By the time Wood died, moreover, nearly thirty years had passed since the organ had been rebuilt and modernized by Willis. The instrument would surely need attention soon.

Plate 1   Matthew Godwin memorial, north nave aisle.

Plate 2   Inscription on Matthew Godwin memorial.

Plate 3   The keyboards that were taken out by Henry Willis in 1891. Note the reversed colour of the keys (ebony naturals and ivory sharps), the rounded sharps and the elegantly carved key cheeks.

Plate 4   Spiral stone staircase to the organ loft.

Plate 5   The organ as it now appears from the quire. Notice that the relative heights of the Chair and main cases are now the same as they were before 1870. The main case was raised five feet when Henry Willis rebuilt the organ in 1891.

Plate 6   The lowest sixteen pipes of the Pedal Organ's Contra Violone rank were moved to the south transept in 1891. Note the ingenious calculation that enabled the longest pipes to fit so neatly within the architectural constraint. Although not particularly loud in terms of volume, the rich harmonic development of the notes produced by these pipes means that the notes can be heard and felt throughout the building. Three of the sixteen pipes are behind the pipes which are visible in this picture.

Plate 7   Part of the Exeter Blitz commemoration window by Christopher Webb in the south nave aisle, showing a stone mason and an organ-builder.

Plate 8   The Chair case today, with the inscription above it: 'John Loosemore made this organ 1665'. The lettering of the inscription was gilded in 1965.

Plate 9   Pipework of the Minstrels' Gallery division. The principal and flute ranks can be seen in the foreground, while the pipes of the impressive Trompette stop occupy the middle. Note how the larger pipes are tied with black cotton tape to support the body of the pipe structure, and also how the largest pipes are 'mitred' (not dissimilar from an orchestral instrument where the resonating tube is folded over to lend rigidity and to save space). One of the wind reservoirs, complete with metal weights, can be seen behind the Trompette on the left. Note the wooden enclosure of the whole division on the back, top and sides to promote sound projection and climatic control.

Plate 10   The organ under construction in Durham in the Harrison & Harrison workshop during 2014. Here we are looking from the south side to the north. The different levels upon which the organ departments will sit can be clearly seen. Sited prominently on the left is the Solo division that occupies the Willis case on the lower order of the west façade of the organ. Here we see it side on. The height from floor level to the top of the organ is 8.1 metres (26.6 feet).

Plate 11   The restored console in 2014, showing the small revisions of some of the stop jambs and piston designations.

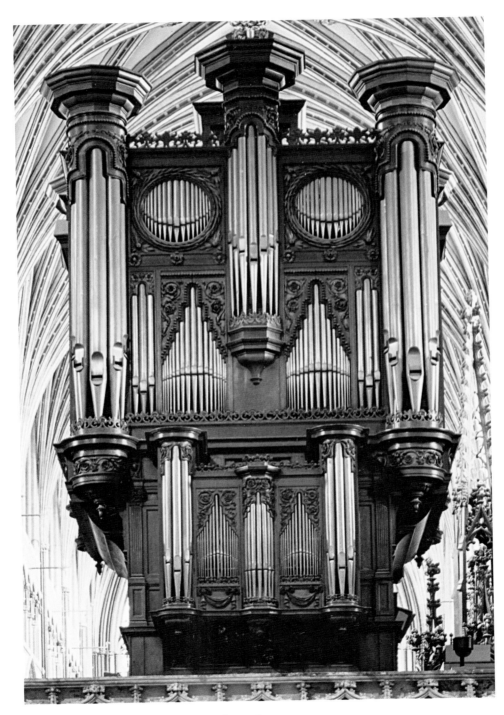

Plate 12   The Solo and main cases from the nave.

Plate 13   The chamber organ built by Kenneth Tickell & Co Ltd in 2007. The details of the display pipes and of the wood carving were designed to complement the existing colour and woodwork patterns of the quire. The organ has four stops: Fifteenth (2), Chimney Flute (4), Principal (4), Stopped Diapason (8).

Plate 14   Andrew Millington (director of music since 1999). Behind him, the organ
in the Lady Chapel, purchased in 1959 through the generosity of the Friends of
Exeter Cathedral. The organ, which has one manual and no pedals, was built in
the nineteenth century by Samuel Parsons of 2 Little Russell Street, Bloomsbury,
London. It has six stops: Fifteenth (2), Principal (4), Stopped Diapason Bass (8),
Twelfth (2⅔), Stopped Diapason Treble (8), Open Diapason (8).

Plate 15   Samuel Sebastian Wesley in the 1830s.

Plate 16   Detail on the east face of the organ case built by John Loosemore in 1665.

CHAPTER 6

The Modern Era

The organ fell silent after Evensong on Sunday 27 January 2013. Two weeks later, the case still towered above the pulpitum, but now empty. Another renovation of the organ had begun, this one costing nearly one million pounds. Loosemore would have been astonished at the cost and could never have imagined what tools and design techniques would be used for creating the instrument that was built in the latter part of 2014. We can only speculate on how different the organ of 1665 would have been had computer-aided design been available! In this final chapter, we continue the story of the cathedral's organs and organists to the present day through a period of considerable change and, at times, drama.

Organists Who Served in the Great War

Daniel Wood's successor was appointed on 18 October 1919.[1] He was Ernest James Bullock, organist of St Michael's College, Tenbury Wells, Worcestershire. Born at Wigan, Lancashire, on 15 September 1890, he had been educated at Wigan Grammar School and sung as a boy in the choir of Wigan Parish Church.[2] The organist of the church, Edward Bairstow, had recognized his musical talent and taken him as an articled pupil.[3] When Bairstow had become organist of Leeds Parish Church, in 1906, Ernest had gone with him and become his assistant, as well as organist of two parish churches in Leeds (St Mary the Virgin, Micklefield, and St John the Baptist, Adel). He had gained the FRCO diploma in 1909 and degrees from the University of Durham (Bachelor of Music in 1908 and Doctor of Music in 1914). He had become assistant organist of Manchester Cathedral in 1912 and served in the Great War from 1915 to 1919 (in France, in the King's Own Yorkshire Light Infantry).[4] He had been appointed organist of St Michael's College in February 1919.

At Exeter, Bullock built upon his growing reputation as a composer and became much involved in the musical life of the South West. As his successor at Exeter Cathedral said, he 'put new life into the music of the cathedral, the diocese and the region'.[5] Many must have been disappointed when he resigned, but they surely congratulated him on being appointed organist and master of the choristers of Westminster Abbey. His resignation took effect on 9 January 1928.[6]

After he left Exeter, Bullock continued to compose (mainly sacred choral music, secular songs, fanfares and organ music), but he lost all his property and papers in 1940, when his home was destroyed in a wartime air raid, and his future looked bleak soon afterwards, when the musical establishment of Westminster Abbey was dispersed.[7] However, he was appointed, in 1941, Gardiner Professor of Music in Glasgow University and Principal of the Royal Scottish Academy of Music and Drama; and he was knighted in 1951. He became Director of the Royal College of Music in London in 1953 and retired in 1960. He died on 23 May 1979, at Long Crendon, Buckinghamshire.[8]

The Dean informed the Chapter on 3 December 1927 that 43 people had applied for the post of organist and four had been shortlisted, one of them Thomas Henry Wait Armstrong, organist of St Peter's Church, Eaton Square, London.[9] He was appointed on 17 December and took up the appointment on 1 February 1928.[10] Meanwhile, the Chapter had agreed on 14 January that the assistant organist, Frederick Gandy Bradford, be paid £10 for 'extra duty pending the arrival of the new organist'.[11]

Born at Peterborough on 15 June 1898, Armstrong had been a chorister in the Chapel Royal from 1907 to 1911 and then, until 1915, a pupil of King's School, Peterborough. He had become organist of Thorney Abbey in 1914 and assistant organist of Peterborough Cathedral in 1915.[12] He had served in the Great War from 1917 to 1919 (in France, with the Royal Garrison Artillery) and then resumed the organ scholarship at Oxford's Keble College that he had taken up in October 1916.[13] He had graduated in modern history in June 1922 and music in March 1923 and thereafter become assistant organist of Manchester Cathedral. Later in 1923, he had become organist of St Peter's, Eaton Square.[14] He had also studied composition at the Royal College of Music with, among others, Ralph Vaughan Williams.[15]

As well as cathedral organist, Armstrong became director of music in the University College of the South West (now the University of Exeter) and also gained an Oxford doctorate in music (in December 1928). In addition to his cathedral and university duties, he conducted concerts, gave lectures, took part in radio broadcasts of services and concerts from the cathedral, and served as an examiner at home and abroad.[16] He also made a gramophone record in 1928, a delightful recording of the cathedral choir singing the Christmas carol 'O Little Town of Bethlehem'.[17]

The Chapter heard on 18 February 1933 that Armstrong had tendered his resignation. He had been appointed organist of Christ Church Cathedral, Oxford, with effect from September 1933.[18] He remained at Christ Church until 1955 and then became Principal of the Royal Academy of Music, a post he held until 1968, when he retired. He was knighted in 1958. After he left Exeter, he published books, articles and musical compositions, including songs, anthems, chamber music, and descants for Christmas carols. He died at his home at Olney near Milton Keynes on 26 June 1994.

A Major Renovation of the Organ

In October 1921, Bullock invited organ-builders Harrison & Harrison of Durham to examine the organ. It had become unreliable. Other than tuning and minor repairs and the addition of a coupler and reversible pedals, the only attention it had received since the reconstruction by Willis in 1891 had been dusting and cleaning (in October 1901 and July 1915). The work had all been carried out by Hele & Co, the firm which had maintained the organ since 1891.

Arthur Harrison duly examined the organ and submitted a report dated 4 November 1921.[19] As these extracts from the report show, the organ's state left much to be desired:

> The whole instrument is now in an unsatisfactory condition. It is very dirty and much out of repair. The mechanism is old-fashioned, very noisy and almost worn out, many parts showing signs of breaking down. The key-board arrangements are clumsy and out of date, and the control, a most important feature of any large organ, is totally inadequate. . . . Many of the reeds have become rough and uneven from dirt and lack of attention, and these should now be re-voiced. . . . The organ is not as efficient for accompanying the services as it might be, considering the number of its stops. The Pedal particularly is deficient in soft stops.

Harrison went on to comment that the interior of the organ was overcrowded, with a considerable portion of the mechanism 'practically inaccessible for purposes of tuning and adjustment'. He commented, too, that the pitch of the organ was high but advised that lowering it to the new French pitch of C=517 Hz at a temperature of 60°F would be costly.

Harrison proposed that the organ be thoroughly cleaned and overhauled, the Pedal and Choir departments placed on the ledges under the arches of the quire nearest the pulpitum, a 'new system of tubular-pneumatic mechanism introduced', and a new set of pistons, couplers and balanced swell pedals provided. He also proposed that the tonal scheme be remodelled. The total cost would be £5,660.

John Calvert Hele examined the organ, too, and submitted a report dated 28 August 1922, accompanied by a covering letter of the same date signed by the firm's managing director, Kenneth Hele.[20] J.C. Hele's opinion was much the same as that of Arthur Harrison. The organ was excessively dirty and noisy and in need of modernization. In particular, the draw-stop and composition actions were 'heavy and cumbersome in the extreme, being quite incompatible with modern organ playing'. He did not believe, however, that any re-voicing was necessary.

Hele explained that 'defects in the leather portions of the organ' had been caused to some extent by the blowing apparatus. Prior to 1906, when the gas engine had been replaced by an electric motor, harmful fumes from the engine had reached the organ through the bellows, but there had been a beneficial effect of the engine, too, in that it had kept the blowing chamber dry. With the electric motor, however, air in the chamber was not being dried, so damp air was reaching the organ. This, he said, was 'largely the cause of the heavy pressure bellows giving out in October 1921'.

Kenneth Hele advised Bullock that the total cost of the work his firm recommended would be much less than stated 'in alarmist reports in newspapers', but he did not give a specific figure. This came in a covering letter dated 2 September 1925, when the report of August 1922 was re-submitted.[21] Cleaning the organ thoroughly and replacing valves in the windchests would cost between £250 and £350. The modernization that he considered was badly needed would cost significantly more, but he did not say how much more.

The Chapter did not act upon the reports of Harrison & Harrison and Hele. Perhaps they were reassured by a comment in the letter Kenneth Hele wrote to Bullock on 28 August 1922. An overhaul of the organ was certainly needed, but, 'excepting accidents, there need be no anticipation of collapse'.[22]

The first time the Chapter considered the state of the organ was 5 September 1925, when they discussed Kenneth Hele's letter of 2 September and ordered the Chapter Clerk to 'ask the Succentor for an expression of his views and those of Dr Bullock on the question of an entire renovation of the organ'.[23] But no action was taken until 17 September 1932, when the Chapter heard from Armstrong that Bullock and other eminent organists had examined the estimates submitted by a considerable number of firms in 1931 and 1932 and recommended that the estimate of Harrison & Harrison should be accepted.[24] The cost would be £3,500.

The proposed renovation of the organ sparked correspondence in *The Times* newspaper, beginning with a letter from a former chorister of Exeter Cathedral, J.J. Tinsley, published on 21 July 1932:[25]

I observe that it is proposed to spend money on improving the organ of Exeter Cathedral, no doubt a very laudable object. Before that money is spent would it not be well for the Chapter to remove it from the splendid screen and rebuild it elsewhere? In its present position it completely spoils the view of the great church from east to west or vice versa and mars the effect of the great unbroken vault. I know it is a puzzle what to do with cathedral organs, but solution has been found in many cathedrals, to the great benefit of architectural effect. Where they stand on the screens in too many of our great churches they are invariably an eyesore.

The idea of moving the organ had not, after all, been consigned to history in the 1870s.

Tinsley's letter brought a reply from Armstrong, published on 23 July.[26] There was, he said, 'a scale model of the cathedral in which the organ is not included; and its absence has an unexpected and undesirable effect upon the general proportions of the building as seen from the west end'.[27] Furthermore, he added, the triforium of the cathedral provided no space for an organ, and the instrument could not be placed at the west end of the nave. In his view, moving the organ to either of the transepts would be 'musically ineffective and undesirable on other grounds', and remodelling or dividing Loosemore's case would be 'vandalism'. The Provost of Eton College thought likewise, saying in a letter published the same day in *The Times* that Exeter had an organ case which was 'one of the very best of the best period'. But a Friend of Exeter Cathedral, Sir Francis Newbolt, sided with Tinsley, calling for removal of 'the organ which has for so long disfigured the central arch'.

More letters were published on 25 July, some agreeing with Tinsley, others with the Provost, but one expressed a different point of view.[28] From the Lady Margaret Professor of Divinity at Oxford, it argued that the pulpitum was 'meant to be surmounted by a great rood, and not primarily by an organ'. However, the Dean of Norwich disputed this, saying in a letter published on 26 July that in the greater churches in mediæval times the pulpitum and rood screen were typically not one and the same thing.[29] In his view, the pulpitum was the 'traditional place for a great organ'. Another of the letters on 26 July was from Tinsley. He was unrepentant and asserted that 'organs are a necessary nuisance and their proper placement in any church, great or small, a problem'.

More letters were published in the coming days, one from the Dean of Exeter, another from Herbert Bishop, Exeter Cathedral's Honorary Librarian.[30] They ranged over aesthetic, spiritual and musical aspects, but there was no consensus. The originator of the spate of correspondence had the last word, saying, in a letter published on 11 August, that the organ so dominated the church 'as to spoil the architecture'.[31] Tinsley was adamant the position of the organ on the screen was 'not at all necessary'. He was ignored, though. The organ remained where it had been for centuries.

The instrument was rebuilt by Harrison & Harrison to a specification they and Armstrong drew up. Electric action replaced the tubular-pneumatic, and a new console was provided, complete with up-to-date accessories. The specifications of the Great and Swell Organs were not altered, but the Choir Organ was remodelled and changes were made to the Solo Organ. The orchestral reeds were moved from the Choir to the Solo and the Clarinet moved from the Solo to the Choir. The Wald Flute was also moved from the Solo to the Choir but converted from 4ft to 8ft pitch; and all of the stops on the Solo Organ except the Tuba were enclosed in a swell-box. Enlargement of the Pedal Organ was considered desirable but did not prove possible, owing to lack of space.

Tonal changes were also made. For example, the reeds on the Swell Organ were made, in the words of Laurence Elvin, 'fiery in character and voiced as a contrast to the smoother Great trumpets'.[32] On the Choir Organ, Elvin was pleased 'the old Willis Salicional and Céleste had been retained', and he approved of the voicing of these stops. He approved, too, of the Solo Organ, except that he felt the Dulciana would have been better on the Choir. The Tuba impressed him greatly: 'a stop of considerable clang, superb both as a solo register or in chords, and forms a thrilling climax to full organ'. He thought the action of the organ 'superb, prompt in repetition and attack, and perfectly reliable'. The instrument was, he said, 'magnificent, worthy of the glorious building in which it is placed'.[33]

The organ was reopened on 25 June 1933 with a recital by Ernest Bullock, this being the first event in a week-long festival to mark the 800th anniversary of the dedication of the Romanesque building. Other musical events that week were conducted by Thomas Armstrong, who remained the cathedral's organist until the autumn, when succeeded by Alfred William Wilcock. Indeed, Armstrong helped choose his successor, by drawing up the shortlist of three candidates. They were all interviewed on 19 April 1933, and the Chapter confirmed the appointment of Wilcock at their meeting on 29 April.[34]

Born at Colne, Lancashire, on 21 October 1887, Wilcock had moved to Lytham St Annes by 1901 and attended Lytham College for Boys.[35] He had moved again a few years later, this time to Liverpool, and served as organist of two churches in the city (St John's, Knotty Ash, from 1904 to 1908 and, thereafter, St Nicholas', Blundellsands). He had from 1916 to 1926 served as organist of St Chrysostom's Church, Manchester, and from then until 1930 as organist of Emmanuel Church, Southport. He had taken organ lessons with Kendrick Pyne at Manchester

Cathedral from 1904 to 1908 and studied at the Royal Manchester College of Music (RMCM) from 1906 to 1910. He had become a Licentiate of the Royal Academy of Music in 1905 (in piano teaching), gained the FRCO diploma in 1908, taken a Durham University Bachelor of Music degree in 1913, received a Manchester University Doctor of Music degree in 1917 and served as a teacher of harmony and composition in the RMCM since 1918. He had been organist of Derby Cathedral since 1930.

Wilcock's conditions of employment as organist of Exeter Cathedral were much the same as those of his predecessors, with one significant exception: he was required to 'retire automatically on attaining his sixtieth birthday' but could be 'reappointed at the discretion of the Dean and Chapter'.[36] Bullock's and Armstrong's retirement ages had been 65, and there had hitherto been no retirement age. In the event, he retired at the age of 65.[37]

Difficult Times

Wilcock had not been in post long when faults on the organ developed.[38] Harrison's responded that 'the mechanism would "settle down" after use for a further period' and any work done on the instrument was covered by the guarantee.[39] However, problems continued, so on 24 March 1934 the Chapter Clerk wrote to Harrison's again, this time to say that 'the Chapter were much disturbed at the frequent ciphering and other complaints made by the organist'.[40] Harrison's rectified the defects soon afterwards.

On 23 February 1935, the Chapter heard from W. Shepherd & Son, an Exeter firm of motor engineers, that the organ's blowing apparatus needed to be overhauled.[41] Bearings needed to be tightened up and routine maintenance carried out. The work was carried out satisfactorily, and on 1 June 1935 the Chapter offered the firm 'five guineas for a quarterly overhaul of the organ blowing engine'.[42]

The Chapter heard on 5 February 1938 that the organ blower again needed attention, the problem now being lack of lubrication at certain key points.[43] Installation of automatic oiling cups proved no more than a short-term solution, so the Chapter considered in 1941 whether to buy a new blower motor. The bearings in the old one needed to be replaced, and the Chapter decided on 23 August that, 'in view of the age of the present blower, it might be more economical to purchase a new one'.[44] The cathedral's surveyor reported to the Chapter on 27 September that he had obtained an estimate from Messrs Watkins & Watson of London for supplying a 'Discus' blower 'in the sum of £421, with no guarantee as to time of delivery and with no certainty of obtaining a licence from the Board of Trade for release of certain of the materials required'.[45] Wartime restrictions were in force. A new blower motor for a cathedral organ was not a priority. The Chapter ordered that the existing blower be repaired as soon as possible.[46]

Fate intervened. A bomb destroyed the Chapel of St James off the south quire aisle in an air raid in the early hours of 4 May 1942. The blower was in the room below the chapel and was buried under tons of rubble. The pipes and action of the organ were badly damaged by the blast and flying debris, and the Loosemore case was damaged, too.[47] Alfred Wilcock sent a telegram to Harrison's on 6 May: 'Exeter Chapter desire expert re dismantling organ – immediate please – severe raid damage'.

The Chapter resolved on 9 May that the mechanism, pipework and console be dismantled by Harrison's and taken to Durham for repair and storage, and that Harrison's be asked to prepare the war damage claim in respect of the mechanism.[48] They also instructed Herbert Read (an Exeter designer and craftsman in wood) to dismantle the organ case 'and prepare the war damage claim in respect of this'. These resolutions proved unduly hasty. The following Saturday, 16th, Read and a representative of Harrison's, Mr R.H. Wood, attended the weekly Chapter meeting. They were now able to give a more considered opinion on the action to be taken in respect of the organ and its case.[49]

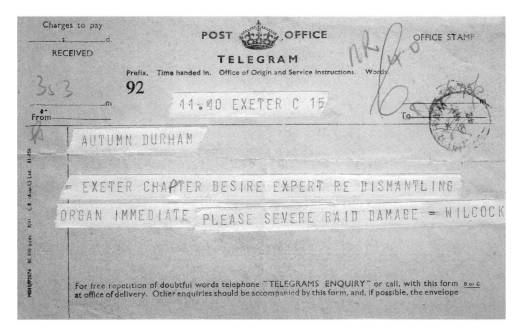

Figure 6.1   The telegram sent by organist Alfred Wilcock to Harrison & Harrison on 6 May 1942, two days after a bomb destroyed one of the cathedral's chapels.

Figure 6.2   The organ case in 1942, soon after the bomb dropped, with pipes missing and others leaning against the north wall of the quire.

Read 'advised that the organ be dismantled and stored in the Chapter House instead of being removed to Durham, also that the organ case be taken down and stored'. The Board of Trade had granted permission through the Ecclesiastical Insurance Office Ltd for the instrument to be dismantled. Wood agreed that the organ be stored in the Chapter House and not taken to Durham. As regards the case, he advised that 'certain parts were out of the perpendicular and in a dangerous condition'. Furthermore, he said, the case would have to be braced once the mechanism had been taken out, as 'there would be nothing left to hold it'.

Wood stated in a letter to Harrison's on 16 May that the organ was 'full of grit and exposed to all weather', there being broken windows in all parts of the cathedral and a gaping hole in the wall of the south quire aisle where the destroyed chapel had stood.[50] Moreover, he noted, the screen itself had moved. His letter also shed light on the initial thoughts of the cathedral authorities as to a suitable place to store the organ. Their preferred choice had been the north transept, but he had persuaded them the Chapter House would provide a more satisfactory location once its windows had been boarded up. His letter also revealed that the Dean had suggested the organ be removed to the country for storage.

A letter from Herbert Read was read at the Chapter meeting on 23 May. He now believed the case could be left as it was. He considered it 'structurally safe and quite as secure as it could be if taken down, repaired and re-erected'.[51] Harrison's agreed but recommended that the swell-box should remain inside the case to aid stability. The rest of the organ was removed to the Chapter House.

After the bombing, Sunday services were held initially in the hall of the Deanery (now the Old Deanery), but as early as St Peter's Day, 29 June, it proved possible to hold sung services with piano accompaniment in the nave.[52] However, the nave was unheated, draughty and often cold and damp, even after the windows had been made weather-tight.[53] The thought of holding services there through the winter was not appealing.

On 12 August 1942, the Dean wrote to Harrison's to say that he and the Chapter were anxious to have the organ removed from the Chapter House because they wanted to fit up that place 'for regular use as a church'.[54] He said that it was not thought necessary that all of the instrument need be removed. The 'very numerous small pipes' which were stored on the window ledges could be left where they were.

The need to use the Chapter House soon became urgent. The floor of the hall in the Deanery broke in September under the weight of too many people. Most of the organ was then moved to the north quire aisle, whereupon the full cathedral choir sang for services in the Chapter House on Sunday mornings, Tuesdays, Thursdays and Saturdays, and the voluntary choir sang on Sunday afternoons.

The organ in the nearby Singing School was also damaged in an air raid, and the Chapter ordered on 30 May 1942 that Hele & Co be 'instructed to inspect and report upon the damage suffered'.[55] A week later, they heard that Hele had quoted £145 17s 0d for the repair and provided a specification of the work required.[56] The Chapter accepted the quotation and decided on 13 June that the organ should be re-erected in the nave and covered with tarpaulins until that part of the building had been made more weather-tight.[57] It was eventually erected on the north side of the nave in December 1942, near the pulpit.[58] However, Wilcock was reluctant to use it, considering it inadequate for accompanying congregational singing. He preferred to use a piano.

The Chapter resolved on 18 September 1943 that the Chapter Clerk should write to Harrison's to ask what priority could be given for repair of the main organ after the

Figure 6.3   Alfred Wilcock (organist 1933–1952).

war.[59] They replied that the organ was on their priority list, provided it 'remained on the screen and no structural alterations were required'.[60] Yet again, as in 1932, there had been calls for the organ to be removed from the pulpitum. The Chapter Clerk wrote to Harrison's on 27 September to assure them there was no intention of re-erecting the organ in a different position, nor did the Dean and Chapter consider such an idea at all likely.[61]

The question of repairing the organ was next raised in October 1944, when the Dean and Chapter broached the subject with Harrison's. There were technical and administrative issues to be resolved.[62] Could it be repaired before its case had been restored? Would the Board of Trade sanction the repair? If so, would the War Damage Commission pay for it? Was the pulpitum in its damaged state fit to take the weight of the renovated organ?

The Chapter heard on 11 November that the organ could indeed be rebuilt before damage to the pulpitum had been made good, and also that 'reconstruction of the mechanism could take place independently of the woodwork of the case'.[63] However, optimism was soon dashed. As recorded in the Chapter minutes for 9 December 1944:[64]

> The Chapter Clerk asked for a decision to enable him to inform Messrs. Harrison & Harrison whether they could commence work on the organ early in the New Year. He mentioned the fact that the blowing apparatus was completely destroyed by enemy action; that Messrs Watkins & Watson in 1941 had quoted the sum of £421 for a new 'Discus' blower; that the exact method of the future supply of electric current to the cathedral was still unsettled; and that the Board of Trade had up to the present given no indication as to whether they would make immediate payment of insurance moneys for the restoration of the organ and the blowing plant. They decided that, as these matters were interdependent, Harrison's must be advised that they would be unable to commence work on the organ early in the New Year.

A letter from Watkins & Watson to Harrison's dated 4 December 1944 shows that they had presumed the organ blower had been made to work again, for they had not heard from the cathedral since 1941.[65] In fact, the blower was beyond repair, and there appeared to be no prospect of an adequate replacement in the foreseeable future. The organ was unplayable without a blower.

Months passed, and then, at the Chapter meeting on 7 July 1945, after the war in Europe had ended, the Chapter Clerk was instructed to write to Watkins & Watson 'to enquire whether a new or second-hand "Discus" blower was obtainable'. He was also to write to Harrison's to ask 'whether the restoration of the organ at an early date could be commenced'.[66] Replies from both firms were reported at the Chapter meeting on 4 August.[67] Watkins & Watson wished to visit Exeter and inspect the site. Harrison's made it plain their work was dependent on there being a suitable supply of electricity and adequate blowing apparatus, but, in any event, they could not start work for four months. The blower required a three-phase supply of electricity, or at least a two-phase supply (as before the bombing), and there were no plans to provide anything more than a single-phase supply.[68] Meanwhile, Herbert Read had begun to repair the organ case, work he completed on 9 March 1946.[69]

The blower proved to be the Achilles' heel of the organ's restoration. The Chapter heard on 6 October 1945 that Watkins & Watson could not manufacture and supply a blower for at least six months, but this was not all. The Chapter learned on 3 November 1945 that the cost of a new blower would be £892, including £386 purchase tax.[70] They refused to pay this much and asked Myles Drury, the cathedral's surveyor, to 'enquire whether some temporary blowing system could not be arranged until it was possible for the new blower to be provided'. Harrison's rejected the Chapter's suggestion that the blower for the Singing School organ might be used, as it would not be sufficient for purpose, but said they would 'consider whether any temporary blowing apparatus could be arranged'.[71]

The Chapter heard from Drury on 1 December 1945 that Harrison's had commenced work on the organ on 27 November, but 'the amount of work they would be able to do without the blowing apparatus was very limited and would probably be finished by Christmas'.[72] He added that he had asked Harrison's to discuss with Watkins & Watson the possibility of obtaining a temporary blower and suggested that 'an order for a new blower be placed now, on condition that delivery be deferred to a time when the purchase tax had been removed'. A temporary blower was indeed provided, but it proved frustratingly incapable of supplying sufficient wind for more than a few stops at a time.

A letter from Drury to Harrison's dated 29 April 1946 shows that Harrison's had suggested moving the organ blower to a new location outside the north tower.[73] Drury objected, pointing out that a new dust-proof chamber would have to be constructed and a licence for doing so obtained from the Ministry of Works, with the possibility of the application being refused. Moreover, ducts would have to be cut through the wall of the tower, which was 'immensely thick', and also under the floor of the north quire aisle, to connect with the ducts from the organ loft. Harrison's reconsidered the idea and then advised, as reported at the Chapter meeting on 4 May 1946, that the blowing plant 'must take up its original position' in the room below the Chapel of St James.[74] But rebuilding of that room had not yet begun.

The organ was protected against dust and grit in October and November 1949 while restoration work in the quire was being carried out, and only the Choir Organ was then playable.[75] After this, for a week in early December, while the new blower was being installed, none of the organ could be used. But eventually, on 7 January 1950, Drury was able to report to the Chapter that installation of the blower had been completed.[76] His request to Watkins & Watson in March 1949 that it be installed in time for the enthronement of Bishop Mortimer on 27 May 1949 had proved impossible to meet.[77] At least, though, the organ was available in its fully restored state for the visit of King George VI with the Queen and Princess Margaret on 10 July 1950 (to mark the 900th anniversary of the See of Exeter).

The end of Wilcock's tenure of office as organist was recorded thus in the Chapter minutes for 26 January 1952:[78]

> Mr Dean informed the organist that the Chapter had decided his appointment as organist would terminate at the age of 65 years and would not be renewed. He was asked to confirm date of his birth.

One cannot help but feel sorry for Wilcock. This wording seems overly terse for someone who had served so loyally through difficult times and not been able to enjoy the cathedral's splendid organ for so many years.[79] However, he duly produced his birth certificate, and the Chapter decided on 22 March that he must retire on his 65th birthday, 21 October 1952.[80] Furthermore, he was informed that possession of his quarters in Church House would be required, but he could remain until Christmas 1952 if it did not suit him to leave earlier. However, he was informed that payment of his pension was dependent upon him vacating his apartment.[81] After retirement, he remained in Exeter but died all too soon, on 26 October 1953, in the Royal Devon and Exeter Hospital.[82]

Organists Who Served in the Second World War

Wilcock's successor was appointed on 27 September 1952 and took up his duties on 1 January 1953.[83] He was Reginald Moore, assistant music master of Winchester College. Born at Bramley, Yorkshire, on 19 May 1910, he had joined the choir of Leeds Parish Church in 1917 and attended the Central High School, Leeds.[84] He had taken organ lessons with Edward Bairstow at York Minster and in 1926 become organist of St Saviour's Church, Leeds. He had been awarded an organ scholarship to Peterhouse, Cambridge, in 1929, but his family had been unable to support him and he had turned to teaching the piano and organ as a source of income. He had become the organist and choirmaster of Bramley Parish Church in 1929, gained his FRCO diploma in 1931, and proceeded in 1933 to become assistant organist of Salisbury Cathedral and music master of Salisbury Cathedral School. He had served in the Royal Air Force from 1941 to 1945 and returned to Salisbury when the war ended. He had taken the job at Winchester in 1947 and gained a Bachelor of Music degree from Durham University as an external student while working at Winchester.[85]

A gentle giant of six feet four inches, Moore inspired respect, affection and loyalty and worked tirelessly to raise standards, not only in the cathedral but also as lecturer in music in the University College of the South West (from 1955 Exeter University).[86] He was equally well respected as conductor of the Exeter Musical Society and choirmaster of the Exeter Diocesan Choral Association. However, difficult relations with the cathedral's authorities developed and complaints were made, as we find in

Figure 6.4   Reginald Moore (organist 1953–1957).

the Chapter minutes for 25 February 1956, when it was recorded that two clergymen had objected to 'the grinding of the solo' at the Eucharist on St Matthias's Day (24 February) and 'the playing of the organ as a display of bad temper on Tuesday (21 February)'.[87] He resigned in early 1957 and concentrated thereafter on his university work. He died (of lung cancer) on 25 May 1968, and his funeral took place four days later in the University Chapel, followed by cremation.

Moore's successor was Lionel Frederick Dakers, appointed on 6 April 1957.[88] He, too, had served his country in the Royal Army Pay Corps, in York, from 1943 to 1945, and then, until 1947, in the Royal Army Education Corps in Egypt, where he had been organist of Cairo Cathedral. While in York, he had, like Bullock and Moore, studied the organ under Edward Bairstow, gaining the FRCO diploma in 1945. Born at Rochester on 24 February 1924, he had been educated in Rochester Cathedral Choir School and Gravesend County School For Boys. He had been organist of All Saints' Church, Frindsbury, Rochester, from 1940 to 1942 and had studied at the

Royal Academy of Music from 1947 to 1951, gaining, in 1951, a Bachelor of Music degree from Durham University as an external student. Before becoming organist of Ripon Cathedral, in 1954, he had been organist of Finchley Parish Church from 1948 to 1950, sub-organist of St George's Chapel, Windsor, from 1950 to 1954, and a music master at Eton College from 1952 to 1954.[89]

The Chapter minutes for 17 August 1957 show that Moore had continued to live in Church House, for it was then decided that he be informed possession of the flat was required on 9 September, 'on which day cleaners would be moving in, so as to have the flat ready for his successor'.[90] Dakers did indeed take possession of the flat on the 10th but moved soon afterwards to No. 11 Cathedral Close.

Problems with the Organ

By early 1957, the trunking which carried wind from the organ blower to the organ loft was leaking badly at joints. The matter was taken up with Harrison & Harrison and with Watkins & Watson. Myles Drury wrote to Harrison's on 8 March 1957 to suggest that the blowing plant be moved from the room below the Chapel of St James to 'a new chamber just outside the north quire aisle', the main benefit being that the length of trunking would be greatly reduced. Neither firm was enthusiastic but nevertheless quoted costs and considered practicalities.[91] A specific question was that of how to supply wind to the pipes in the south transept, some distance from the north quire aisle. The conclusion was that a separate blower would be needed.

Drury reported to Harrison's in a letter dated 27 March 1958 that he had not been able to convince the Chapter a new blower chamber was necessary, not least because of the cost (about £1,300).[92] However, the Chapter had agreed they would not drop the idea without first consulting Harrison's once more. In the end, the idea was indeed dropped and the existing trunking renewed (at a cost of £500). The work was carried out in November 1958, by which time the need to renew the trunking had become urgent.[93]

By 1960, the organ itself was giving cause for concern. Dakers wrote to Harrison's on 26 May:[94]

> For some time now I have been mildly agitating in the right quarters for the re-building of the cathedral organ. Now the Secretary of the Friends of Exeter Cathedral has asked me to go one stage further and submit some recommendations unofficially.

He brought the matter of the organ's condition to the attention of the Chapter on 18 June, and they ordered that Harrison's should examine the instrument.[95] Their report, dated 8 July, indicated that the organ needed to be cleaned, all pipework and action regulated, wind trunks and reservoirs repaired, and mechanical and tonal improvements made.[96] And they proposed that a Trompette Militaire be placed in the Minstrels' Gallery.

The organ's condition was discussed at Chapter meetings in July and August 1960 without progress being made. Indeed, the Canon Treasurer was dismissive at the Chapter meeting on 2 July, saying that he understood from the tuner that 'only cleaning and minor repairs were really necessary and no major operation was needed'.[97] The Chapter decided on 16 July that consideration of Harrison's estimate be deferred and suggested on 30 July that Bullock be consulted as to the work needed.[98] They noted at the latter meeting that Armstrong had given a recital on 28 July and afterwards reported that a new set of pedals was needed. Finally, the Chapter decided on 6 August that further consideration of the organ's condition 'should await the arrival of the new Dean' and agreed that Bullock should indeed be asked for his advice.[99] And there the matter rested for more than two years.

Meanwhile, Dakers consulted Francis Jackson, the organist of York Minster, who submitted a report of his own, dated 21 September 1960.[100] He broadly agreed with Harrison's scheme but suggested alternative ways of achieving the same tonal effects as they proposed and rejected their idea of a Trumpet in the Minstrels' Gallery. Instead, he suggested a chorus of three or four stops in the gallery, but he really did not consider any part of the organ need be placed there at all if the main organ was given more brightness. Dakers put Jackson's ideas to Harrison's, who responded on 5 October.[101] They agreed with some of Jackson's ideas but not with others, particularly those which concerned replacement of some stops in the Pedal Organ with others that were brighter.

At the Chapter meeting on 12 January 1963, Dakers described in detail the unsatisfactory and deteriorating condition of the organ.[102] He was asked to ascertain from Harrison's how much more than the £8,500 quoted in their report of July 1960 the work would now cost, and he was also to enquire how soon the work could be carried out, and how long it would take. In reply, Harrison's estimated 'roughly £12,000' and stated that the work could not be carried out before 1965.[103] Whether or not the Chapter had seen the letter Dakers wrote to Harrison's on 12 January is not known.[104] He had asked them to 'paint as black a picture as possible', because the organ appeared to the listener to be in order, thus giving the impression that all was well. And he had also asked them to warn the Chapter that the organ may 'all pack up one day before so very long'! Renovation of the organ was approved by the Chapter at their meeting on 19 January and Dakers was asked to obtain a detailed specification.

The Chapter heard on 30 March 1963 that a provisional estimate of £11,500 had been received from Harrison's, this figure not including the cost of scaffolding or the cost of cleaning the case.[105] The work would be carried out in 1965 and take eight months. The Chapter agreed that renovation was essential and decided that 'a sum of £15,000 must be envisaged as the probable total cost'; and they also heard on 13 April that Harrison's could start work on Easter Tuesday 1965 'if given a definite order in the near future'.[106] The Chapter Clerk was asked to write to Harrison's to this effect. Dakers wrote to Harrison's on 21 May 1963 to say that the Chapter Clerk had been away rather a lot in recent weeks but assured them they would be hearing from him 'any time now'.[107] He stressed that the organ was now 'behaving very badly' and reported that the Belgian organist Flor Peeters had commented to the Dean at the end of a recital that the organ was 'très fatigué'!

Dakers went further in a letter to Harrison's dated 26 July 1963:[108]

> We are having a little trouble with one or two of the typical people who frequent cathedrals, and gossip. They say that the organ was rebuilt after the war and why should it need doing again, etc, etc. We feel it would be a good thing if we could have something official with which to disarm these people. . . . Sorry to bother you, but none of us here want any gossipers to start putting round a garbled version of facts.

He asked Harrison's to send him information 'in plain language stating exactly what was done after the bombing and why a total rebuild was required now'. Harrison's duly obliged.

A contract was signed in January 1965, and rebuilding of the organ, at a cost of £12,920, began on Easter Tuesday, 20 April.[109] As agreed by the Chapter on 30 January, storage and working space was provided for Harrison's in the Chapter House.[110] Meanwhile, the Chapter had decided on 2 January that 'maintenance of the organ blower be put in the hands of Mr Dalley' (of Willey & Dalley, electrical engineers, Palace Gate, Exeter).[111] However, Watkins & Watson remained responsible for repairing, and supplying parts for, the blower.

Rebuilding of the organ was completed in time for a recital by the Italian virtuoso Fernando Germani on 27 October 1965, but it was a close call. Dakers wrote to Harrison's on 6 October expressing concern and disappointment that it seemed 'more than probable' that the work would not be completed in time; 800 tickets had been sold and the BBC would be recording the recital.[112] In the event, the whole organ was available, including the new Trompette Militaire, but Harrison's rescued the situation by using old reeds in the Swell Organ for the occasion and returning these to Durham after the recital for re-voicing.[113]

Figure 6.5   The Chapter House being used as a workshop when the organ was overhauled in 1965.

Figure 6.6   Cleaning the woodwork above the Chair case, 1965.

Drury mentioned in an article published in 1966 that advantage had been taken of the scaffolding erected for the organ renovation 'to make a measured survey of the whole organ case'.[114] He said there had previously been no drawings of it. During the renovation, the cathedral's carpenter, Percy Webber, had treated the woodwork of the case with a preservative and then wax-polished the wood. The canvas that backed the pierced carving of the case, which had been painted red in 1819, had faded 'until all colour had gone'. It had been restored, and the inscription 'John Loosemore made this organ 1665' on the eastern face of the case had been gilded.

Figure 6.7   Lionel Dakers (organist 1957–1972).

Dakers wrote to Harrison's on 7 November 1965 to say 'how delighted' he was with the rebuilt organ.[115] Everything could now be heard 'with a clarity unknown before', and the console was 'a delight to play'. Norman Sterrett was impressed with the organ, too, saying that the more one tried to criticize the stop-list, the more convincing it became.[116] The new specification showed, he said, 'the transition from a very Romantic Victorian cathedral organ to a scheme influenced by modern thought'. He mentioned Loosemore in his article but did not point out, and nor did anyone else, that 1965 was the 300th anniversary of Loosemore's masterpiece. Sterrett reviewed the rebuilt organ and wrote approvingly of all the changes made. During Germani's recital, he said, 'there was no scream and there were no harsh, snarling reeds; the tone was warm and yet had a new sparkling vitality'.

On 8 May 1966, however, Dakers wrote to Harrison's. He was now far from satisfied.[117] There was 'running' on the Swell which affected all the soft stops and made that division of the organ 'virtually useless'; one of the pipes on the Great Organ rattled so much that he had had to disconnect it; the wind supply was 'gasping'; and the reeds refused to stay in tune for more than a day or two. 'Today', he said, the organ sounded 'like a fair-ground instrument'. The 'strange noises emitting from the organ' were, he went on, 'obvious to the most unmusical of people', and questions were being asked as to 'why this should be happening to a rebuilt organ on which so much money was spent'. He believed that 'something must be basically wrong with the wind supply' and had, as requested by Harrison's, written to Watkins & Watson about it but not received a reply. In fact, Watkins & Watson had not ignored the matter. They had written to Harrison's on 24 April, suggesting that the separate blower for the Trompette Militaire may be a cause of the intermittent noise reported by Dakers, and they had asked that this suspicion be not passed on to him, lest it 'affected his judgement' in answering questions about organ symptoms they wished him to answer.[118]

When an instrument as complex as an organ is taken apart and rebuilt, it is almost inevitable that a settling-in period will be required. And so it was with the rebuild of 1965. The teething problems were soon overcome and the organ thereafter functioned well for years to come. It was heard many times in broadcasts on radio and television and recorded for gramophone records, some of which have been reissued recently as compact discs.

The Musical Centre of Exeter

When it was announced, in April 1972, that Dakers would be leaving Exeter, many were disappointed. As Sterrett had said in 1966, 'a musical Renaissance' had taken place in the city from the time Dakers had been appointed to the cathedral in 1957.[119] Exeter, he went on, 'had been starved of music since the concert hall in Queen Street with its Father Willis organ was destroyed at the beginning of the century, and it would appear that Mr. Dakers was the first to see the cathedral as the new musical centre of the city'. Thanks to him, the numbers of people singing at diocesan choral festivals had grown to many hundreds, and other musical events had grown in frequency and popularity, particularly organ recitals and concerts.

Dakers had been not only the cathedral's organist and master of the choristers but also lecturer in music in St Luke's College of Education, conductor of both the Exeter Musical Society and the Exeter Chamber Orchestra, an examiner for the Associated Board at home and abroad, and a special commissioner for the Royal School of Church Music (RSCM). Moreover, he had found time to write articles and a book and compose church music, including *Missa Exoniensis*. As a special commissioner, he had become concerned about changes that were taking place in parish churches and discussed them in his book *Church Music at the Crossroads*, published in 1970. Some were surprised he should leave the world of cathedral music to become Director of the RSCM, but it proved an inspired choice, for he brought administrative ability, a friendly approach, educational experience, a desire to foster good relations between clergy and musicians, and acceptance of the need to embrace change in church music, while at the same time retaining his love of all that was best in the sacred music of earlier times.

Dakers retired to Salisbury in 1989 and died there on 10 February 2003.[120] While with the RSCM and in retirement he wrote books and edited hymnals and collections of anthems and maintained a close association with various organizations, notably Hymns Ancient and Modern, the Royal College of Organists, the Royal Academy of Music, and the Incorporated Association of Organists. He was awarded a Lambeth doctorate of music in 1979 and appointed a Commander of the Order of the British Empire in 1983.[121]

To succeed Dakers, the Chapter elected Lucian Alaric Nethsingha, organist of St Michael's College, Tenbury Wells, Worcestershire.[122] Born on 3 May 1936, in Colombo, Ceylon (now Sri Lanka), Lucian had been educated at St Thomas's College, Colombo, and entered the United Kingdom on 17 July 1954. He had studied at the Royal College of Music for two years before proceeding, in 1956, to King's College, Cambridge, where he had gained a degree in music. He had gained the FRCO diploma in 1958 and graduated at Cambridge in 1959, moving immediately thereafter to Tenbury.[123]

Dakers left Exeter in December 1972 and Nethsingha succeeded him as the cathedral's organist and master of the choristers on 1 January 1973. Under Lucian, there were many broadcasts by the cathedral choir, and a number of recordings were made, invariably with him directing the choir and the assistant organist, Paul Morgan,

Figure 6.8   Lucian Nethsingha (organist 1973–1999).

accompanying.[124] Indeed, throughout his time at Exeter, he usually left the organ-playing to Paul, but he did give organ recitals and also served as Diocesan Organ Advisor. Like his predecessors, he conducted the Exeter Musical Society.

Julian Sutton mentioned in an appreciation that the choir Lucian established was not only one of high quality but also 'a remarkably happy and firmly established group of singers' who often enjoyed his hospitality at No. 11 Cathedral Close.[125] His many gifts and qualities 'inspired commitment, loyalty and a strong desire to sing well'. He knew his choir well, said Sutton, even if he could not always remember their names! His rehearsals, Sutton added, were 'always relaxed, good-humoured and efficient, no matter what the circumstances', and his gift of perfect pitch 'caused terror in the heart of many a flat-sounding singer'! There was 'no place for a casual or slack approach'.

Further Renovations of the Organ

By the time Lucian retired, on 11 July 1999, further work on the organ had been carried out. The story had begun in 1982, when manifestations of normal wear and tear had been reported to Harrison's.[126] Gussets in wind reservoirs needed to be replaced. Wooden wind trunks were leaking. A number of keys and pedals needed to be refaced. Pallets of the Contra Violone pipe actions in the south transept were noisy. And there was a potentially serious problem in the Minstrels' Gallery not caused by normal wear and tear. Rainwater was running down a wall onto the soundboard of the Trompette Militaire. This was remedied in 1984 by moving the soundboard, providing a new wind trunk from the reservoir, and re-voicing the pipes. Overall, however, the condition of the organ's action was, as Lucian stated in a letter to Harrison's on 21 May 1984, 'very reliable indeed and still functioning exceedingly well'.[127] Nevertheless, 'a stitch in time' was needed. The organ was dismantled in 1985 for repairs, cleaning, re-regulation of pipework and minor improvements. The work cost £50,605 and was paid for by the Friends of Exeter Cathedral, using the major part of a legacy from the late Miss Ruby Arnold, to whom the music of the cathedral had meant so much.[128]

The work included re-leathering and other repairs to wind reservoirs, overhaul of soundboards, re-facing of Great and Swell keys in ivory, replacing the sides and back of the Solo box (affected by woodworm), and providing a new Tremulant for the Solo Organ. It also included replacement of the pedalboard with one of standard dimensions and standard relationship to the manual keys. Harrison's Bristol tuner had reported to his superiors at Durham on 15 February 1975 that the pedalboard was, in his words, 'flatter and straighter' than Harrison's 'usual radiating and concave', and Lucian was not comfortable with it.[129]

Renovation began soon after Easter 1985 and was sufficiently far advanced for the organ to be used for the installation of Bishop Thompson on 12 October that year. Indeed, a note from Mark Venning of Harrison's dated that day said that 'the enthronement went splendidly – no ciphers! – especially L.N., who gave me the thumbs up from the choir stalls when the organ got into its stride'.[130] While the organ was out of action, electronic instruments were used in the nave and the quire.

Venning mentioned in his note that there had been television cameras in the cathedral for the enthronement. This had not been without incident, as we find in a letter written by the Canon Chancellor, John Thurmer, to Television South West Ltd, drawing to their attention damage to organ pipes caused by their cameramen.[131] They had, he said, placed heavy objects on the pipes, despite a warning by the organist. Harrison's wrote to Lucian on 15 November to say that the overhaul of the organ had been completed, including repairs to the pipes damaged by the television crew.[132]

As with all previous renovations of the organ, there were teething troubles. Lucian wrote to Harrison's on 18 December 1985 to say that the organ was, by and large, behaving well.[133] He was, he said, '_very_ pleased with the present state of things – except for the Swell Mixture (bad!) and a few minor matters'. In particular, he mentioned the Pedal Trombone, which was '<u>very</u> elusive', refusing to come on when required but making its presence known when not required! Overall, though, 'the Dean and Chapter were very thrilled with the results', and so was he.

A problem that was not associated with normal wear and tear occurred in 1998. In the words of a note from one of Harrison's tuners, dated 9 May:

> Water damage on the Choir has occurred from a workman testing a water stand-pipe in the roof. The 8ft and 4ft flutes are affected. Their two slides are locked solid. . . . Lucian is anxious that it is sorted out as soon as possible.

Exeter Cathedral possesses a sophisticated fire and smoke detection system which includes dry risers to convey water to the roof-space above the nave and quire vaults in the event of fire in that part of the building.

By the time any further renovation work on the organ was carried out, Lucian's successor was in post. He was Andrew Thomas Seager Millington, organist and master of the choristers of Guildford Cathedral (see Plate 14). Born at Willenhall in the West Midlands on 2 May 1952, he had received his musical education at The King's School, Worcester, before proceeding to Downing College, Cambridge, where, from 1971 to 1974, as Organ Scholar, he had read Music. As a boy, he had been a chorister in the Priory Church at Great Malvern and begun organ lessons there when 13 years of age, with the church's organist, John Durham Holl. He had gained his FRCO diploma in 1972, become assistant music master at Malvern College in 1974 and assistant organist of Gloucester Cathedral a year later, before moving to Guildford in 1983.[134]

When Andrew was appointed at Exeter, tradition was broken. The title he was given was 'director of music', not 'organist and master of the choristers'. And to confuse matters, the title of Paul Morgan was altered from 'assistant organist' to 'organist', while Stephen Tanner, who had founded the cathedral's girls' choir in 1994, became 'assistant organist'! However, Andrew's duties were the same as those of his predecessors. He was the principal organist and master of the choristers and remained so in 2014, when this book was completed. Some clarification was provided in 2010, when Paul retired. His successor, David Davies, was appointed 'assistant director of music', and Stephen Tanner retained the title 'assistant organist'. Paul was given the title 'organist emeritus'.

When Andrew took up his appointment, in August 1999, he inherited a programme of work on the organ which had been discussed with Harrison's but not yet given the go-ahead by the Chapter. That came in September 2000.[135] There were two parts to the work, as summarized by Andrew in the annual report of the Friends of Exeter Cathedral for 2001: firstly, 'updating of the technology side of the instrument and some enhancement of its tonal scope'; secondly, additional pipework installed in the Minstrels' Gallery.[136] He was 'particularly grateful to the cathedral's Music Foundation Trust for their support in funding this project'.

The work carried out in 2001 and the expansion of the Minstrel Organ in 2002 (see Plate 9) were reviewed by Andrew in 2003 in the annual report of the Friends of Exeter Cathedral.[137] On the technical side, he said, a new solid-state system had replaced the couplers and relays which had been installed in 1965 and become badly worn. And a new piston system had replaced the previous 'cumbersome and obsolete arrangement', allowing the organist to 'select combinations of stops more easily and use the colours of the instrument to maximum effect'. Parts of the action had been re-leathered and the console refurbished. As regards tonal changes, he drew attention particularly to the new 32-foot Contra Trombone in the Pedal Organ. The idea of expanding the Minstrel Organ was, Andrew explained, to support congregational singing. This part of the organ now had eight stops, one of them in the Pedal division, and the original stop had been renamed Trompette.

Overall, the work carried out in 2001 and 2002 cost close to £200,000, funded by the cathedral's Music Foundation Trust. While the organ was being overhauled, two 'Eminent' digital organs were used, a two-manual instrument in the quire and a three-manual instrument in the nave. They were provided by Cathedral Organs Ltd of Hertfordshire.

And So to the Future

At Exeter, Andrew has expanded the repertoire of the cathedral choir greatly, introducing Mass settings, anthems, psalm chants and descants he himself has composed, as well as music of various genres, including jazz settings of the Mass and orchestral Masses. He has also taken the choir on tour at home and abroad, including visits to Russia, the USA, the Canary Isles and Vienna; and he has broadcast on Radio 3 many times, as a solo organist and as director of the choir for Choral Evensong. In addition, he has taken the choir to parishes around Devon on a regular basis as part of the cathedral's outreach commitment. And, like his predecessors, he has made recordings of the cathedral organ and cathedral choir and become involved in the musical life of Exeter and further afield. He is, for example, director of the Exeter Philharmonic Choir, an inspirational leader of festivals and other events for the Royal School of Church Music, an examiner for the Associated Board of the Royal Schools of Music, a former president of the Cathedral Organists' Association, and an honorary member of the Exeter and District Organists' Association. He is a most approachable person with a great sense of humour and almost certainly the first organist of Exeter Cathedral who has supported Aston Villa Football Club!

In 2013 and 2014, Andrew has overseen a complete redesign and renovation of the cathedral's organ. As we have seen in this book, the lack of space in Loosemore's case has long been an issue, and it has been literally true for many years that some pipes have been inaccessible for tuning and others difficult to reach safely. Moreover, the positioning of ranks of pipes within the case has been musically far from ideal. The weather of December 2010 helped bring matters to a head. There are many services and concerts in the cathedral in December. The extra heating that was needed in that exceptionally cold month dried out parts of the organ to such an extent that joints in the wind trunking under the floor of the cathedral opened up, so much so that visitors sometimes reported 'gas leaks' when the organ blower was switched on! And in the organ loft, the sound of air escaping was reminiscent of a steam engine of old waiting in a railway station.

The time had come for another overhaul of the organ, and on this occasion the rebuilt instrument had to conform to health and safety legislation in respect of access for tuning and maintenance.[138] The organ was dismantled at the end of January 2013 and removed by Harrison's to Durham, leaving only the case and display pipes on the pulpitum, along with the Contra Violone pipes in the south transept and the pipes in the Minstrels' Gallery. Harrison's have undertaken the first complete rebuilding of the organ since 1933 and the most radical since 1891 (see Plate 10). They have redesigned the instrument and made entirely new soundboards, wind conveyances and other components, but re-using most of the pipes. The change in specification is small, with only two new stops, a Gemshorn on the Choir Organ and a Sesquialtera on the Swell, the latter formed from the old Twelfth joined by a new Tierce.

Since February 2013, a three-manual digital instrument by Copeman Hart has been used, its speakers in a scaffolding tower at the north-west corner of the pulpitum. This instrument has proved effective for accompanying services in both the quire and the nave. With its console in the nave, however, communication between organist and the conductor of singers in the quire has not been ideal. During 2013 and 2014, the usual programmes of organ recitals had to be put in abeyance. Instead, the digital instrument has been used in imaginative ways which have shown just how much fun concerts can be when an organ is coupled with human voice, piano, saxophone, trumpet, cello, drums or other musical devices. Full advantage has been taken of opportunities to promote the organ as a versatile and exciting instrument. Heavenly harmony has been maintained in 2013 and 2014, but a digital instrument can never produce the natural sounds of a pipe organ fully. We look forward to the return of the cathedral's great musical asset and to marking the 350th anniversary of Loosemore's organ in 2015.[139]

The King of Instruments

There are two types of organ pipe: flue and reed. In a flue pipe, air is forced through a slit (the flue) which is in the mouth of the pipe. The air in the pipe is thus made to vibrate, and the note which is produced is that corresponding to the natural frequency of the pipe. The longer the pipe, the lower the pitch of the note. In a reed pipe, a metal tongue is made to vibrate when air is blown over it. A resonator focuses and refines the sound. Pipes are normally made of wood or metal, an alloy of lead and tin.

Pipes with a common timbre are arranged in rows, called ranks, with pipes of various lengths in each row, each one producing a different pitch. Pipes are mounted on a windchest into which air is fed under pressure. Groups of ranks form partial organs, which are usually today called divisions, and each division is played by a separate keyboard.

A keyboard which is played with the hands is called a manual, while one played with the feet is called a pedalboard. Keys on mediæval organs were typically much wider than those of today, sometimes as wide as eight to ten centimetres (cm) in the thirteenth and fourteenth centuries. Widths decreased from around 1400, when keys began to be played by the finger rather than the whole hand, and reached the modern width of about 2.2 cm soon after 1500. The compasses of manuals have increased over the centuries, from about an octave and a half in the fourteenth century to more than three octaves by about 1450 and more than four octaves by the eighteenth century. Pedalboards have a shorter compass, typically two and a half octaves today, whereas manuals now extend over five octaves, give or take a note or two.[1]

The Great Organ is the primary manual division, containing the so-called foundation (or chorus) pipes which produce the grand and solid sounds that are quintessentially those which most people associate with a church organ. The Choir Organ is the division that provides sweet-toned softer stops which are useful for accompanying singers. However, Choir is actually a corruption of Chair (or Chaire or Chayre), so-called from the old practice of placing this division behind the organist's seat. The Swell Organ is so-called because its pipes are placed inside a box which has shutters like large Venetian blinds on one or more sides. By opening and closing these shutters, the sounds of the pipes can be made to swell and diminish. The Solo Organ that is found on larger instruments contains ranks of pipes which are suitable for playing solo lines of music.

Below each rank of pipes there is a slider (or slide) which has holes in it, and these holes become aligned with the pipes when that rank is selected by means of a stop. Sliders were always made of wood until very recently but are sometimes now made of rigid foam (PVC) board. Valves prevent notes from sounding until played by the organist. When a key is depressed, the associated valve opens and thus allows air to pass through the hole in the slider to the pipe, which then produces the required note. Electric blowers are generally used today, but the air was previously fed from bellows that were pumped by hand or foot, from which it follows that an organ remained silent if no one was available to blow it. Linkages from keyboards to valves were always mechanical before the nineteenth century, when tubular-pneumatic action was introduced. Even though there are several types of action these days, mechanical (tracker) action is still favoured by many organists and organ-builders for the precise response it provides.

The origins of the pipe organ are lost in the mists of time but are surely to be found in the pan-pipes of antiquity which were made from reeds that grew by the water-side. A very early form of pipe organ was the *hydraulis* (water organ) of Ancient Greece, in which, in the third century BCE, the supply of air to pipes was produced by hydraulic means. Bellows that were pumped by hand or foot were introduced in the first century or two CE, and most of the sounds which are available on a modern organ had been developed by about 1600. By then, the organ had become the most complex device made by humans, and so it remained until it lost that distinction to the telephone exchange in the late nineteenth century. The French poet and composer Guillaume de Machaut (*c*.1300–1377) called the organ 'the king of instruments', and so, too, did Wolfgang Amadeus Mozart (1756–91).

The Organ Specification in 1859

The organ as found by 'Father' Willis before his work in 1859. Within a short space of time Willis had been contracted to undertake work that was to be ready by Divine Service in the Nave on Easter Day, 24 April 1859. Willis's initial recommendation consisted of six proposals that included the alteration of compasses and making new keyboards to be sited on the south side of the case. The question of altering compasses generated some debate with the then organist, Alfred Angel, and the Chapter Clerk (D&C 7062/1859; see also Chapter 5). This touched on the lack of available space for extending compasses within the organ case; indeed, this issue of the lack of space has been a constant factor during the life of the organ, even in 2014 where the most modern and ingenious techniques have made the organ both ergonomically impressive and space efficient to an optimum degree.

The standardization of manual and pedal compasses at Exeter did not come about until 1891 (Appendix 4).

GREAT ORGAN
Double Diapason
Open Diapason
Open Diapason
Stopped Diapason
Principal
Twelfth
Fifteenth
Sesquialtera V
Cornet (middle C) V
Bassoon
Trumpet

CHOIR ORGAN
Stopped Diapason
Dulciana (TC)
Principal
Flute
Cremona

PEDAL ORGAN
Open Diapason

COUPLERS
Swell to Great
Swell to Choir

SWELL ORGAN
Open Diapason
Stopped Diapason
Principal
Sesquialtera III
Hautboy
Trumpet

Pedals to Great
Pedals to Choir
Octave pedal

ACCESSORIES
Four composition pedals

The Organ as Built by Henry Speechly in 1876

GREAT ORGAN
Double Stopped Diapason
Open Diapason
Open Diapason
Stopped Diapason
Clarabella
Principal
Flûte Harmonique
Twelfth
Fifteenth
Sesquialtera II
Mixture III
Trumpet
Clarion

SWELL ORGAN
Double Diapason
Open Diapason
Stopped Diapason
Salicional
Principal
Mixture III
Cornopean
Oboe
Clarion

CHOIR ORGAN
Gamba
Lieblich Gedact
Dulciana
Gemshorn
Wald Flute
Corno di Bassetto

PEDAL ORGAN
Double Open Diapason (32)
Open Diapason (16)
Bourdon (from Great) (16)

COUPLERS
Swell to Pedal
Great to Pedal (unison)
Great to Pedal (sub octave)
Choir to Pedal
Swell to Great
Swell to Choir

ACCESSORIES
Four composition pedals to Great Organ
Four composition pedals to Swell Organ
One double action pedal to Great to Pedal
and Pedal Open Diapason 16

The Organ as Rebuilt by Henry Willis in 1891

PEDAL ORGAN

1	Double Open Diapason	32
2	Open Diapason	16
3	Violone	16
4	Bourdon	16
5	Octave	8
6	Violoncello	8
7	Bass Flute	8
8	Trombone	16
i	*Choir to Pedals*	
ii	*Solo to Pedals*	
iii	*Swell to Pedals*	
iv	*Great to Pedals*	

SWELL ORGAN

34	Double Stopped Diapason	16
35	Open Diapason	8
36	Stopped Diapason	8
37	Echo Gamba	8
38	Voix Célestes (TC)	8
39	Principal	4
40	Celestina	4
41	Twelfth	$2\frac{2}{3}$
42	Fifteenth	2
43	Mixture	III
44	Contra Hautboy	16
45	Hautboy	8
46	Cornopean	8
47	Clarion	4
x	*Tremulant*	
xi	*Swell Octave*	
xii	*Swell Sub Octave*	

CHOIR ORGAN

9	Lieblich Gedact	16
10	Lieblich Gedact	8
11	Salicional	8
12	Vox Angelica (TC)	8
13	Gemshorn	4

SOLO ORGAN

48	Gamba	8
49	Dulciana	8
50	Claribel Flute	8
51	Gemshorn	4
52	Viola	4

14	Salicet	4
15	Lieblich Gedact	2
16	Vox Humana (enc)	8
17	Orchestral Oboe (enc)	8
18	Corno di Bassetto (enc)	8
v	*Tremulant*	
vi	*Swell to Choir*	
vii	*Solo to Choir*	

53	Wald Flute	4
54	Harmonic Flute	4
55	Piccolo	2
56	Clarionet	8
57	Tuba	8

GREAT ORGAN

19	Double Open Diapason	16
20	Open Diapason	8
21	Open Diapason	8
22	Open Diapason	8
23	Stopped Diapason	8
24	Clarabella	8
25	Octave	4
26	Principal	4
27	Harmonic Flute	4
28	Twelfth	$2\frac{2}{3}$
29	Fifteenth	2
30	Mixture	III
31	Double Trumpet	16
32	Trumpet	8
33	Clarion	4
viii	*Swell to Great*	
ix	*Solo to Great*	

ACCESSORIES

Choir Flue Work Ventil
Choir Reeds Ventil
Five composition pedals to Great Organ
Four composition pedals to Swell Organ
Ventil reverser to cancel all Pedal
stops except Bourdon
Great to Pedal reverser
Crescendo pedals to Choir and Swell

The Organ as Rebuilt by Harrison & Harrison in 1933

PEDAL ORGAN

1	Contra Violone (from 3)	32
2	Open Diapason	16
3	Violone	16
4	Bourdon	16
5	Stopped Diapason (from 34)	16
6	Octave (from 2)	8
7	Violoncello	8
8	Bass Flute (from 4)	8
9	Trombone	16
i	*Choir to Pedal*	
ii	*Great to Pedal*	
iii	*Swell to Pedal*	
iv	*Solo to Pedal*	

SWELL ORGAN

34	Double Stopped Diapason	16
35	Open Diapason	8
36	Stopped Diapason	8
37	Echo Gamba	8
38	Voix Célestes (TC)	8
39	Principal	4
40	Celestina	4
41	Twelfth	2⅔
42	Fifteenth	2
43	Mixture (17.19.22)	III
44	Contra Fagotto	16
45	Hautboy	8
x	*Tremulant*	
46	Cornopean	8
47	Clarion	4
xi	*Swell Octave*	
xii	*Swell Sub Octave*	

CHOIR ORGAN

10	Lieblich Bourdon	16
11	Lieblich Gedackt	8
12	Wald Flute	8
13	Salicional (enclosed)	8
14	Vox Angelica (TC) (enclosed)	8
15	Salicet	4

SOLO ORGAN (48–55 enclosed)

48	Claribel Flute	8
49	Viole d'Orchestre	8
50	Dulciana	8
51	Harmonic Flute	4
52	Piccolo	2
53	Corno di Bassetto	8

16 Lieblich Flute	4
17 Lieblich Piccolo	2
18 Clarinet (enclosed)	8
v *Swell to Choir*	
vi *Solo to Choir*	

GREAT ORGAN

19 Double Open Diapason (from 3)	16
20 Open Diapason No 1	8
21 Open Diapason No 2	8
22 Open Diapason No 3	8
23 Stopped Diapason	8
24 Claribel Flute	8
25 Octave	4
26 Principal	4
27 Harmonic Flute	4
28 Twelfth	2⅔
29 Fifteenth	2
30 Mixture (17.19.22)	III
31 Double Trumpet	16
32 Trumpet	8
33 Clarion	4
vii *Choir to Great*	
viii *Swell to Great*	
ix *Solo to Great*	

54 Orchestral Oboe	8
55 Vox Humana	8
xiii *Tremulant*	
56 Tuba (harmonic)	8
xiv *Solo Octave*	
xv *Solo Sub Octave*	
xvi *Solo Unison Off*	

COMBINATION COUPLERS
Great and Pedal Pistons
Pedal to Swell Pistons

ACCESSORIES
Six toe pistons to Pedal Organ
Four thumb pistons to Choir Organ
Seven thumb pistons to Great Organ
Seven thumb pistons to Swell Organ
Four thumb pistons to Solo Organ
One adjustable general piston
General Cancel
Doubles Off piston
Pedal Trombone reverser
Reversible pistons to:
Choir to Pedal, Great to Pedal, Swell to
Pedal, Solo to Pedal, Swell to Great and
Solo to Great.
Three balanced swell pedals to Choir,
Swell and Solo organs.

The Organ as Rebuilt by Harrison & Harrison in 1965

PEDAL ORGAN

1	Contra Violone (from 3)	32
2	Open Diapason	16
3	Violone	16
4	Bourdon	16
5	Quintadena (from 39)	16
6	Octave (from 2)	8
7	Violoncello	8
8	Flute (from 4)	8
9	Fifteenth	4
10	Octave Flute	4
11	Mixture	II
12	Trombone	16
i	Choir to Pedal	
ii	Great to Pedal	
iii	Swell to Pedal	
iv	Solo to Pedal	

CHOIR ORGAN

13	Lieblich Bourdon (12 from 4)	16
14	Lieblich Gedackt	8
15	Viola	8
16	Open Flute	4

SWELL ORGAN (enclosed)

36	Quintadena	16
37	Open Diapason	8
38	Stopped Diapason	8
39	Salicional	8
40	Voix Célestes (12 from 42)	8
41	Principal	4
42	Flute	4
43	Twelfth	2⅔
44	Fifteenth	2
45	Mixture	IV
46	Contra Fagotto	16
47	Hautboy	8
x	Tremulant	
48	Cornopean	8
49	Clarion	4
xi	Swell Octave	
xii	Swell Sub Octave	
xiii	Swell Unison Off	
xiv	Solo to Swell	

SOLO ORGAN (50–57 enclosed)

50	Viole d'Orchestre	8
51	Claribel Flute	8
52	Viole Octaviante	4
53	Harmonic Flute	4

17	Nazard	$2\frac{2}{3}$	54	Piccolo	2
18	Lieblich Piccolo	2	55	Corno di Bassetto	8
19	Tierce	$1\frac{3}{5}$	56	Orchestral Oboe	8
20	Twenty Second	1	57	Vox Humana	8
21	Cimbel	III	*xv*	*Tremulant*	
v	*Swell to Choir*		58	Tuba	8
vi	*Solo to Choir*		59	Trompette Militaire	8
			xvi	*Solo Octave*	
			xvii	*Solo Sub Octave*	
			xviii	*Solo Unison Off*	

GREAT ORGAN

22	Double Open Diapason	16
23	Open Diapason I	8
24	Open Diapason II	8
25	Stopped Diapason	8
26	Dulciana	8
27	Principal	4
28	Harmonic Flute	4
29	Twelfth	$2\frac{2}{3}$
30	Fifteenth	2
31	Mixture	IV
32	Sharp Mixture	III
33	Double Trumpet	16
34	Trumpet	8
35	Clarion	4
vii	*Choir to Great*	
viii	*Swell to Great*	
ix	*Solo to Great*	

ACCESSORIES
Great and Pedal Combinations Coupled
Pedal to Swell Pistons
Eight toe pistons to Pedal Organ
Eight toe pistons to Swell Organ
Eight thumb pistons to Great Organ
Eight thumb pistons to Choir Organ
Eight thumb pistons to Solo Organ
Eight thumb pistons to Swell Organ
Six general pistons and general cancel to each division
One general cancel piston
Two general pistons to couplers
Reversible thumb pistons to all couplers and Pedal Trombone
Reversible toe pistons to *ii*, *iii* and *viii*
Balanced swell pedals to Swell and Solo organs
All pistons adjustable

The Organ after Renovation by Harrison & Harrison in 1985

PEDAL ORGAN

1	Contra Violone (from 3)	32
2	Open Diapason	16
3	Violone	16
4	Bourdon	16
5	Quintadena (from 39)	16
6	Octave (from 2)	8
7	Violoncello	8
8	Flute (from 4)	8
9	Fifteenth	4
10	Octave Flute	4
11	Mixture	II
12	Trombone	16
i	*Choir to Pedal*	
ii	*Great to Pedal*	
iii	*Swell to Pedal*	
iv	*Solo to Pedal*	

SWELL ORGAN (enclosed)

36	Quintadena	16
37	Open Diapason	8
38	Stopped Diapason	8
39	Salicional	8
40	Voix Célestes (12 from 42)	8
41	Principal	4
42	Flute	4
43	Twelfth	2⅔
44	Fifteenth	2
45	Mixture	IV
46	Contra Fagotto	16
47	Hautboy	8
x	*Tremulant*	
48	Cornopean	8
49	Clarion	4
xi	*Swell Octave*	
xii	*Swell Sub Octave*	
xiii	*Swell Unison Off*	
xiv	*Solo to Swell*	

CHOIR ORGAN

13	Lieblich Bourdon (12 from 4)	16
14	Lieblich Gedackt	8
15	Viola	8
16	Open Flute	4

SOLO ORGAN (50–57 enclosed)

50	Viole d'Orchestre	8
51	Claribel Flute	8
52	Viole Octaviante	4
53	Harmonic Flute	4

17	Nazard	2⅔		54	Piccolo	2
18	Lieblich Piccolo	2		55	Corno di Bassetto	8
19	Tierce	1⅗		56	Orchestral Oboe	8
20	Twenty Second	1		57	Vox Humana	8
21	Cimbel	III		*xv*	*Tremulant*	
v	*Swell to Choir*			58	Tuba	8
vi	*Solo to Choir*			59	Trompette Militaire	8
				xvi	*Solo Octave*	
				xvii	*Solo Sub Octave*	
				xviii	*Solo Unison Off*	

GREAT ORGAN

22	Double Open Diapason	16
23	Open Diapason I	8
24	Open Diapason II	8
25	Stopped Diapason	8
26	Dulciana	8
27	Principal	4
28	Harmonic Flute	4
29	Twelfth	2⅔
30	Fifteenth	2
31	Mixture	IV
32	Sharp Mixture	III
33	Double Trumpet	16
34	Trumpet	8
35	Clarion	4
vii	*Choir to Great*	
viii	*Swell to Great*	
ix	*Solo to Great*	

ACCESSORIES
Great and Pedal Combinations Coupled
Pedal to Swell Pistons
Eight toe pistons to Pedal Organ   Eight thumb pistons to Choir Organ
Eight toe pistons to Swell Organ   Eight thumb pistons to Solo Organ
Eight thumb pistons to Great Organ   Eight thumb pistons to Swell Organ
Six general pistons and general cancel to each division
One general cancel piston
Two general pistons to couplers
Reversible thumb pistons to all couplers and Pedal Trombone
Reversible toe pistons to *ii, iii* and *viii*
Balanced swell pedals to Swell and Solo organs
All pistons adjustable

The Organ as Rebuilt by Harrison & Harrison in 2002

PEDAL ORGAN

1	Contra Violone (from 3)	32
2	Open Diapason	16
3	Violone	16
4	Bourdon	16
5	Quintadena (from 39)	16
6	Octave (from 2)	8
7	Violoncello	8
8	Flute (from 4)	8
9	Fifteenth	4
10	Octave Flute	4
11	Mixture	II
12	Contra Trombone (from 13)	32
13	Trombone	16
14	Tromba (from 13)	8
i	*Choir to Pedal*	
ii	*Great to Pedal*	
iii	*Swell to Pedal*	
iv	*Solo to Pedal*	

CHOIR ORGAN

15	Lieblich Bourdon (12 from 4)	16
16	Lieblich Gedackt	8
17	Viola	8
18	Lieblich Flute	4

SWELL ORGAN (enclosed)

39	Quintadena	16
40	Open Diapason	8
41	Stopped Diapason	8
42	Salicional	8
43	Voix Célestes (12 from 42)	8
44	Principal	4
45	Flute	4
46	Twelfth	$2\frac{2}{3}$
47	Fifteenth	2
48	Mixture	IV
49	Hautboy	8
xiv	*Tremulant*	
50	Contra Fagotto	16
51	Cornopean	8
52	Clarion	4
xv	*Swell Octave*	
xvi	*Swell Sub Octave*	
xvii	*Swell Unison Off*	
xviii	*Solo to Swell*	

SOLO ORGAN (53–60 enclosed)

53	Viole d'Orchestre	8
54	Claribel Flute	8
55	Viole Céleste (tenor C)	8
56	Harmonic Flute	4

19	Nazard	2⅔
20	Open Flute	2
21	Tierce	1⅗
22	Larigot	1⅗
23	Clarinet	8
v	*Tremulant*	
vi	*Octaves Alone*	
vii	*Swell to Choir*	
viii	*Solo to Choir*	

57	Piccolo	2
58	Corno di Bassetto	8
59	Orchestral Oboe	8
60	Vox Humana	8
xix	*Tremulant*	
61	Tuba	8
62	Trompette (from 69)	8
xx	*Solo Octave*	
xxi	*Solo Sub Octave*	
xxii	*Solo Unison Off*	

GREAT ORGAN

25	Double Open Diapason	16
26	Open Diapason No 1	8
27	Open Diapason No 2	8
28	Stopped Diapason	8
29	Octave	4
30	Principal	4
31	Harmonic Flute	4
32	Twelfth	2⅔
33	Fifteenth	2
34	Mixture	IV
35	Sharp Mixture	III
36	Double Trumpet	16
37	Trumpet	8
38	Clarion	4
ix	*Great Reeds on Choir*	
x	*Great Reeds on Pedal*	
xi	*Choir to Great*	
xii	*Swell to Great*	
xiii	*Solo to Great*	

MINSTREL ORGAN

63	Bourdon (12 from 70)	16
64	Open Diapason	8
65	Stopped Diapason	8
66	Principal	4
67	Fifteenth	2
68	Mixture	V
69	Trompette	8
70	Pedal Bourdon	16
xxiii	*Minstrel on Choir*	
xxiv	*Minstrel on Great*	
xxv	*Minstrel on Solo*	

ACCESSORIES

Eight toe pistons to Pedal Organ
Eight toe pistons to Swell Organ
Eight thumb pistons to Great Organ
Three thumb pistons to Minstrel Organ
Two general pistons to couplers

Eight thumb pistons to Choir Organ
Eight thumb pistons to Solo Organ
Eight thumb pistons to Swell Organ
Eight general pistons and general cancel
Reversible toe pistons *ii, xiv, 12*

Combination couplers to Great and Pedal pistons, Pedal to Swell pistons, Generals on Swell toe pistons
Sequencer operating general pistons
Balanced expression pedals to Swell and Solo organs

APPENDIX 9

The Organ as Rebuilt by Harrison & Harrison in 2014

PEDAL ORGAN

1	Contra Violone (from 3)	32
2	Open Diapason	16
3	Violone	16
4	Bourdon	16
5	Quintadena* (from 39)	16
6	Octave (from 2)	8
7	Violoncello	8
8	Flute (from 4)	8
9	Fifteenth	4
10	Octave Flute	4
11	Mixture	II
12	Contra Trombone (from 13)	32
13	Trombone	16
14	Tromba (from 13)	8
i	*Choir to Pedal*	
ii	*Great to Pedal*	
iii	*Swell to Pedal*	
iv	*Solo to Pedal*	

SWELL ORGAN (enclosed)

39	Quintadena*	16
40	Open Diapason	8
41	Stopped Diapason	8
42	Salicional	8
43	Voix Célestes (12 from 42)	8
44	Principal	4
45	Flute	4
46	Fifteenth	2
47	Sesquialtera (2014)	II
48	Mixture	IV
49	Hautboy	8
xvi	*Tremulant*	
50	Contra Fagotto	16
51	Cornopean	8
52	Clarion	4
xvii	*Swell Octave*	
xviii	*Swell Sub Octave*	
xix	*Swell Unison Off*	
xx	*Solo to Swell*	

CHOIR ORGAN

15	Lieblich Bourdon (12 from 4)	16
16	Lieblich Gedackt	8
17	Viola	8

SOLO ORGAN (53–60 enclosed)

53	Viole d'Orchestre	8
54	Claribel Flute	8
55	Viole Céleste (tenor C)	8

18	Gemshorn (2014)	4	56	Harmonic Flute	4
19	Lieblich Flute	4	57	Piccolo	2
20	Nazard	2⅔	58	Corno di Bassetto	8
21	Open Flute	2	59	Orchestral Oboe	8
22	Tierce	1⅗	60	Vox Humana	8
23	Larigot	1⅗	*xxi*	*Tremulant*	
24	Clarinet	8	61	Tuba	8
v	*Tremulant*		62	Trompette (from 69)	8
vi	*Choir Octave*		*xxii*	*Solo Octave*	
vii	*Choir Sub Octave*		*xxiii*	*Solo Sub Octave*	
viii	*Choir Unison Off*		*xxiv*	*Solo Unison Off*	
ix	*Swell to Choir*				
x	*Solo to Choir*				

GREAT ORGAN

MINSTREL ORGAN

25	Double Open Diapason	16	63	Bourdon (12 from 70)	16
26	Open Diapason No 1	8	64	Open Diapason	8
27	Open Diapason No 2	8	65	Stopped Diapason	8
28	Stopped Diapason	8	66	Principal	4
29	Octave	4	67	Fifteenth	2
30	Principal	4	68	Mixture	V
31	Harmonic Flute	4	69	Trompette	8
32	Twelfth	2⅔	70	Pedal Bourdon	16
33	Fifteenth	2	*xxv*	*Minstrel on Choir*	
34	Mixture	IV	*xxvi*	*Minstrel on Great*	
35	Sharp Mixture	III	*xxvii*	*Minstrel on Solo*	
36	Double Trumpet	16			
37	Trumpet	8			
38	Clarion	4			
xi	*Great Reeds on Choir*				
xii	*Great Reeds on Pedal*				
xiii	*Choir to Great*				
xiv	*Swell to Great*				
xv	*Solo to Great*				

ACCESSORIES

Eight toe pistons to Pedal Organ
Eight toe pistons to Swell Organ
Eight thumb pistons to Great Organ
Three thumb pistons to Minstrel Organ
Two general pistons to couplers

Eight thumb pistons to Choir Organ
Eight thumb pistons to Solo Organ
Eight thumb pistons to Swell Organ
Eight general pistons and general cancel
Reversible toe pistons *ii, xiv, 12*

Combination couplers to Great and Pedal pistons, Pedal to Swell pistons, Generals on Swell toe pistons

Sequencer operating general pistons

Balanced expression pedals to Swell and Solo organs, with dual electro-mechanical switching operation of Solo shutters.

* This rank was revoiced as a Lieblich Bourdon in 2014, its tonal character reverting to that of a Double Stopped Diapason of earlier specifications.

Notes

D&C – documents in the Exeter Cathedral Library and Archives.

Chapter 1

1 'A relation of a short survey of the Western Counties made by a Lieutenant of the Military Company in Norwich in 1635', transcribed from British Library Lansdowne MS 213 and edited by L.G. Wickham Legg, Camden Third Series Vol. 52 (*Miscellany Vol. 16*), 1936, pp. 1–128. Extracts from the MS first appeared in *The Gentleman's Magazine* in November 1858, Vol. 205 (New Series Vol. 5), pp. 479–487. Lieutenant Hammond began his journey on 4 August 1635 and visited several cathedrals before he reached Exeter. It seems likely that he visited Exeter Cathedral in late August or early September 1635.

2 The grant has been reproduced in full, in Latin, in Appendix D of a paper by the Rev H.T. Ellacombe on 'The church bells in the towers of all the parish churches of Devonshire' (*Transactions of the Exeter Diocesan Architectural Society*, 1867, Vol. 1, Second Series, pp. 221–410. A section of this paper is called 'The bells of the Cathedral Church of St Peter, Exon' (pp. 292–298). Appendix D can be found on pp. 383–384.

3 'The accounts of the fabric of Exeter Cathedral, 1279–1353', edited and translated by Audrey M Erskine (*Devon & Cornwall Record Society*, New Series, Vols 24 and 26, 1981 and 1983). February 1286/87 would have been 1287 by today's reckoning, for in those days the number of the year was changed on 25 March, not 1 January. New Year's Day was Lady Day (25 March) from the twelfth century until 1751. It has been the first day of January in England and Wales since 1752 (1600 in Scotland).

4 Alan Mould, 2007, *The English Chorister* (London: Hambledon Continuum, 366 pages).

5 National Archives document reference C143/108/15 (8 Edward II). See also the note by Ethel Lega-Weekes on 'Exeter Cathedral bell-founders' in *Devon Notes and Queries*, Vol. 4 (1906–1907), pp. 106–107.

6 The original of the grant has been lost. However, an inspeximus and confirmation of it for Robert, son of Walter de Ropford, bell-founder, can be found in the *Calendar of Patent Rolls*, 11 Edward II, Part 1, Membrane 5, dated 6 January 1318 (See *Calendar of the Patent Rolls preserved in the Public Record Office*, Edward II, Vol.III, AD1317–1321, London: HMSO, published 1903, p. 72).

7 D&C 3550, f. 60 and D&C 3586, p. 129.

8 'The accounts of the fabric of Exeter Cathedral, 1279–1353', *op.cit.*

9 Details of the bars were given in the report of a visit by Scott to Exeter published in *Trewman's Exeter Flying Post* on 26 July 1871 and also in *The Morning Post* (a London newspaper) on 30 September 1871.

10 N. Orme, 1978, 'The early musicians of Exeter Cathedral', *Music and Letters*, Vol. 59, No. 4, pp. 395–410.

11 D&C 3550, f. 85b and D&C 3586, p. 432.

12 D&C 3550, f. 115a and D&C 3586, p. 432.

13 D&C 2704/7.

14 S. Bicknell, 1996, *The History of the English Organ* (Cambridge: Cambridge University Press, 407 pages).

15 D&C 3551, f. 38a and D&C 3586, p. 294. Chagford is a village about fifteen miles west of Exeter.

16 B. Matthews, not dated but certainly published in 1965, *The Organs and Organists of Exeter Cathedral* (Exeter: Exeter Cathedral Dean and Chapter, 30 pages).

17 D&C 3552, f. 47b and D&C 3586, p. 294.

18 'Surveys of church goods, jewels, bells, vestments, &c., 6 Edward VI, A.D. 1552, recently discovered among the archives of the Exeter Corporation', *The Ecclesiologist*, 1868, Vol. 29 (New Series Vol. 26), pp. 39–44.

19 There has been much debate over the meaning of 'a pair of organs'. The view which prevails today is that 'pair' meant something which consisted of two parts that were joined or corresponded but were not used separately (such as a pair of scissors or a pair of trousers).

20 D&C 3552, f. 60a and D&C 3498/80. Holwill appears to have been the Chapter Clerk.

21 Bicknell, *op. cit.*

22 W. Shaw, 1991, *The Succession of Organists of the Chapel Royal and the Cathedrals of England from c. 1538* (Oxford: Clarendon Press, 445 pages).

23 See N. Orme, 2009, *Exeter Cathedral: The first thousand years, 400–1550* (Exeter: Impress Books, 244 pages), Chapter 12.

24 Queen Elizabeth had been baptized a Roman Catholic.

25 N. Orme, 1986, *Exeter Cathedral as it was, 1050–1550* (Exeter: Devon Books, 122 pages).

26 Mould, *op. cit*, pp. 96–97. See also T. Roast, 2012, *The Organs and Organists of Norwich Cathedral* (Norwich: Gateway Music, 43 pages).

27 For a detailed account of changing attitudes to sacred music in England in the sixteenth century, see 'The Prayer Book and the musicians, 1549–1662', by Roger Bowers (*Cathedral Music*, April 2002, pp. 36–44).

28 The date of appointment is given in a document in the Devon Heritage Centre (formerly Devon Record Office). Its reference is CC181/5(a)/1.

29 The memorial was originally in the Chapel of St John the Evangelist and moved from there to the north transept in the nineteenth century. It was moved to its present position in the middle of the twentieth century.

30 Regarding the number of the year, see note 3 above.

31 Canterbury Cathedral Chapter Book CA1 (1581–1607), f. 28. Selby had been organist at Canterbury since the 1540s and therefore would have been quite old in 1584.

32 I. Payne, 1983, 'Two early organists of Exeter Cathedral: Matthew Godwin and Arthur Cocke', *Devon and Cornwall Notes and Queries*, Vol. 35, Part 4, pp. 133–142.

33 See, for example, Payne, 1983, *op. cit.*, and Payne's biography of Matthew Godwin in the *Oxford Dictionary of National Biography* (2004, Oxford: Oxford University Press).

34 Payne, 2004, *op. cit.*

35 See pages 20, 54 and 70 in *The Blazon of Episcopacy* by WK Riland Bedford (London: John Russell Smith, 1858, 144 pages).

36 Canterbury Cathedral Chapter Book CA1 (1581–1607), f. 80.

37 D&C 7155/1, f. 146, and Devon Heritage Centre document CC181/5(a)/1.

38 D&C 7155/1, f. 2.

39 Devon Heritage Centre document CC181/5(a)/1, and Payne, 1983, *op. cit.*

40 E.F. Rimbault, 1872, *The old cheque-book, or book of remembrance, of the Chapel Royal, from 1561 to 1744* (London: Camden Society, New Series, 3, 250 pages), pp. 6, 37. As organist of the Chapel Royal, Cocke succeeded George Waterhouse, who died on 18 February 1602.

41 Rimbault, *op. cit.*, p. 230.

42 D&C 3801.

43 Edward Gibbons was baptized at Cambridge on 21 March 1568 and died in or before 1650. He was an elder brother of the celebrated musician Orlando Gibbons (1583–1625). According to John Harley, in his article on Edward Gibbons in the *Oxford Dictionary of National Biography* (2004), Edward was from 1592 to 1598 a lay clerk and instructor of the choristers at King's College, Cambridge, where, for a time, Orlando was one of the choristers.

44 D&C 3801.

45 Peter Chambers was an assistant organist and choirmaster.

46 The name of the custos is often not given after 1610, when Paunchard last appeared in the accounts. The registers of Exeter Cathedral show that John Paunchard was buried on 8 August 1616.

47 D&C 3553, p. 78, D&C 3554, and D&C 3586, p. 294.

48 D&C 3586, p. 389.

49 See the article on John Chappington by Roger Bowers in the *Oxford Dictionary of National Biography* (2004). See also Bicknell, *op. cit.*, p. 55.

50 D&C 3553, p. 83, and D&C 3554.

51 Compare D&C 3554 with D&C 3553, p. 84.

52 His will was proved on 5 May 1620.

53 For information about Thomas Dallam, see the article about him by Christopher Kent in the *Oxford Dictionary of National Biography* (2004). See also pp. 72–80 of Bicknell, *op.cit.*, and pp. 114–118 of W L Sumner, 1962, *The Organ* (London: Macdonald, 544 pages).

54 D&C 3553, p. 87, and D&C 3554.

55 D&C 3553, p. 93, and D&C 3554.

56 D&C 3553, p. 111, D&C 3555 and D&C 3586, p. 384.

57 D&C 3553, p. 117, D&C 3555 and D&C 3586, p. 394.

58 D&C 3553, p. 125, and D&C 3555.

59 S. Jeans, 1958, 'The musical life of Exeter Cathedral (1600–1650)', *Quarterly Record of the Incorporated Association of Organists*, Vol. 43, pp. 103–113.

60 William Cotton was Bishop of Exeter from 1598 to 1621. Both of his sons became canons of Exeter Cathedral, William in 1607, Edward in 1611. Moreover, William became the cathedral's Precentor in 1607 and remained so until 1646. Edward became the cathedral's Chancellor in 1613. Gibbons was not only an accomplished musician but also a wealthy man who owned an estate of more than 1,000 acres near Tiverton. Lugge was a very competent organist, but he was comparatively poor.

61 D&C 3586, p. 389.

62 See particularly Mould, *op. cit.*, pp. 107–111.

63 Kalendarhay was the row of houses near the cathedral which were mostly occupied by vicars choral.

64 See Jeans, *op. cit.*, and the article about John Lugge by Ian Payne in the *Oxford Dictionary of National Biography* (2004).
65 C. Maxim, 2001, 'Hugh Facy's Ave Maris Stella: a postcard from Rome?', *The Musical Times*, Vol. 142, No. 1876, pp. 33–38.
66 The fact that John Lugge wrote voluntaries for double organ (i.e. for two keyboards) suggests that the organ of Exeter Cathedral then had two divisions, Great and Chair.
67 Payne, 2004, *op. cit.*

Chapter 2

1 *An exact diary of the late expedition of His Illustrious Highness the Prince of Orange (now King of England) from his Palace at the Hague to his landing at Torbay and from thence to his arrival at Whitehall*, by John Whittle, Chaplain in the Army (London: printed for Richard Baldwin, 1689, 75 pages). See p. 48.
2 *The History of England from the Accession of James the Second*, by Thomas Babington Macaulay, first published in 1848. The words quoted can be found in Vol. 2, Chapter 9. Macaulay based his account on Whittle's diary and other contemporary sources.
3 D&C 3802.
4 D&C 3787.
5 We noted in Chapter 1 that Lugge was from Barnstaple. He may have known Loosemore, or known of him.
6 Mark Stoyle, 1996, *From Deliverance to Destruction: Rebellion and civil war in an English city* (Exeter: University of Exeter Press, 232 pages).
7 D&C 3557, p. 196
8 D&C 3787.
9 The first quarter ended on 25 March (Lady Day), the second on 24 June (Nativity of St John the Baptist), the third on 29 September (Michaelmas Day), the fourth on 25 December (Christmas Day).
10 D&C 3557, pp. 319–320.
11 *Journals of the House of Lords*, Vol. 5 (18 Charles I, 1642–43), p. 487.
12 See Stoyle, *op. cit.*, p. 73.
13 *Mercurius Rusticus, or The Countries Complaint of the Sacriledges, Prophenatians, and Plunderings, Committed by the Schismatiques on the Cathedrall Churches of this Kingdome*, by the Rev Bruno Ryves (Oxford, 1646, 224 pages). Section IV of this compilation of tracts (pp. 214–223) is concerned with Westminster Abbey and Exeter Cathedral. The pages concerned with Exeter are pp. 217–223.
14 D&C 3557, p. 324.
15 Mayne was a vicar choral.
16 D&C 2542/7.
17 Much in the cathedral had to be repaired in the autumn of 1643 (see D&C 3787).
18 D&C 3558, p. 15.
19 *Journals of the House of Lords*, Vol. 6 (20 Charles I, 1644), 9 May 1644, p. 546.
20 D&C 3787. The book cost five shillings.
21 D&C 2542/7. The secondaries (men of the choir) and choristers (boys) were paid in total £9 12s 0d a month.
22 D&C 3558, pp. 69–70. The meeting was held at the home of Canon Chancellor Laurence Burnell, because a committee convened by the Parliamentary Commissioners had taken possession of the Chapter House. The Chapter Acts contain a reference to 'Parliamentary vulgarities'.

23 See the biographies of John Lugge by Ian Payne and Edward Gibbons by John Harley in the *Oxford Dictionary of National Biography* (2004, Oxford: Oxford University Press).

24 D&C 3499/179. The Treaty of Surrender has been reproduced in full by Stoyle, *op. cit.*, pp. 214–218.

25 See W. Cotton and Henry Woollcombe, 1877, *Gleanings from the Municipal and Cathedral Records Relative to the History of the City of Exeter* (Exeter: James Townsend, 246 pages), in particular p. 115, where it is stated that there was 'no evidence whatever that any damage was done to our Cathedral during the rebellion' and that 'the best evidence that no desecration worth mentioning took place is the fact that Izacke the Royalist Churchman, who suffered so much during the rebellion, and lived for many years afterwards, mentions not a word on the subject'.

26 *Act Book of the Chamber* number 10 (9 March 1652 to 30 June 1663), f. 79b. See *The City of Exeter: Act Books of the Chamber, Report on the Records of the City of Exeter* (1916), pp. 302–339. The decision to purchase the Cloisters was made by the City Chamber on 15 January 1656. See *Act Book of the Chamber* number 10 (9 March 1652 to 30 June 1663), f. 70a. By 11 March 1656, £1600 had been raised by subscription for the purpose. See *Act Book of the Chamber* number 10 (9 March 1652 to 30 June 1663), f. 71b.

27 Cotton and Woollcombe, *op. cit.*, p. 175.

28 Cotton and Woollcombe, *op. cit.*, p. 171.

29 *Act Book of the Chamber* number 10 (9 March 1652 to 30 June 1663), f. 90a. See *The City of Exeter: Act Books of the Chamber, Report on the Records of the City of Exeter* (1916), pp. 302–339.

30 *Calendar of State Papers, Domestic Series*, 1655–66, preserved in the State Papers Department of Her Majesty's Public Record Office, edited by M.A.E. Green (London: Longmans & Co., 1882, see p. 117).

31 Percy Morris, 1940, 'Exeter Cathedral. Two studies, Part 2: the cathedral during the Reformation and the Interregnum – the weapon and its effect' (typescript in the Exeter Cathedral Archive). See pp. 205–208.

32 See Ernest Law, 1888, *The History of Hampton Court Palace, Vol. 2 – Stuart times* (London: George Bell and Sons, 311 pages).

33 D&C 3787.

34 Word would surely have spread that the Chapter were prepared to pay for the return of organ pipes. The fact that only one such payment was made may indicate that very little of any previous organ was in fact in the possession of members of the public. Otherwise, more people would have surely come forward with pipes, hoping for some reward. The cathedral's accounts for the months and years after the Restoration are very full. Had there been other payments for the return of pipes, it is likely they would have been recorded.

35 William Leslie Sumner, 1962, *The Organ* (London: Macdonald & Co., 3rd Edition, 544 pages). See p. 137.

36 D&C 3559, pp. 1*ff.*

37 D&C 3787. The Dean and Chapter appointed Blechyndon clerk of the works on 22 September 1660 (see D&C 3559, p. 15).

38 *Journals of the House of Lords*, Vol. 11 (12 Charles II, 1660), 1 September 1660, p. 152. The Lords ordered that the wall be removed 'forthwith' by the Chamber of Exeter 'at their own charge'.

39 The 'disbursements about pulling downe the partition wall' listed in D&C 3787 show that payments were made to a 'heliar' (i.e tiler) in November and December 1660.

40 D&C 3559, p. 47; and D&C 3787.

41 D&C 3559, p. 104; and D&C 3787.
42 D&C 3787. On 25 March 1661, Mr Blechyndon was paid 2s 6d for a curtain for the organ.
43 Samuel Loosemore was born in 1577 and died in November 1642. John Loosemore was baptized at Barnstaple on 25 August 1616.
44 See I.L. Gregory, 1950, *Hartland Church Accounts 1597–1706* (Frome and London: Butler and Tanner Ltd., 372 pages). For the household accounts of Tawstock House, see T. Gray (ed.), 1996, *Devon Household Accounts, 1627–59, Part II: Henry, fifth Earl of Bath, and Rachel, Countess of Bath, 1627–1655* (Exeter: Devon and Cornwall Record Society, 337 pages).
45 John Loosemore's daughter Joan was baptized in Barnstaple in September 1642. Winifred Loosemore was baptized in Exeter (Parish of St Paul) in July 1645.
46 The Poll Tax of 1660 shows that John and his wife and their daughter Joan were then living in the Parish of St Stephen, near the Cathedral Close.
47 As Loosemore had worked on the cathedral's organ in 1638 and possibly repaired it in 1643, it is reasonable to suppose that he would have wished to acquire some or all of it, especially if he thought there was a possibility such a fine instrument might otherwise be lost.
48 D&C 3559, p. 275.
49 D&C 3802.
50 D&C 3559, p. 125
51 D&C 3559, p. 2
52 D&C 3559, p. 138
53 D&C 3559, p. 175
54 D&C 3802.
55 We may wonder if choral services actually recommenced on 14 April 1661, which was Easter Day and therefore a most appropriate occasion to celebrate new life.
56 D&C 3787. See also D&C 3559, p. 542, where it is mentioned that Williams was 'him that blows the organs'.
57 D&C 3559, p. 23.
58 William Hopwood Senior died in March 1661 and was buried on the tenth of that month (see H.T. Soper and W.U. Reynell-Upham, 1910, *The Registers of Baptisms, Marriages and Burials of the City of Exeter, Volume 1: The Registers of the Cathedral* (Exeter: Devon and Cornwall Record Society), p. 147). See also D&C 3559, p. 125.
59 D&C 3787.
60 D&C 3802.
61 E.F. Rimbault, 1872, *The old cheque-book, or book of remembrance, of the Chapel Royal, from 1561 to 1744* (London: Camden Society, New Series, 3, 250 pages)., p. 14. In this book, Hopwood was described as 'a basse from Exeter'. It was recorded in Rimbault's book (pp. 17 and 213) that he died on 13 July 1683 and was buried four days later in the east cloister of Westminster Abbey.
62 D&C 3559, p. 474, and D&C 3787.
63 D&C 3559, p. 102.
64 D&C 3559, p. 141.
65 D&C 3559, p. 184.
66 Most sources state that Thomas was a son of the John Mudd who was born in 1555 and served as organist of Peterborough Cathedral from 1583 to 1631. See, for example, the entry on the Mudd family by Ian Payne in the *Oxford Dictionary of National Biography* (2004) and the piece about Exeter's Thomas Mudd on pages 110 and 111 in Watkins Shaw, 1991, *The Succession of Organists* (Oxford: Clarendon Press, 445 pages). It is more likely, however, that he was a son of the Thomas Mudd who was born at Peterborough in 1585 and thus a grandson or great-nephew of John Mudd. The Thomas Mudd who

was employed in Exeter was born *c.*1610, became a chorister in Peterborough Cathedral in 1619, and played the organ in Peterborough Cathedral in 1631 and 1632 after the death of John Mudd.

67 D&C 3787.

68 See D&C 3559, p. 566. Thomas Mudd became master of the choristers of York Minster on 20 August 1666, but that appointment was short-lived, possibly less than a month. He died at Durham the following year and was buried on 2 August 1667. The authorities clearly believed he was still York's organist, for it was stated in the burial register of Durham Cathedral that he was 'Thomas Mudd, Ecclesiae Cathedralis Eboracensis Organista' (organist of York Minster). See Shaw, *op. cit*, p. 317.

69 D&C 3559, p. 542. It is generally believed that Colby was German, for he was so described by Anthony Wood, who had been resident in Oxford in the 1660s. See A. Wood, 1692, *Athenæ Oxonienses*, Vol. II, Column 848. 'German' may have been an assumption based on a thick Germanic accent. He could have been Austrian, Swiss or even Dutch.

70 D&C 3559, p. 529. Loosemore had personal financial difficulties in 1664 and a number of years thereafter. The Chapter agreed on 9 January 1664 that he be lent £20, 'to be repaid (to Archdeacon Cotton) within convenient time' (D&C 3559, p. 464). Some of this appears to have been paid back fairly quickly, for on 28 March 1664 Cotton was paid £10 'lent by him to Mr Loosemore', but a further loan was made to Loosemore on 24 December 1664, when he was lent £20 'for the rent of his house for the year' (D&C 3559, p. 528). On this occasion, the Dean lent him £10 and Mr Wright, the Cathedral's Treasurer, the other £10.

71 This suggestion has been made by a member of the Loosemore family who has researched the family in great detail. See Chapter 6 of the family history at http://www.loosemore.co.uk (accessed 26 August 2014).

72 D&C 3559, p. 543.

73 D&C 3559, pp. 380 and 391.

74 Interestingly, the arms of John Grenville, first Earl of Bath (1628–1701) were *gules, three clarions or*. The ancient clarion was a type of mouth-organ, a wind instrument similar to a pan flute with a curved mouthpiece. This earldom of Bath is not to be confused with the one associated with Tawstock House. That earldom (Second Creation) became extinct in 1654 on the death of Henry Bourchier, the fifth earl. John Grenville was created Earl of Bath (Third Creation) in 1661.

75 D&C 3559, pp. 406–407.

76 D&C 3559, p. 445.

77 B. Matthews, 1972, *The Organs and Organists of Salisbury Cathedral* (Salisbury: Maidments Publicity Ltd, 20 pages).

78 D&C 3787. The Staverton fine was the Staverton Manor rental income.

79 D&C 4683

80 D&C 6000/1

81 The Stannary hundredweight was 120 lb (i.e. six score pounds weight). See G.R. Lewis., 1908, *The Stannaries: A study of the English tin miner* (Boston and New York: Houghton, Mifflin & Co., 299 pages). Loosemore appears to have made a slip when stating six score and two lb. The imperial hundredweight was in 1663 the same as it is today, 112 lb.

82 D&C 3559, p. 549.

83 D&C 3787. The use of the term 'syde-organ' appears to confirm that the organ built in 1660–61 was not on the pulpitum. The most likely location for it was the north side of the quire almost opposite the bishop's throne.

84 The eastern face of the case bears the date 1665, which may be an original feature. It also

bears a label which reads 'John Loosemore made this organ 1665', but the label's date is uncertain.

85 A. Freeman, 1921, *English Organ Cases* (London: George Augustus Mate & Son, 132 pages).

86 See p. 23 of D. Gwynn, 2009, 'How organs and organists survived the Commonwealth', *Organists' Review*, Vol. 95, No. 1, pp. 21–27.

87 E.J. Hopkins and E.F. Rimbault, 1855, *The Organ: Its history and construction* (London: Robert Cocks & Co., 581 pages).

88 J. Sutton, 1847, *A Short Account of Organs built in England from the Reign of Charles the Second to the Present Time* (London: J. Masters, 117 pages).

89 See M. Wilson, 1968, *The English Chamber Organ: History and development 1650–1850* (Columbia: University of South Carolina Press, 148 pages).

90 D&C 3560, p. 367.

91 D&C 3787 and 3788, and D&C 3559, p. 669.

92 D&C 3788.

93 D&C 3788.

94 D&C 3560, p. 169.

95 D&C 3788.

96 D&C 6000/2.

97 Moiety, i.e. half the cost.

98 D&C 6000/3 and 4.

99 D&C 4724/a

100 D&C 3561, p. 205.

101 D&C 3561, p. 219.

102 It is not there now. It was moved to the north quire aisle in the 1970s.

103 Translated, the ledger stone reads: 'Here lies in hope of the Resurrection, John Loosemore, sometime the very faithful Keeper to the Dean and Chapter of this Church and easily the chief among craftsmen of his kind. May this majestic organ placed nearby be a perpetual monument to his art and genius. He died 18 April 1681 in the 68th year of his age.' The stone, of Purbeck 'marble', was recut in 1909 by E.G.S. Luscombe (D&C 7001/1909).

104 D&C 3561, p. 222. John Shearme died on 12 July 1686 and was buried alongside his father-in-law.

105 R. North, 1826, *The Lives of the Right Hon. Francis North, Baron Guilford, &c* (London: Henry Colburn, Volume 1, 442 pages), see pp. 246–247.

106 These large pipes were comparable in size to 'the fair pipes of an extraordinary length' described by the Lieutenant from Norwich in 1635 (see Chapter 1). Knowing that Loosemore saw those pipes in 1638, we may wonder if he resolved (or was asked) to provide pipes that were equally, or maybe more, impressive. Is it possible, indeed, as suggested by S. Bicknell, 1996, *The History of the English Organ* (Cambridge: Cambridge University Press), p. 115, that some or all of the pipes that were seen by the Lieutenant survived the Civil War and Interregnum and were then re-used by Loosemore?

107 North, *op. cit.*, p. 247.

108 D&C 3788 and 3803.

109 See, for example, J.R. Bloxam, *A Register of the Presidents, Fellows, Demies, Instructors in Grammar and in Music, Chaplains, Clerks, Choristers, and other members of Saint Mary Magdalen College in the University of Oxford*, eight volumes (Oxford, 1853–85). See Vol. 2, p. 192.

110 D&C 3560, p. 176.

111 D&C 3560, pp. 292–293.

112 D&C 3560, p. 69 and 145.

113 D&C 3560, p. 270.

114 See the biography of Hall by Oliver Pickering in the *Oxford Dictionary of National Biography* (2004).

115 D&C 3788. Edward Cotton was Archdeacon of Cornwall and Exeter Cathedral's Treasurer. He died in 1675.

116 D&C 3561, p. 111–112.

117 D&C 3788 and 3803.

118 See Pickering, *op. cit.*, and the entry on Hall by Bruce Wood in *The New Grove Dictionary of Music and Musicians* (ed. Stanley Sadie, 1980, London: Macmillan, pp. 699–700). See also Shaw, *op. cit.*, pp. 137–138.

119 See the Chapter Acts for 21 December 1676 (D&C 3560, pp. 406–407).

120 Shaw, *op. cit.*, p. 111.

121 D&C 3561, pp. 347. Hodge in fact studied under a pupil of Blow, Henry Purcell, who became the organist of Westminster Abbey in 1680. We see from a letter written by Purcell on 27 October 1686 (D&C 6077/1) and a Chapter Act of three days later (D&C 3562, p. 57) that Hodge got into debt. In the words of the Chapter Act, 'they ordered Mr Purcell to be paid his demand for Robert Hodge being as by his letter 27th'. Hodge became a vicar choral of Wells Cathedral in January 1687, organist of Wells Cathedral in April 1688, a lay clerk of Durham Cathedral in April 1691, a vicar choral of St Patrick's Cathedral in Dublin in April 1693, organist of that cathedral in October 1694, and organist of St Patrick's Cathedral in Armagh in June 1695. See A.G. McCartney, 1999, *The Organs and Organists of the Cathedral Church of Saint Patrick, Armagh, 1482–1998* (Armagh: The Friends of St Patrick's Church of Ireland Cathedral, 101 pages). See also Shaw, *op. cit.*, pp. 288, 403 and 420.

122 D&C 3561, p. 434.

123 D&C 3561, p. 184–185.

124 D&C 3562, p. 45.

125 D&C 3562, p. 21.

126 Whittle, *op. cit*, p. 48.

Chapter 3

1 Alan Mould, 2007, *The English Chorister* (London: Hambledon Continuum, 366 pages).

2 D&C 3562, p. 152.

3 D&C 3789.

4 D&C 3562, p. 162, and D&C 3789. On 11 May 1689, the Chapter 'order'd the Bills for the funeral charges of Richard Williams late custos organorum to be paid *ex gratia Capti*'. A week later (D&C 3562, p. 163), they declared Williams's room in the cloister 'voide by his death' and granted it to Katherine Kerswell, a widow.

5 D&C 3562, p. 383.

6 D&C 3789.

7 D&C 3562, p. 380.

8 D&C 3562, p. 387.

9 Mortimore was buried on 26 June 1744. See H.T. Soper and W.U. Reynell-Upham, 1910, *The Registers of Baptisms, Marriages and Burials of the City of Exeter, Volume 1: The Registers of the Cathedral* (Exeter: Devon and Cornwall Record Society), p. 169.

10 D&C 3562, p. 208. A posse was a body of people who enforced law and order and helped repel hostile forces.

11 D&C 3562, p. 209. A Cornet was the lowest commissioned officer in a cavalry troop who carried the standard.

12 D&C 3789.

13 D&C 3562, p. 355.

14 D&C 3562, pp. 370–371. He was admitted to the position of priest vicar on 15 September 1694 (D&C 3562, p. 376) and installed on 3 November 1694 (D&C 3562, p. 382).

15 He was Clerk of the Works until April 1708, when succeeded by Robert Burrington (D&C 3563, pages 614 and 616). As recorded in Soper and Reynell-Upham, *op. cit.*, p. 159, he died in April 1713.

16 D&C 3562, p. 377.

17 R. Ford, 1986, 'Henman, Humfrey and *Have Mercy*', *The Musical Times*, Vol. 127, pp. 459–462. In this article, Robert Ford discusses 'Have mercy upon me, O God', a setting of the first eight verses of Psalm 51 attributed to Richard Henman and possibly composed before he went to Exeter.

18 D&C 3562, p. 404a.

19 D&C 3563, p. 115.

20 D&C 3563, pp. 417–418.

21 D&C 3563, p. 548. Hicks was a priest vicar.

22 D&C 3564, p. 388.

23 D&C 3564, pp. 439–442.

24 D&C 3566, p. 336.

25 D&C 3566, p. 351. Sanders became a chorister in 1730 and remained so until June 1740 (D&C 3806).

26 D&C 3566, p. 369.

27 D&C 3566, p. 390.

28 D&C 3789, 3790 and 3806.

29 D&C 3566, p. 503.

30 D&C 3566, p. 545.

31 D&C 3567, p. 115.

32 D&C 3567, p. 79.

33 Winchester Cathedral DC/B3/4, p. 136, and Exeter Cathedral D&C 3567, pp. 80–81. He was baptized in St Thomas's Church, Winchester.

34 D&C 3567, p. 227.

35 D&C 3566, p. 177.

36 D&C 3790.

37 D&C 3566, p. 182.

38 D&C 3566, p. 321. Creswell became clock keeper towards the end of 1744 and held the post for eleven years.

39 John Hicks was paid £3 4s 6d in May 1708 'by Mr Dean's order for tuning the organ' (D&C 3789). This was a substantial amount of money and may indicate that more work than tuning was carried out. The fact that the money was paid to a priest vicar does not necessarily mean that he himself tuned the organ. He may have been responsible for paying the person who actually did the work.

40 D&C 4684.

41 D&C 4685.

42 D&C 3564, p. 287.

43 D&C 3564, p. 297.

44 D&C 4690/1.

45 D&C 4690/2. There is a reference in this document to the Bishop of Rochester. This refers

to Dr Atterbury, who was nominated Bishop of Rochester on 14 June and consecrated three weeks later.

46 D&C 4690/3.

47 D&C 3564, pp. 307–308.

48 See Chapter 2.

49 D&C 4690/4.

50 D&C 4689.

51 An additional payment of £10 15s 0d was made to Nicholas Webber 'for Mr Shrider the Organ Builder' on 29 June 1713 (D&C 3789), presumably to cover the costs incurred by Shrider when visiting Exeter to inspect the organ.

52 Gamut is the note on the bottom line of the bass staff. The word is a combination of *gamma* (the third letter of the Greek alphabet) with *ut*, in which *gamma* denotes the first note of a six-note ascending scale (hexachord) which begins on G and *ut* is the first note of that scale (now usually called *doh*). The term 'long octave' indicated that all the lowest notes were present (except perhaps the lowest G sharp), as distinct from 'short octave', in which some notes were omitted for reasons of space, economy or tonality. Swarbrick proposed to put the organ 'in the proper pitch' and Shrider proposed to make it Gamut Proper, terms that were used in accordance with the emerging practices of relating vocal and organ pitches that were themselves regional interpretations that eventually culminated, hundreds of years later, in our modern understanding of a standard pitch. The pitch favoured by Loosemore was considered unduly high by the early eighteenth century. For a discussion of pitch, see the section by Christopher Kent (pp. 51–54) in *The Cambridge Companion to the Organ*, ed. N. Thistlethwaite and G. Webber (Cambridge: Cambridge University Press, 1998, 340 pages).

53 Until 1823, when the organ of York Minster was provided with a Double Diapason that extended down to the F one tone below the lowest note of Loosemore's organ, the Exeter Cathedral Double Diapason pipes were the largest in England. Loosemore's Double Diapason pipes were of pure tin.

54 Respectively, D&C 3565, p. 482, and D&C 3567, p. 61.

55 D&C 3567, p. 84.

56 D&C 3567, p. 85.

57 For information about Jordan Father and Son, see the entry on them by Joan Jeffery in the *Oxford Dictionary of National Biography* (2004). See also S. Bicknell, 1996, *The History of the English Organ* (Cambridge: Cambridge University Press, 407 pages), pp. 151–156.

58 See Bicknell, *op. cit.*, p. 164. See also p. 524 in D. Burrows, 2008, *Handel and the English Chapel Royal* (Oxford: Oxford University Press, 656 pages).

59 D&C 4686

60 *Ibid.*

61 Jordan used a hexachord notation. 'D la sol in Alt' is the D next above the treble staff, i.e. the D a little over two octaves above middle C.

62 D in Alt is the D a little over two octaves above middle C.

63 D&C 4687.

64 D&C 4688. Mr Bridge was probably his foreman.

65 *Ibid.*

66 D&C 3567, p. 157.

67 D&C 4687.

68 D&C 3567, p. 206. John Hicks became informator choristarum in June 1741 in succession to John Vinicombe, who had died (D&C 3567, pp. 104 and 114).

69 D&C 3567, p. 258.

70 D&C 3567, p. 331.
71 D&C 3567, pp. 224–225.
72 D&C 3567, p. 228.
73 D&C 3567, p. 362.
74 D&C 3567, p. 361.
75 D&C 3568, p. 33.
76 D&C 3568, pp. 49–50.
77 D&C 3568, pp. 68, 82, 83 and 154. On 15 November 1746, he was ordered 'to attend the Chapter with the rest of the choir'.
78 D&C 3568, p. 165.
79 D&C 3567, p. 257. William Hooper was baptized on 21 February 1730 (see Soper and Reynell-Upham, *op. cit.*, p. 93).
80 D&C 3790.
81 Hooper had been a chorister since 1741 (D&C 3806).
82 D&C 7062/18th c.
83 D&C 3568, p. 220.
84 D&C 3790.
85 Westcott had been a chorister of Exeter Cathedral from 1710 to 1718 (D&C 3805). Richards signed for the organist's stipend in December 1744 and March 1745.
86 D&C 3568, p. 220.
87 D&C 3568, p. 332.
88 D&C 3568, p. 334.
89 D&C 3569, p. 1.
90 D&C 3568, p. 65.
91 D&C 3568, p. 95.
92 D&C 3568, p. 96.
93 D&C 3806.
94 Could he have been a relative of John Sanders, the chorister who played the organ in the 1730s?
95 D&C 3569, p. 6.
96 D&C 3569, p. 4.
97 D&C 3567, p. 361.
98 John Hicks replaced Tobias Langdon as master of the choristers in September 1712.
99 D&C 3790.
100 D&C 3790 and 3807.
101 D&C 3790.
102 D&C 3570, p. 432.
103 D&C 3569, p. 591.
104 D&C 3569, p. 353.
105 *Alumni Oxonienses (1715–1886): their parentage, birth-place and year of birth, with a record of their degrees* (Joseph Foster, 1891), Vol. 3, p. 815.
106 Respectively, D&C 3570, p. 253, and D&C 3571, pp. 23, 147, 171, 373 and 439.
107 Soper and Reynell-Upham, *op. cit.*, p. 270. The officiating priest was former chorister and deputy organist Simon Westcott and the witnesses were William Luscombe and former custos organorum and clock keeper Isaac Creswell.
108 Hicks died on 14 August 1762, aged 80, and was buried in the cathedral. See page 13 of *The Family of Hicks*, by the Marquis de Ruvigny et Raineval (London: privately printed, 1902, 45 pages). See also Soper and Reynell-Upham, *op. cit.*, p. 174. Langdon's salary for being master of the choristers was £20 *per annum*.

109 Edward Gibbons was appointed informator choristarum towards the end of 1608 (see Chapter 1).

110 D&C 3569, pp. 329.

111 See the entries for Richard Langdon by Watkins Shaw in *The New Grove Dictionary of Music and Musicians* (edited by Stanley Sadie, 1980, London: Macmillan) and J.C. Hadden and K.D. Reynolds in the *Oxford Dictionary of National Biography* (2004, Oxford: Oxford University Press).

112 D&C 3572, p. 44.

113 'William Jackson, of Exeter, musician. An autobiography', published in several parts long after his death, in *The Leisure Hour* (1882, Vol. 31). The quotation can be found on page 361. The autobiography, in manuscript form, had never previously been published.

114 There is no evidence that Jackson received any money from the cathedral, unless a payment of 9s 3d to him in the fourth quarter of 1777 is not all it seems: 'To Mr Jackson for necessaries for the Music School' (D&C 3791).

115 Watkins Shaw, 1991, *The Succession of Organists* (Oxford: Clarendon Press, 445 pages), pp. 103 and 39.

116 A.G. McCartney, 1999. *The Organs and Organists of the Cathedral Church of Saint Patrick, Armagh, 1482–1998* (Armagh: Friends of St Patrick's Cathedral, 101 pages); see p. 79. See also Shaw *op. cit.*, p. 404. The Chapter minutes of Peterborough Cathedral show that Langdon was appointed their organist in July 1784 in succession to James Rodgers, and they also record his resignation the following year. It appears, however, that he never in fact took up the appointment at Peterborough. See Shaw, *op. cit.*, p. 222.

117 D&C 3568, p. 15.

118 D&C 3568, p. 155.

119 D&C 3569, p. 467.

120 See J.D.C. Hemsley, 2007, 'Crang & Hancock: the eighteenth-century London organ-builders', *The Galpin Society Journal*, Vol. 60, pp. 229–232.

121 He died in London in May 1774 and his will is held by the National Archives at Kew. This will shows that Crang had cousins with the surname Langdon.

122 D&C 3569, p. 493.

123 D&C 3569, p. 494.

124 D&C 3569, p. 503.

125 D&C 3569, p. 505.

126 *Loc. cit.*

127 D&C 3569, p. 512.

128 D&C 3569, p. 520.

129 D&C 3569, p. 591.

130 D&C 3569, p. 605.

131 *The Journal of the Reverend John Wesley* (London: J.M. Dent & Co, 1906, Vol. 3, p. 113).

132 Micheau was baptized at Barnstaple on 23 October 1734.

133 Obituary of Micheau published in *Trewman's Exeter Flying Post*, 18 November 1824, Issue No. 3109, p. 4.

134 D&C 3570, p. 313.

135 D&C 3570, p. 317.

136 D&C 3570, p. 334.

137 D&C 3570, p. 369.

138 D&C 3570, p. 403.

139 D&C 4691.

140 D&C 3570, p. 420.

141 D&C 7062.
142 *Ibid.*
143 D&C 3791.
144 Mould, *op. cit.*, pp. 145–165.
145 Jackson, *op. cit.*, p. 361.

Chapter 4

1 Entry on Milles by Peter Thomas in the *Oxford Dictionary of National Biography* (2004, Oxford: Oxford University Press).
2 The practice was eventually forbidden under the 1838 Pluralities Act.
3 For details of his autobiography, see note 113, Chapter 3. For a summary of Jackson's autobiography, see G. Townsend, 1882, 'A Devonshire worthy – William Jackson, of Exeter', *Report and Transactions of the Devonshire Association for the Advancement of Science, Literature and Art*, Vol. 14, pp. 695–701.
4 D&C 3806.
5 See, for example, the entry about William Jackson by Richard McGrady in *The New Grove Dictionary of Music and Musicians* (ed. Stanley Sadie, 1980, London: Macmillan, pp. 724–726) and the entry about him by Robert Farquharson Sharp in the *Dictionary of National Biography, 1885–1900* (Volume 29).
6 'William Jackson, of Exeter, musician. An autobiography', *The Leisure Hour* (1882, Vol. 31), p. 274.
7 Travers was organist of the Chapel Royal from 1737 until his death in 1758.
8 Entry on William Jackson by Paul Williamson in the *Oxford Dictionary of National Biography* (2004, Oxford: Oxford University Press).
9 See McGrady, *op. cit.*
10 Jackson's autobiography, *op. cit.*, p. 276. He married when 23 years of age. By his wife, Mary (née Bartlett), he produced at least twelve children; and he also produced an illegitimate son through a liaison with the daughter of an Exeter clergyman (see Williamson, *op. cit*).
11 D&C 3572, pp. 47–48.
12 Jackson's autobiography, *op. cit.*, p. 361.
13 T. Busby, 1803 (1 September), 'Memoirs of Mr Jackson, of Exeter', *Monthly Magazine*, Vol. 16, pp. 139–143. Busby (Mus.Doc., Cantab) was a composer of music, author and journalist based in London.
14 Entry on William Jackson by W.H. Husk in *A Dictionary of Music and Musicians*, Vol. 2 (ed. Sir George Grove, 1890, London: Macmillan & Co., p. 27).
15 McGrady, *op. cit.*
16 None of the music Jackson composed for Exeter Cathedral was published in his lifetime. The man who succeeded him as the cathedral's organist, James Paddon, remedied this deficiency in 1819, when he published privately, in three volumes, *Anthems and Church Services by the late William Jackson of Exeter*.
17 Jackson's autobiography, *op. cit.*, p. 362.
18 D&C 3574, p. 187.
19 William Jackson of Exeter, 1791, *Observations on the present state of music in London* (London: Harrison & Co, 33 pages).
20 The memorial was commissioned by his daughter Mary and designed by John White Abbott of Exeter, a surgeon and amateur painter. The date of Jackson's death can be found on p. 445 of D&C 3575; and he appears to have died at his home, No. 1 Bedford Circus, Exeter.

21 Busby, *op. cit.*

22 A. Chalmers, 1814, 'William Jackson of Exeter', *The General Biographical Dictionary*, Vol. 18 (London: J. Nichols & Son), pp. 425–426.

23 29 May was the anniversary of the restoration of the monarchy in 1660.

24 Townsend, *op. cit.*, p. 700.

25 'England Births and Christenings, 1538–1975'. Available online through https://familysearch.org (accessed 27 August 2014).

26 The Ordinary Solutions show that he was certainly a chorister by Christmas 1777 (D&C 3809). Unfortunately, the book of Ordinary Solutions for the period 1758 to 1777 has been lost. His appointments as secondary and lay vicar were recorded in D&C 3573, pp. 264 and 280, and D&C 3574, p. 170.

27 D&C 3572, pp. 164, 239, 306 and 385.

28 D&C 3575, p. 5.

29 D&C 3575, p. 445. When appointed organist he was a Volunteer Fourth Class in the Exeter Militia (Parish of Holy Trinity). See page 119 in the *Exeter Militia List 1803*, compiled by W.G. Hoskins (1972, London and Chichester: Phillimore, with the Devon and Cornwall Record Society, 145 pages).

30 D&C 3575, p. 527.

31 *Trewman's Exeter Flying Post*, Thursday 21 April 1814, Issue 2537.

32 D&C 3577, p. 10.

33 D&C 3579, p. 29.

34 D&C 3580, pp. 313–315

35 D&C 3581, p. 222.

36 D&C 3581, p. 256.

37 *Trewman's Exeter Flying Post*, Thursday 18 June 1835, Issue 3639.

38 See, for example, Alan Mould, 2007, *The English Chorister* (London: Hambledon Continuum, 366 pages), p. 173.

39 It was reported in *Trewman's Exeter Flying Post* on Thursday 8 January 1835 (Issue 3614) that she had died 'suddenly, aged 55, on Tuesday evening the 6th of January, about 9 o'clock, after having sustained a severe fright'. She and her husband had been married almost 34 years. *Trewman's Exeter Flying Post* (Thursday 25 June 1835, Issue 3640) reported that 'Mr Gedye of Dawlish' played the organ for James Paddon's funeral.

40 The stone is unfortunately now quite worn and only partly legible.

41 D&C 3577, p. 431.

42 D&C 3577, p. 463. The mediæval cloisters were demolished in the 1650s and houses and other buildings then constructed between the buttresses of the cathedral and on other sides of the Cloister Garth, including a serge market. For many years, the Singing School was on the first floor of a building across the west front of the Chapter House. The buildings on the western, northern and eastern sides of the cloisters were demolished in the early nineteenth century, Paddon's house included. Columns of the former serge market can still be seen on the southern side of Cloister Garth.

43 D&C 3577, p. 456.

44 D&C 3577, p. 637.

45 D&C 3572, p. 200.

46 D&C 3572, p. 468.

47 D&C 4692.

48 D&C 7062/1800–15.

49 *Ibid*.

50 George Pyke England was born in 1767, son of John England, organ-builder. This

is confirmed by the record of his baptism in St James's Church, Clerkenwell, and an indenture dated 1782 (when he was apprenticed to a skinner).

51 D&C 7062/1800–15.

52 D&C 3577, p. 406.

53 D&C 3577, p. 413.

54 D&C 3577, p. 422.

55 D&C 3577, p. 455.

56 D&C 3792.

57 *Trewman's Exeter Flying Post*, Thursday 18 November 1824, Issue 3109, p. 4.

58 This was George England, an uncle of George Pyke England, the latter's father being a brother of George. It is stated in several sources that George Pyke England was son of George England, but this was not so. The father of George Pyke England was called John. See note 50.

59 D&C 7062/1800–15.

60 William Alfred Adolphus Nicholls succeeded his father-in-law, but not for long. He was declared bankrupt on 10 March 1821. See G. Elwick, 1843, *The Bankrupt Directory from December 1820 to April 1843* (London: Simpkin, Marshall & Co., 468 pages).

61 D&C 7062/1818.

62 *Ibid.*

63 D&C 3578, p. 92.

64 D&C 7062/1818.

65 *Ibid.*

66 *Ibid.*

67 D&C 3578, p. 126.

68 D&C 3578, p. 131.

69 D&C 3578, p. 137. Mr Carter was presumably an employee of Cole in his carving and engraving business.

70 D&C 3578, p. 139.

71 D&C 7062/1818.

72 D&C 3578, p. 144, and D&C 7062/1818.

73 D&C 3578, p. 147.

74 D&C 7062/1818.

75 D&C 3578, p. 167.

76 D&C 3578, p. 247.

77 D&C 7062/1819.

78 These sundry items included £3 5s 0d on 'Holwell and Halsey's account', £1 10s 0d for charcoal and coke, and 7s 6d for corks, making a total of £5 2s 6d.

79 D&C 7062/1819.

80 *Ibid.*

81 *Ibid.*

82 *Ibid.*

83 D&C 3578, p. 264.

84 D&C 7062/1819.

85 For a breakdown of these sundry items, see note 78.

86 D&C 3578, p. 267.

87 It was recorded in the timber accounts (D&C 7081, p. 121) that Cole had been paid £228 8s 6d. This was a mistake in the accounts.

88 D&C 3578, p. 114.

89 D&C 7062/1818.

90 D&C 3578, p. 129.

91 'Apollonicon' by William H. Husk in *A Dictionary of Music and Musicians* (1879, ed. Sir George Grove, London: Macmillan & Co., Vol. 1, pp. 74–75). A full description of the Apollonicon, with several diagrams, was provided by C. Davy, 1828, 'The Apollonicon', *Mechanics' Magazine*, Vol. 9, pp. 97–104.

92 D&C 7062/1818.

93 Wesley was the son of hymn-writer Charles Wesley, nephew of John Wesley and father of Samuel Sebastian Wesley, who features later in the story of Exeter Cathedral's organists.

94 D&C 7062/1818.

95 *Ibid.*

96 *Ibid.* The letter from Whitfield was dated 18 October 1818.

97 *Ibid.*

98 At the time, this could have been either John Lincoln or his son Henry Cephas Lincoln. The latter had once been apprenticed to Flight & Robson.

99 D&C 7062/1818.

100 D&C 3578, p. 135.

101 Landon had been Provost since 1795 and remained so until his death in 1838. He was also (from 1818 until his death) rector of Croft with Yarpole in Herefordshire and later, from 1821 until his death, a prebendary of Salisbury, being also, from 1822 to 1826, rector of Bishopstone near Salisbury and from 1827 to 1830 vicar of Branscombe in Devon. He died at his rectory in Herefordshire.

102 D&C 7062/1818.

103 *Ibid.*

104 D&C 7062/1818. 'Lincoln's partner' would have been his son, Henry Cephas Lincoln.

105 D&C 3578, pp. 152–153.

106 D&C 7062/1819.

107 D&C 3578, pp. 169–170.

108 D&C 7062/1819.

109 *Ibid.* The letter from Johnes was dated 6 February and that from Heberden 11 February.

110 D&C 7062/1819.

111 *Ibid.*

112 D&C 3578, pp. 186–187.

113 D&C 3578, p. 196, and D&C 4693.

114 D&C 7062/1819.

115 *Ibid.*

116 D&C 3578, p. 251.

117 D&C 3578, p. 254. It was recorded in the timber accounts (D&C 7081, p. 121) that Lincoln received £430 on 23 October and £110 10s 0d on 27 November, a total of £540 10s 0d. The receipt Lincoln signed (D&C 4693) shows, however, that he received £100 10s 0d on 27 November. It appears, therefore, that a mistake was made in the timber accounts.

118 D&C 3578, p. 494.

119 D&C 7062/1820–26. The meeting took place on 14 February 1822 and the proceedings of that meeting were confirmed at a Chapter meeting two days later (D&C 3578, p. 528).

120 D&C 3578, p. 529.

121 D&C 3578, p. 216.

122 D&C 3578, p. 275.

123 D&C 7062/1820–26.

124 D&C 7061/1820–26. Vicary thus resigned with effect from 2 February, which is the half or cross quarter day between Christmas Day and Lady Day.

125 D&C 3578, p. 433.
126 D&C 7062/1820–26.
127 D&C 3578, pp. 466 and 468.
128 D&C 3578, p. 531, and D&C 7062/1820–26.
129 D&C 7062/1820–26.
130 *Ibid.*
131 D&C 3579, p. 21.
132 D&C 3579, p. 46.
133 D&C 7062/1820–26.
134 D&C 3579, pp. 65–66.
135 D&C 7062/1820–26.
136 D&C 3579, p. 68.
137 D&C 7062/1820–26.
138 *Ibid.*
139 D&C 3579, pp. 82–83.
140 D&C 7062/1820–26.
141 D&C 3579, p. 138.
142 D&C 3579, p. 352.
143 D&C 3579, p. 358.
144 D&C 7062/1820–26.
145 D&C 3579, p. 458.
146 D&C 3579, p. 464.
147 D&C 3580, p. 491.
148 D&C 7062/1832.
149 *Ibid.*
150 *Ibid.*
151 D&C 3580, p. 509. Also D&C 7062/1832.
152 D&C 7062/1832.
153 *Ibid.*

Chapter 5

   1 D&C 7170/26.
   2 Wesley married Mary Anne Merewether on 4 May 1835.
   3 D&C 7170/26.
   4 *Ibid.*
   5 We may wonder why neither Barnes nor Bull nor anyone else at Exeter had informed him of Paddon's death.
   6 Landon said in his letter to Barnes that Bull had written to the Dean of Westminster for advice as to a successor to Paddon and seen in an Exeter paper that the organist of the Chapel Royal, Sir George Smart, 'was disposed to accept the appointment'. However, the reference to Smart in the newspaper seems to have been pure speculation. He did not apply for the job, and no evidence has been found that he was ever considered for it.
   7 D&C 7170/26
   8 *Ibid.*
   9 *Ibid.*
  10 D&C 7061/S.S. Wesley/1a. Wesley was interviewed at Dawlish.
  11 D&C 7061/S.S. Wesley/1.

12 D&C 3581, pp. 273–276.
13 D&C 7061/Wesley papers/4b.
14 D&C 3581, p. 280.
15 Peter Horton, 2004, *Samuel Sebastian Wesley: a life* (Oxford: Oxford University Press, 385 pages). Young Wesley's mother was Sarah Suter, his father's housemaid and long-term partner after separation from his wife. Samuel Sebastian was Samuel's fourth child, his first by Sarah Suter.
16 Horton, *op. cit.*, p. 29.
17 Horton, *op. cit.*, p. 17.
18 W. Spark, 1909, *Musical Memories* (London: W Reeves, Third Edition, 366 pages). See pp. 67–68.
19 D&C 3581, pp. 290 and 292–293.
20 Horton, *op. cit.*, pp. 115–116.
21 D&C 7061/S.S. Wesley/1b and 2.
22 Horton, *op. cit.*, p. 111.
23 He was later considered for university posts in Edinburgh (1844) , Oxford (1848) and Cambridge (1856) universities. See Horton, *op. cit.*
24 Horton, *op. cit.*, pp. 117–119. See also D&C 7061/S.S. Wesley/3, D&C 7061/Wesley papers/3 and D&C 7061/Wesley papers/7.
25 D&C 3582, p. 238.
26 D&C 3582, p. 243.
27 D&C 3582, p. 352.
28 Spark, *op. cit.*, p. 70.
29 D&C 3582, p. 392.
30 D&C 7061/ S.S. Wesley/4.
31 D&C 7061/Wesley papers/10.
32 D&C 7061/S.S. Wesley/15.
33 D&C 7061/Wesley papers/8.
34 For details, see Horton, *op. cit.*
35 Horton, *op. cit.*, p. 307. The cemetery in question is now known as the Lower Cemetery. Wesley's grave is near the Catacombs.
36 Horton, *op. cit.*, p. 112.
37 D&C 7062. Brooking had been the cathedral's organ tuner from 1814 to 1819, when he was dismissed and subsequently contested his dismissal (see Chapter 4).
38 'Helpers' had long been used to make the Double Diapasons speak. They were noticed by Baron Guilford when he visited in 1683 (see Chapter 2).
39 D&C 3581, p. 357. The Chapter also noted on 4 June 1836 that the organ which had been used in the Music School had belonged to James Paddon and been taken away by his executors. However, it had since been 'put into good order' and purchased by the Chapter for the sum of £21. The Chapter resolved, too, on 4 June 1836 that 'the engagement of Mr Turner to tune the organ be discontinued from and after the end of the present Quarter'. As noted in Chapter 4, Turner had been employed in 1823 to 'tune and take care of the organ'.
40 D&C 3581, p. 369.
41 D&C 3581, pp. 410–411.
42 D&C 3582, p. 402.
43 Horton, *op. cit.*, pp. 112–113.
44 D&C 7061/S.S. Wesley/1b and 2.
45 Vicary died on 7 December 1842, aged only 44, less than a year after Wesley left Exeter.
46 D&C 3581, pp. 513 and 528.

47 *The Musical World*, 1838, Vol. 10, p. 152.
48 D&C 7062.
49 D&C 3582, p. 15.
50 *The Times*, 9 September 1844, p. 4, Issue 18710, column G.
51 D&C 7062/1841–2.
52 D&C 7061/1841–2.
53 D&C 3582, p. 404.
54 D&C 3582, p. 417.
55 D&C 3582, p. 431.
56 D&C 3582, pp. 429–430.
57 D&C 3582, p. 432.
58 Chichester Cathedral Chapter Act Book F, WSRO Cap I/3/6, page 179. This Act Book is held by the West Sussex Record Office. See also p. 258 in M. Hobbs (ed.), 1994, *Chichester Cathedral: An historical survey* (Chichester: Phillimore & Co. Ltd, 362 pages).
59 Wells Cathedral Archives: DC/FI/127, DC/FI/128, p. 12, DC/CF/7/1, pp. 43–44, and DC/CF/7/2, p. 40.
60 D&C 3582, p. 431.
61 Angel's keen interest in madrigals was shown on 9 February 1847, when he delivered a lecture about them to the Exeter Scientific and Literary Institution, with 'vocal illustrations sung with great taste and precision by ten trebles, seven altos, six tenors and eight basses'(as it was put in *Trewman's Exeter Flying Post* on Thursday 11 February 1847, Issue 4233). Though not expressly stated in the newspaper, it may be assumed the singers were members of the cathedral choir.
62 The Gresham Prize was a gold medal of five guineas value awarded annually from 1831 for about a decade for the best original composition in sacred vocal music. It was awarded by Gresham College, London.
63 Anne died on 12 November 1870. Her father was the organist of Salisbury Cathedral from 1804 to 1863, like his father before him, from 1792 to 1804. One of Anne's brothers, Joseph Corfe, was a priest vicar of Exeter Cathedral from 1836 to 1878, and another, John David Corfe, became organist of Bristol Cathedral. Yet another, Charles William Corfe, became organist of Christ Church, Oxford.
64 D&C 7062 and D&C 3588, pp. 553–554.
65 D&C 3590, p. 302.
66 D&C 3589, p. 545.
67 D&C 7062/1859.
68 *Ibid.*
69 *Ibid.*
70 *Ibid.*
71 It was stated in *Dwight's Journal of Music* (Boston, USA, 23 July 1859, Vol. 15, No. 17, p. 134), in a report on a meeting in London on 'Uniform musical pitch', that Willis found when he tuned the organ in Exeter Cathedral that the pitch was 'a semitone below Mr Hullah's fork, and in accordance with that given by Handel's fork'. Hullah's fork was tuned to A=441.3 Hz, Handel's to A=422.5 Hz.
72 D&C 7062/1859.
73 *Ibid.* The Chapter approved these payments on 7 and 21 May 1859 (D&C 3590, pp. 10 and 15).
74 D&C 7062/1859.
75 D&C 3590, p. 15.
76 D&C 3590, p. 18.
77 D&C 3590, p. 175.

78 D&C 3590, p. 423.

79 D&C 3591, p. 60.

80 D&C 7170/51/1.

81 Nothing came of a proposal put forward by architect John Hayward in 1858 that the pulpitum be moved to the western end of the nave to form an inner porch and the organ moved to the north quire aisle. See 'Exeter Diocesan Architectural Society', *The Architect*, 19 February 1870, Vol. 3, p. 94.

82 See *Trewman's Exeter Flying Post*, Wednesday 3 May 1871, Issue 5472. For Scott's revised suggestions, see D&C 7170/51/1.

83 For details, see *Trewman's Exeter Flying Post*, Wednesday 25 September 1872, Issue 5626. See also D&C 3591, p. 254.

84 Luscombe was a builder, of St Sidwell Street, Exeter. His son, Edwin George Snell Luscombe, was also involved in Scott's restoration of the cathedral and became the cathedral's Clerk of the Works in 1876, succeeding Horatio Richard Snelgrove.

85 D&C 4724.

86 Continuing nervousness over the opening up of the screen can be found in the Chapter Acts for 21 December 1872 (D&C 3591, p. 278), when it was 'resolved that the weakened state of screen and the reparation of the organ imperatively call for the decision of the architect and that at the earliest moment possible'.

87 D&C 3591, p. 514. The work was carried out by Edwin Light Luscombe.

88 The mediæval stalls were removed during the Interregnum and in 1683 given to the church of St Lawrence on the High Street in Exeter. They were destroyed by fire on 4 May 1942 when the church was severely damaged in a German bombing raid.

89 By 1875, when the pipes were remade, the partnership between Speechly and Ingram, formed in 1867, had been dissolved, hence the reference to Speechly only. For details of the decision to remake the Double Diapason pipes and other pipes, with explanations as to why the pipes were in such poor condition, see letters from Speechly to Angel dated 21 January 1874, 31 December 1874 and 14 May 1875, all found in D&C 7170/51/3.

90 T.B. Worth, 1878, *Exeter Cathedral and its Restoration* (Exeter: William Pollard, 136 pages).

91 D&C 7170/51/3.

92 *Personal and Professional Recollections* by the late Sir George Gilbert Scott, 1879, edited by his son, George Gilbert Scott junior (London: Sampson Low, Marston, Searle and Rivington, 436 pages). See p. 349.

93 D&C 7170/51/3.

94 D&C 3591, p. 277.

95 D&C 3591, p. 280.

96 D&C 7170/51/3. Speechly & Ingram were appointed the cathedral's organ-builders in the autumn of 1872.

97 CC is the key two octaves below middle C, GG the key a fifth above it. The F in question is that two and a half octaves above middle C.

98 D&C 7170/51/3.

99 *Ibid.*

100 *Trewman's Exeter Flying Post*, Wednesday 28 June 1876, Issue 5811. The specification listed by Worth (*op. cit.*) has thirteen stops on the Great Organ, the extra one being a small Open Diapason, but this may be a mistake (perpetuated by later authors).

101 D&C 3591, p. 499.

102 D&C 3591, p. 534.

103 D&C 3592, p. 9.

104 *Trewman's Exeter Flying Post*, Wednesday 31 May 1876, Issue 5807.

105 Vinnicombe was appointed assistant organist on 15 February 1873, 'in the place of Frank Pinney deceased, the Chapter agreeing to pay £30 *per annum* towards his salary' (D&C 3591, p. 288). On 12 February 1875, in recognition of Angel's 'long and efficient services as organist of Exeter Cathedral', the Chapter relieved him of the payment of £20 *per annum* he had been making to the assistant organist and increased Vinnicombe's stipend to £50 *per annum*, the additional £20 being paid by the Chapter (D&C 3591, p. 428).

106 D&C 3591, p. 542.

107 D&C 7170/51/3.

108 *Ibid.*

109 Ouseley was professor of music in the University of Oxford and titular precentor of Hereford Cathedral.

110 D&C 7170/51/3.

111 D&C 3592, p. 37.

112 *The Times*, 19 October 1877, Issue 29077, p. 10, Column D.

113 D&C 7062.

114 *Ibid.*

115 D&C 3593, p. 24.

116 D&C 3593, p. 232.

117 D&C 7062. A quotation for a similar organ from Willis's costing £170 was not accepted.

118 The note was published in the 1926–27 volume of *The Organ* (Vol. 6, No. 23, p. 192). Hele said that he remembered finishing the organ in January 1889 on the way home from his FRCO examination.

119 D&C 7062.

120 *Exeter Cathedral Organ – description of the instrument, statement of account and list of subscriptions* (Exeter: printed at the 'Gazette' Office, High Street, by order of the Organ Restoration Committee for distribution to subscribers, published 1891, 12 pages). Copy in the Exeter Cathedral Archive (D&C 7062).

121 A. Freeman, 1926, 'The organs of Exeter Cathedral', *The Organ*, Vol. 6, No. 22, pp. 100–112.

122 D&C 3591, p. 528.

123 Wood married Louisa Sharp in Boston in early 1873, but she died on 25 July of that year. He married his second wife, Elizabeth Matilda Wren, in late 1876, in Bromley, Kent. They had three children, of whom one had died by the time of the 1881 census. Two daughters survived to adulthood, Kathleen Clare (born 1877) and Dorothy Charlotte (born 1878).

124 D&C 3591, p. 529.

125 D&C 3591, pp. 552–555. See also D&C 7062.

126 D&C 3592, pp. 12–13.

127 D&C 3592, p. 17. Neither of them was named in the Chapter Acts. They were the first of his many pupils while he was Exeter's organist. Among others, he took Walter Clarke on 28 April 1877 (D&C 3592, p. 29), Edward West and Ernest Slater on 19 January 1878 (D&C 3592, p. 75), and William Arthur Ellis on 30 March 1878 (D&C 3592, p. 88). A number of his pupils went on to hold prestigious appointments, notably Walter Hoyle, who was appointed assistant organist of Exeter Cathedral on 13 February 1892 (D&C 3593, p. 471) and was later, from 1898 to 1927, organist of the church in Coventry which became the city's cathedral in 1918. Another pupil of Wood was Edward Ellis Vinnicombe, son of Edward Moxhay Vinnicombe.

128 *Hymnal Companion to the Book of Common Prayer*, 1890 (London: Sampson Low and Marston & Co., 482 pages). *Chant Book Companion to the Book of Common Prayer*, 1894 (edited by Charles Vincent, London: Sampson Low and Marston & Co.).

129 *Trewman's Exeter Flying Post*, Saturday 24 June 1899, Issue 9968.

130 *Report of Her Majesty's Commissioners for Inquiring into the Condition of Cathedral Churches in England and Wales upon the Cathedral Church of Exeter*, 1885 (London: Eyre and Spottiswoode, 15 pages). See p. 13.

131 Wood was living in Cathedral Yard at the time of the 1881 census. He was living at 'Holmdale' on Denmark Road in 1891 and 1901 and 9 Cathedral Close in 1911.

132 D&C 3594, p. 178.

133 Procacious: 'insolent or arrogant in attitude or tone; forward, cheeky; provocative' (*Oxford English Dictionary*).

134 Obituary in *The Western Times*, Thursday 28 August 1919, Issue 21885, p. 2. The obituary mentioned that Wood had suffered a nervous breakdown about nine years beforehand and taken a cruise in the Mediterranean lasting three months, accompanied by his elder daughter. He had made a full recovery and thereafter continued his work at the cathedral without a break until the beginning of the month he died.

135 *The Western Times*, Tuesday 2 September 1919, Issue 21889, p. 3.

136 *The Western Times*, Tuesday 2 September 1919, Issue 21889, p. 4.

137 Wood left £582 15s 8d, with probate granted to his widow.

Chapter 6

1 D&C 3595/3, p. 206.

2 Ernest's father, Thomas Bullock, died on 5 May 1902. Sources which state that his mother, Eliza Eleanor Bullock, also died while he was still a schoolboy are incorrect. She died on 3 April 1920.

3 Edward Bairstow was organist of York Minster from 1913 until his death in 1946. He was knighted in 1932.

4 Bullock was promoted to Captain on 11 September 1917, made Adjutant of the 4th Battalion King's Own Yorkshire Light Infantry on 25 October 1918. He was mentioned in despatches in December 1917.

5 Entry on Ernest Bullock by Thomas Armstrong (revised by Mervyn Cooke) in the *Oxford Dictionary of National Biography* (2004, Oxford: Oxford University Press).

6 D&C 3596/6, pp. 378 and 389.

7 Armstrong, *op. cit.*

8 Bullock married Margery Newborn in December 1919 and they had two sons and a daughter. His wife survived him for only a few months.

9 D&C 3596/6, p. 383.

10 D&C 3596/6, pp. 386, 389 and 404.

11 D&C 3596/6, p. 397. Bradford resigned as assistant organist in August 1929, when appointed Music Master of Exeter School (D&C 3596/7, p. 41). William Harry Gabb succeeded him the following month (D&C 3596/7, p. 53) but resigned in December 1936, when appointed organist of Llandaff Cathedral (D&C 3596/8, p. 419). His successor was John Hind, appointed in January 1937 (D&C 3596/8, p. 429). Hind was appointed organist of St Leonard's Church in Exeter in September 1938 (D&C 3596/9, pp. 109–110) but on a shared basis with the cathedral. He was required to play at the cathedral on six Sundays a year and be available should any emergency arise, such as illness of the organist or a vacancy.

12 Entry on Thomas Henry Wait Armstrong by Richard Stoker in the *Oxford Dictionary of National Biography* (2004).

13 Armstrong was promoted from Officer Cadet to Second Lieutenant on 17 September 1917.

14 Armstrong married, in 1926, Hester Draper, daughter of the Master of the Temple Church, London. They had a son and a daughter, Robert (born 1927) and Helen (born 1930). Hester died on 11 May 1982.

15 Obituary of Armstrong by Ursula Vaughan Williams published in *The Independent* newspaper on 4 July 1994.

16 Armstrong was granted leave of absence by the Chapter in 1931 to 'go to Canada for a tour of adjudication in 1932, after Easter' (D&C 3596/7, pp. 206 and 207).

17 *The Times*, Friday 21 December 1928, Issue 45082, p. 12. The record was produced by Columbia.

18 D&C 3596/7, pp. 396 and 422.

19 D&C 7062.

20 *Ibid.*

21 *Ibid.*

22 *Ibid.*

23 D&C 3596/6, pp. 167–168.

24 D&C 3596/7, pp. 368–369. For the estimates of the various firms, see D&C 7062/1932. Arthur Harrison inspected the organ on 11 July 1932.

25 *The Times*, Thursday 21 July 1932, Issue 46191, p. 8, column C.

26 *The Times*, Saturday 23 July 1932, Issue 46193, p. 11, column E.

27 For an article about this model, see Malcolm Walker, 2012, 'A curious model of St Peter's Cathedral', *Annual Report of the Friends of Exeter Cathedral*, pp. 26–27.

28 *The Times*, Monday 25 July 1932, Issue 46194, p. 13, column E.

29 *The Times*, Tuesday 26 July 1932, Issue 46195, p. 8, column A.

30 The letter from the Dean was published on 4 August (*The Times*, Issue 46203, p. 6, column A), the letter from Herbert Bishop the following day (*The Times*, Issue 46204, p. 6, column D).

31 *The Times*, Thursday 11 August 1932, Issue 46209, p. 6, column A.

32 Laurence Elvin, 1937, 'The organ at Exeter Cathedral', *The Organ*, Vol. 17, No. 66, pp. 97–99.

33 The Chapter awarded the tuning contract to Harrison & Harrison on 2 September 1933 at a cost of £35 *per annum* (D&C 3596/7, p. 491).

34 D&C 3596/7, pp. 440 and 448.

35 Alfred Wilcock's father, Joseph, was a police officer.

36 D&C 7188/2.

37 For information about Wilcock's salary, see D&C 3596/7, p. 427, D&C 3596/8, p. 272, D&C 3596/10, p. 124, and D&C 3596/10, p. 387.

38 D&C 3596/8, pp. 12–13 and 29.

39 D&C 3596/8, pp. 32 and 34.

40 D&C 3596/8, p. 59.

41 D&C 3596/8, p. 189.

42 D&C 3596/8, p. 221.

43 D&C 3596/9, p. 45.

44 D&C 3596/9, p. 400.

45 D&C 3596/9, p. 410.

46 Copies of correspondence in 1941 between Watkins & Watson, Harrison & Harrison and the cathedral's architect on the subject of a new blower are held in Harrison's archive at Durham.

47 S.C. Carpenter, 1943, *Exeter Cathedral, 1942* (London: Society for Promoting Christian Knowledge, 50 pages). See p. 22. This must be considered a definitive account of the air

raid and the damage sustained by the cathedral, written by an eyewitness, the Dean of Exeter.

48 D&C 3596/9, pp. 448–449. The letter sent by the Chapter Clerk to Harrison's on 21 May 1942 is held in Harrison's archive at Durham, along with other correspondence concerned with this claim.

49 D&C 3596/9, p. 450.

50 Letter from Wood to Harrison & Harrison dated 16 May 1942, in Harrison's archive at Durham.

51 D&C 3596/9, pp. 452.

52 Carpenter, *op. cit*, p. 27.

53 Carpenter, *op. cit*, p. 29.

54 The letter from the Dean is held in Harrison's archive at Durham.

55 D&C 3596/9, p. 453.

56 D&C 3596/9, pp. 454–455.

57 D&C 3596/9, pp. 456–457.

58 D&C 3596/9, p. 487.

59 D&C 3596/10, p. 32.

60 D&C 3596/10, p. 33.

61 Letter in Harrison's archive.

62 See letters in Harrison's archive, also D&C 3596/10, p. 106.

63 D&C 3596/10, p. 108.

64 D&C 3596/10, p. 113.

65 Letter in Harrison's archive.

66 D&C 3596/10, p. 159.

67 D&C 3596/10, pp. 166–167. Copies of letters from the Chapter Clerk to Harrison & Harrison about blower and electricity requirements for the organ are held in Harrison's archive.

68 The decision of the Dean and Chapter to have a three-phase supply provided was reported to Harrison's by the cathedral's surveyor in a letter dated 4 March 1946. There is a copy of this letter in Harrison's archive.

69 In Harrison's archive, there are several letters from Read to Harrison's about his restoration of the organ case. See also the note from Read on page 9 of the 16th *Annual Report of the Friends of Exeter Cathedral*, which covered the year ending 31 March 1946.

70 D&C 3596/10, p. 188.

71 D&C 3596/10, pp. 190–191.

72 D&C 3596/10, pp. 195–196.

73 There is a copy of this letter in Harrison's archive.

74 D&C 3596/10, p. 231.

75 D&C 3596/11, p. 1.

76 D&C 3596/11, pp. 8 and 12.

77 There is in Harrison's archive a copy of a letter dated 23 March 1949 from Watkins & Watson to Harrison's which refers to Drury's letter.

78 D&C 3596/11, p. 140.

79 Wilcock was said by many to prefer playing the piano to the organ.

80 D&C 3596/11, p. 147.

81 D&C 3596/11, pp. 170–171 and 172. Church House is on the south side of the cloisters.

82 Alfred Wilcock married Isabel Ruth (née Gadd) in Exeter Cathedral on 6 November 1945, and their daughter, Mary, was born in 1947. Isabel was his second wife. He had married

Nora Lindop in 1922, in Chester, and she had died on 8 December 1941. There was one child of that marriage, Philip Geoffrey Joseph Wilcock, born in 1926.

83 D&C 3596/11, p. 178. Howard Stephens deputized after Wilcock's retirement. He had been assistant organist since 15 January 1951 (D&C 3596/11, pp. 51, 52 and 70), succeeding J.L. Birley. He remained assistant organist until the end of December 1954 (D&C 3596/11, pp. 137, 154 and 304), when Gandy Bradford was re-appointed on a monthly basis (D&C 3596/11, p. 315). Stuart Marston Smith was appointed assistant organist in 1956.

84 Moore's father, Leonard, was a railway fitter.

85 For information about Moore, see *Who Was Who, 1961–70* (1971, London: A & C Black) and the article about him published by his daughter, Christine Ford, in *Cathedral Music* (the magazine of the Friends of Cathedral Music), May 2010, pp. 48–49. Moore married Grace Estelle Houghton at Bramley in 1939, and Christine was their only child.

86 Moore widened the cathedral choir's repertoire. For lists of new music sung, see the annual reports of the Friends of Exeter Cathedral for 1953, 1954 and 1955 (24th report, p. 5, 25th report, p. 5, and 26th report, p. 6).

87 D&C 3596/11, p. 402.

88 D&C 3596/11, p. 469.

89 For information about Lionel Dakers, see *Who's Who in Music and Musicians' International Directory*, Sixth Edition, 1972 (London: Burke's Peerage), also *Who's Who*, 2002 (London: A & C Black). He married Mary Elisabeth Williams in 1951.

90 D&C 3596/11. p. 494.

91 There are copies of letters concerning this matter in Harrison's archive.

92 There is a copy of this letter in Harrison's archive.

93 See letter from Drury to Harrison's dated 7 November 1958, in Harrison's archive.

94 There is a copy of this letter in Harrison's archive.

95 D&C 3597/1/1960/minute 343.

96 There is a copy of this report in Harrison's archive.

97 D&C 3597/1/1960/minute 374.

98 D&C 3597/1/1960/minutes 402 and 411.

99 D&C 3597/1/1960/minute 433.

100 There is a copy of Jackson's report in Harrison's archive.

101 There is a copy of Harrison's response in their archive.

102 There is a copy of the report by Dakers in Harrison's archive. A shortened version of the report was published in the *Annual Report of the Friends of Exeter Cathedral* for 1963 (34th Report, pp. 3–4).

103 D&C 3597/2/1963, minute 11.

104 There is a copy of the letter from Dakers in Harrison's archive.

105 D&C 3597/2/1963/minute 48.

106 D&C 3597/2/1963/minute 64.

107 There is a copy of the letter from Dakers in Harrison's archive.

108 *Ditto.*

109 See D&C 3597/3/1964/minute 150, and D&C 3597/3/1965/minute 11. Letters from the Chapter Clerk to Harrison's about the contract are in Harrison's archive. Payment of the £12,920 was made in stages, in four instalments of £3,230 each.

110 D&C 3597/3/1965/minute 12.

111 D&C 3597/3/1965/minute 3.

112 There is a copy of the letter from Dakers in Harrison's archive.

113 This information can be found, handwritten in pencil by one of Harrison's staff, at the end of the letter Dakers sent to Harrison's on 6 October.

114 36th *Annual Report of the Friends of Exeter Cathedral* (for the year 1965, pp. 25–27).
115 There is a copy of this letter from Dakers in Harrison's archive.
116 N. Sterrett, 1966, 'Exeter Cathedral organ', *The Organ*, Vol. 46, No. 182, pp. 49–61.
117 There is a copy of this letter from Dakers in Harrison's archive.
118 There is a copy of this letter from Watson & Watkins in Harrison's archive.
119 Sterrett, *op. cit.*, p. 53.
120 Elisabeth Dakers died in 1997. Their four daughters survived him.
121 Full obituaries of Dakers were published in *The Daily Telegraph* and *The Independent* on 14 March, *The Times* on 19 March and *The Guardian* on 22 March 2003.
122 D&C 3597/6/1972, minute 44. Lucian was indeed elected, there being a vote at the Chapter meeting on 24 July 1972 to choose between him and one other candidate.
123 Lucian Nethsingha married Jane Symons in London on 4 September 1965 and they had two children: Andrew, born 1968, and Alison, born 1974. Andrew was a chorister in the choir of Exeter Cathedral under his father from 1976 to 1981 and has been since 2007 Director of Music at St John's College, Cambridge.
124 Paul Morgan was appointed assistant organist in 1969, when his predecessor, Christopher Gower, was appointed organist of Peterborough Cathedral. Gower had been assistant organist since 1961.
125 'Lucian Nethsingha – a personal appreciation from the Punctator', by Julian Sutton, *Annual Reports of the Friends of Exeter Cathedral*, 69th Report, 1999, pp. 9–13. The Exeter choir's Punctator is the senior lay vicar.
126 There is in the archive of Harrison's a list of faults, dated 25 November 1982.
127 There is a copy of this letter in Harrison's archive.
128 See the 56th *Annual Report of the Friends of Exeter Cathedral*, the report for 1985, p. 5.
129 There is a copy of this report in Harrison's archive, including detailed diagrams of the pedalboard.
130 This note is in Harrison's archive.
131 There is a copy of this letter in Harrison's archive.
132 *Ditto.*
133 *Ditto.*
134 Andrew Millington married Madeleine Cooke at Malvern in 1978 and they had two daughters and a son, Anna (born 1985), Sophie (born 1987) and Thomas (born 1988).
135 Details of the work and costings of the various components of the project can be found in a letter from Mark Venning to Andrew Millington dated 5 October 2000. There is a copy of this letter in Harrison's archive.
136 71st *Annual Report of the Friends of Exeter Cathedral*, the report for 2001, p. 26.
137 73rd *Annual Report of the Friends of Exeter Cathedral*, the report for 2003, pp. 29–35.
138 See David Davies, 'The cathedral organ restoration project', 83rd *Annual Report of the Friends of Exeter Cathedral*, the report for 2013, pp. 14–15.
139 It was announced as this book was going to press that Andrew Millington will retire as Exeter Cathedral's director of music in the summer of 2015.

Appendix 1

1 The manuals of the organ in Exeter Cathedral today extend from the C two octaves below middle C to the A nearly three octaves above middle C. The pedalboard extends from the C two octaves below middle C to the F above middle C. As there are twelve notes per octave, this means that the manuals have 58 notes and the pedalboard has 30.

Glossary

Action – The type of mechanism that transmits the input of the organist's hands and feet from the organ manuals (*q.v.*) and pedalboard to the windchest (*q.v.*) in order to activate the pallets (*q.v.*), or equivalent, that admit air into the organ pipes. The actions most commonly found in pipe organs are mechanical (direct transmission), pneumatic (transmission achieved via pneumatic assistance), electromagnetic (transmission achieved via electrical switching), or a combination of these (e.g. electro-pneumatic). Within each of these main families of actions are various permutations. A broad analogy with everyday life might be a system such as power-assisted steering on a car: as wind pressures, or sheer number of stops, on an organ increase so, too, must the physical effort of the organist to operate a direct, mechanical linkage with the pallet. By inserting one or more intermediate stages to do the work, the effort of the player can remain constant while the lion's share of the work is executed by the intermediate machine. Such a machine can receive its impulses – and/or discharge its work – mechanically, pneumatically, electromagnetically or electro-pneumatically. In a high-pressure system the amount of physical force required by the organist to open a sprung pallet against such air resistance would be defeating. The introduction of electrical actions has also meant that the distance of the organist from the pipes can be exploited (as is the case with the Minstrels' Gallery division (*q.v.*) of the organ at Exeter Cathedral.)

ARCO – An Associate of the Royal College of Organists (RCO, *q.v.*) is a diploma holder, via written and practical examination, in the skill of organ playing and its associated art. A less demanding examination than that set for FRCO (*q.v.*).

Astragal – In furniture moulding and cabinetry a piece of carving with geometric properties that plays a prominent visual role.

Bourdon – An organ stop name. A member of the flute family, this stop operates the most common rank of pipes found in the Pedal division, its notes sounding one octave lower than piano pitch.

Calvinist – Adherents to the dogmatic, philosophical and theological teaching of John Calvin (1509–1564), the influential French pastor who is chiefly remembered for his leading role in the Protestant Reformation.

Canon – Usually a priest in a Cathedral Foundation who is a member of the Chapter (*q.v.*), and who has a specific named role (e.g. Canon Precentor, Canon Treasurer, Canon Chancellor, Canon Missioner). With the expansion of Cathedral Chapters to include members of the laity, it is not unusual now to find Lay (non-ordained) Canons, either with or without portfolio, sitting on Chapter.

Case – *(as in organ case)* The external structure, usually of wood, that clothes an organ, the façade(s) of which often house the organ pipes that are on display. This is especially significant at Exeter Cathedral where the visual impact of the organ case and the history of its evolution have played a vital role in the unfolding timeline of the organ.

Chapter – The body of canons (*q.v.*) appointed to various roles within the Cathedral foundation; together with the Dean (*q.v.*), this is the group of individuals that collectively takes major decisions on all commercial and legal aspects of the running of the Cathedral. It also determines the institution's ethos in terms of liturgy, worship, Christian education, doctrine and mission.

Chapter House – The building on the south side of Exeter Cathedral originally intended as the formal meeting room of the Dean and Chapter. This function has ceased to exist, and the building is now used for a wide variety of social, musical, artistic and educational events.

Chorus – The combination of various groups of organ stops, usually at different pitches, within the same tonal family (e.g. diapason chorus, reed chorus).

Cipher – The continuous, uncommanded sounding of an organ pipe or pipes due to a technical fault or to the presence of debris that compromises any part of the organ action mechanism. A less obvious cipher is called a *murmur*, and, even though sometimes barely perceptible, can cause irritation to the player and listener alike.

Cloisters – The external area to the south of Exeter Cathedral now enclosed on three and a half sides by the cathedral, the Chapter House (*q.v.*), the Cathedral Café, Church House and the two Cloisters buildings.

College of the Vicars Choral – The group of clergy whose principal role was to assist the offering of cathedral worship on a daily basis. The Hall of the College of Vicars Choral is the now-ruined building visible in Kalendarhay where members of the College lived.

Compass – The range of an organ keyboard or pedalboard from bass to treble. Compass is usually described either by the number of musical notes in this range, or the number of octaves it includes.

Cornet – An organ stop name. This stop can operate multiple ranks, often at the unison, octave, twelfth, fifteenth and seventeenth pitches. See also Chapter 3, note 11.

Cornett – A wind instrument popular from around 1500 onwards through the Baroque period.

Custos of the College of the Vicars Choral – The head (literally 'guardian') of the College of the Vicars Choral (*q.v.*).

Dean – The head of the clergy foundation in a cathedral (as opposed to a bishop, who has oversight of a diocese, or part thereof). The Dean is also often the Senior Priest of the diocese.

Decorated – An expression of the English Gothic architectural style that flourished roughly for a hundred years from about 1250.

Diapason – An organ stop name, the pipes of which produce what is often described as fundamental organ tone within the chorus (*q.v.*). Diapason pipes are members of the 'principal' (*q.v.*) family.

Division – A section of the organ housing a particular set of pipes. Often, although not always, these sections correspond to the different manuals (*q.v.*) and pedalboard of the organ (e.g. the Great division, the Swell division, the Pedal division etc.). A 'floating' division refers to organ stops that do not necessarily have a fixed keyboard from which they are always played: the Minstrels' Gallery division at Exeter Cathedral is an example of this. Therefore the organist has to select not only the required stop or stops of the Minstrels' Gallery division but also a separate stop to select a keyboard from which to play those stops. The selector stop *Minstrel on Choir* enables the organist to play the Minstrels' Gallery division from the lowest keyboard of the four manuals, for example.

Double chant – Influenced by the plainsong tones (melodies) used for the singing of the psalms, the music for singing psalms and other portions of the scriptures in the Anglican choral tradition developed into a format of a series of harmonized chords organized in a particular structure. A 'double chant' refers to a structure of twenty chords divided into four quarters, the first and third quarters containing four chords each, the second and fourth quarters containing six chords each. The lines of text are *pointed* (i.e. made to fit this structure) accordingly.

Echo Organ – A division (*q.v.*) of the organ traditionally comprising quiet ranks of pipes often situated in a part of the organ structure (or building) to achieve remoteness of sound.

English Reformation – The turning tide against the supremacy of the Roman Catholic Church in England was fuelled both by Henry VIII's desire to marry again and by the rise of reforming thought in northern Europe. The establishment of a Protestant state Church of England, together with Calvinist influence that laid the ground for a Presbyterian Church in Scotland, played a significant part in the current Christian denominational heritage of the UK.

Fifteenth – An organ stop name. The pipes belong to the 'principal' (*q.v.*) family of organ tone, the notes sounding two octaves higher than piano pitch.

FRCO – A Fellow of the Royal College of Organists (RCO, *q.v.*) is a diploma holder, via written and practical examination, in the skill of organ playing and its associated art. Candidates for this diploma must already have passed the ARCO (*q.v.*) and this qualification is traditionally regarded as the highest benchmark of achievement within the profession. In some circles the FRCO diploma is regarded as an academic degree equivalent.

Gothic – The type of architecture that emerged from the Romanesque (*q.v.*) style. L'abbé Suger's iconic Basilica of Saint-Denis (1144) in Paris is often cited as the true beginning of Gothic, a style that lasted into the sixteenth century and which has enjoyed several revivals since.

Independent – During the English Civil War a member of the group that championed independence from the established churches. Oliver Cromwell is one of the most noted Independents.

Informator Choristarum – The Master of the Choristers, a historic title that is still used to this day at Magdalen College, Oxford.

Interregnum – The republican period of the English Civil War between 30 January 1649 and 29 May 1660, defined by the execution of Charles I and the restoration of the monarchy of Charles II. In Exeter, however, a unique definition is required, as the Parliamentarians controlled the city from 5 April 1646 when Charles I was still alive.

Keraulophon – An organ stop name. The sound of the pipes is usually gentle with a slightly stringy quality.

Lady Chapel – A richly decorated chapel dedicated to the Blessed Virgin Mary that is to be found in the easternmost part of the Cathedral.

Lady Day – The Feast of the Annunciation of the Blessed Virgin Mary, celebrated on 25 March.

Lay Vicar – One of the gentlemen of the Cathedral Choir, distinct from a choral scholar by virtue of being more experienced and receiving a higher salary for singing. The Lay Vicar can deputize for a singing member of the clergy in the singing (as *cantor*) of the liturgy (*q.v.*).

Liturgy – Literally 'the work of the people' in praising God, liturgy refers to the provision and execution of worship. Within the English choral tradition liturgy is closely linked to the style of the offering of music in worship, and to the decorum and enactment of the worship itself.

Magnificat – Also known as 'The Song of Mary', the Magnificat is the name for that portion of text found in the first chapter of the Gospel of St Luke (verses 46 to 55) that is the Blessed Virgin Mary's hymn of praise at the Visitation to her cousin Elizabeth. Known as a *canticle*, the text of the Magnificat is central to the Roman Catholic service of Vespers, and retains a centrality in the Anglican service of Evensong. The text has inspired some of the finest liturgical Christian music over the centuries.

Manual – In organ terminology the word for a keyboard. On a typical English organ with four keyboards, such as at Exeter Cathedral, the keyboards from the lowest up control the stops of the Choir Organ, Great Organ, Swell Organ and Solo Organ respectively. This organ would therefore be described as being a four-manual instrument.

Michaelmas – The Feast of St Michael and All Angels, celebrated on September 29. It can also refer to the winter academic term, usually from September to Christmas.

Nason – An organ stop name in the flute family.

Nazard – An organ stop name, playing at the same pitch as a Twelfth (*q.v.*), but of gentler tone.

New Model Army – The formal army raised in 1645 with a membership that often held deeply rooted Puritan views. In opposing the Royalists, the Army had a unique religious conviction and numbered over 20,000 soldiers. It was disbanded at the Restoration of the Monarchy.

Open Diapason – See 'Diapason'. The word 'open' denotes that the pipes are open at the top, as opposed to having a stopper (akin to a bung) placed within the speaking length of the pipe that lowers the pitch of that pipe and changes its tone. ('Stopped Diapason', *q.v.*).

Office – A liturgical Christian service, derived from the Latin word for ceremony, *officium*. In the Church of England, the service of Evensong is classed as the 'Office of Evensong', and has its roots in the cyclical offices of the Roman Catholic Church. Office can also refer to an employed position, e.g. the office of Organist.

Pallet – The valve that physically moves to admit air into the correct part of a windchest (*q.v.*) to sound a pipe.

Parliamentarian – The so-called 'Roundheads' of the English Civil War, Parliamentarians who sought to give Parliament executive powers and control that had, in their mind, been abused by absolutist monarchs who claimed divine right of rule.

Plainsong – Monophonic (single note) melodies that date from the earliest times of the rise of Christianity, with their roots in much older musical forms. Plainsong, also known as plainchant, embodies a large number of chants that adorn the liturgies of the Christian Church in the West, including formal tones used for the singing of the psalms.

Polyphony – Any musical composition written in multiple parts, normally where one part, or 'voice', is echoed by others subsequently, and where the melody of such subsequent voices is the same as, or derived from the first voice. Mediæval and Renaissance liturgical choral music became a highly sophisticated vehicle for this form of composition, raising such music to the level of high art of considerable craft and distinction. Such artistry was felt in some ecclesiastical quarters to distort the sacred text, and the depth of this argument has historically caused significant schismatic tendencies within the Church.

Prayer Book Rebellion – The 1549 uprising in Devon and Cornwall in response to the introduction of the Book of Common Prayer. Roman Catholic sympathies were quashed by a particularly gruesome massacre of at least 2,000 people largely by the forces of Edward VI, an action that was to have long and damaging effects and for which an apology was issued by the Bishop of Truro in 2007.

Precentor – Within the clergy hierarchy of a cathedral administration, the Canon Precentor is primarily responsible for worship and music. The origin of the word can be found in the Latin *praecantor,* the one who 'sings before' (i.e. leads) or 'sings first'.

Presbyterian – The Reformed Church that, for the purposes of this book, is significant in the English Civil War. The roots of the denomination are to be found in the European Reformation.

Principal – The fundamental type of organ tone; also an organ stop name.

Pulpitum – A screen, usually of stone, that divides the body of a church. In larger buildings the pulpitum would necessarily be substantial, as at Exeter Cathedral, and in many cases large enough to support an organ and/or a place set aside for liturgical and/or musical use.

Puritanism – The rising faction within the Church of England that sought to question and change many aspects of the established Church in the sixteenth and seventeenth centuries. In general, Puritans felt that the extent of the English Reformation was not far-reaching enough.

Quarterage – A financial transaction (a payment made or received) that occurs once every three months in a fiscal year.

Quarter Days – The days upon which the cathedral staff were paid.

RAM – The Royal Academy of Music, established in 1822, is one of the premier music conservatoires of Europe, and the oldest in Britain.

RCM – The Royal College of Music, established in 1882, is one of the premier music conservatoires of Europe.

RCO – The Royal College of Organists is a professional body that was founded in 1864 and which gained its royal charter in 1893. Its aim is to promote and reward excellence in organ performance, organ history and theory via competitive examinations and to house a library of important organ-related material.

Reed – The family names for ranks of pipes in the organ that are constructed differently from flue pipes. The nomenclature given to stops that control reed pipes include names such as trumpet, oboe, trombone, clarinet and bassoon. Typically a reed organ pipe will consist of a brass tongue that is fixed in place next to a shallot within a solid block underneath the resonator (*q.v.*).

Reredos – A screen that usually decorates the eastern wall behind an altar. A reredos can have striking and ornate architectural elements on an impressive scale and will often be of iconographic significance.

Resonator – The upper structure of any organ pipe, via which sound resonates. The characteristics of a resonator affect timbre (*q.v.*) and pitch.

Re-voicing – The art of altering the tonal quality of any organ pipe either to suit a new musical taste or to correct any tonal deficiencies that, over time, may have impaired the speech of that pipe. ('Voicing', *q.v.*)

Rollerboard – A component in a mechanical organ action (*q.v.*) as part of the angled transmission from the keyboard to the windchest (*q.v.*).

Romanesque – The medieval style of European architecture that was the precursor of the Gothic. Its principal qualities are symmetry, sturdiness, thick walls and pillars, distinctive arches, substantial towers and arcading.

Rood – The crucifix that adorns the crossing of a church or cathedral, often present as an icon of adoration in the mediæval mind. In many cases, although not always, the rood was either suspended above, or attached to, a rood screen, giving rise to the interesting juxtaposition of screens in cathedrals such as at Exeter. These were possibly separate from existing pulpitum screens. The English Reformation saw the removal and/or destruction of many roods.

Running – Any escape of air within the organ windchest (*q.v.*) that causes air to find its way into another part of the windchest where it should not be. Normally a running is caused by torsional twisting of the windchest, or parts thereof, due to climatic conditions, or wear and tear, or normal deterioration. Such deterioration compromises the necessity that a windchest operates at its optimum air-tightness when all its components sit absolutely true. The effects of a running are usually the unwanted whimpering of certain organ pipes when other notes are intentionally played.

Sackbut(t) – The precursor of the modern trombone, a brass instrument of the Renaissance and Baroque periods.

Secondary – Ordinarily a young male singer whose voice is in transition to a lower pitch. Some all-male choirs continue the practice of encouraging post-voice-break teenagers to provide the alto, tenor and bass parts of a choir. Such singers would still be learning the tradition and gaining more experience and, indeed, their voices would be in the process of developing and maturing. As such, if they were employed, they would not command the same payment as a more mature adult singer.

Sesquialtera – An organ stop that controls two ranks of pipes simultaneously, the Nazard and Tierce (both *q.v.*).

Stopped Diapason – An organ stop that, while containing the word 'diapason' is, in fact, a member of the flute family.

Sub-chanter/Succentor – A member of the cathedral clergy appointed to assist (*succurrere*) the Precentor (*q.v.*).

Supplication – At Oxford and Cambridge Universities the action that is complementary to admission ('matriculation') once studies are completed.

Historically, candidates proceed to a degree and, within a given length of time, can *supplicate* for the higher degree, most commonly now the degree of Master of Arts for which no further work after the Bachelor of Arts degree needs to be submitted. The historical idiosyncrasy of the graduation system in this way stems partly from the tradition that it took several years to complete a first degree in certain disciplines as opposed to the modern period of three or four years.

Tierce – An organ stop name. The pipes usually belong to the flute family of organ tone, the notes sounding seventeen notes higher than piano pitch. The Tierce lends the characteristic sound 'ingredient' of the Cornet (*q.v.*).

Timbre – Any aspect of musical sound that relates to its quality.

Trinity – Trinity Sunday falls one week after Whitsunday, or the Feast of Pentecost. The Trinity term, therefore, equates to the academic summer term.

Tuning – The process of unifying the intonation of the pipes of an organ, with the same goal as tuning a piano, for example. When tuning organ flue pipes, adjustments are made to the length of the pipe which in turn alter the dimensions of the vibrating body of air within the pipe and which thus alter the pitch. In reed pipes a metal spring is adjusted against the vibrating tongue to alter the pitch. Temperature, humidity, foreign body contamination, and even proximity to other organ pipes, can have an effect on whether an organ pipe is in tune.

Twelfth – An organ stop name. The pipes belong to the 'principal' (*q.v.*) family of organ tone, the notes sounding twelve notes higher than piano pitch.

Ventil – A mechanism by means of which air is either shut off or brought into play for a particular section of pipes on a windchest (*q.v.*).

Viol – A fretted instrument of six strings, also known as the viola da gamba, that appears either as a solo instrument or in *consort* (ensemble), often using instruments of different sizes. Anthems such as Orlando Gibbons' famous 'This is the Record of John' would have been accompanied by a consort of viols, for example, demonstrating that viols had a liturgical as well as domestic role.

Voicing – The art of making an organ pipe speak to its correct and optimum ability and quality. The process involves making often minute physical alterations to the organ pipe concerned, thereby creating and elevating the tonal quality from the raw and rough organ pipe that emerged from the pipe-making process. In all types of organ pipes the pipe-voicer works to achieve the most desirable balance of dynamic (loudness/quietness), timbre (quality of sound) and intonation (the phenomenon of an organ pipe speaking 'on pitch' most comfortably given the amount of air pressure admitted into it). The outcome of the laborious, highly skilled and meticulous craft of voicing determines the overall cohesiveness of the instrument's tonal character. The level of specialism of this work often means that pipe-voicers tend to concentrate their skill either on flue or on reed pipes.

Voluntary – A piece of organ music played either before or after a liturgical service, or as part of it.

Windchest – The structure upon which organ pipes sit, the windchest houses the final stages of the mechanism that admits air into the pipes. Sometimes referred to as 'soundboard', the word 'windchest' is a better description of the structure, as it includes the hollow chamber that is filled with the 'wind' that is supplied from a pressurised reservoir of air.

Index

*Page numbers in **bold** refer to figures and plates.*